Defining Neomedievalism(s)

Studies in Medievalism XIX

2010

Studies in Medievalism

Founded by Leslie J. Workman

Previously published volumes are listed at the back of this book

Defining Neomedievalism(s)

Edited by
Karl Fugelso

Studies in Medievalism XIX 2010

Cambridge
D. S. Brewer

© Studies in Medievalism 2010

First published 2010
D. S. Brewer, Cambridge

ISBN 978–1–84384–228–6

ISSN 0738–7164

D. S. Brewer is an imprint of Boydell & Brewer Ltd
PO Box 9, Woodbridge, Suffolk IP12 3DF, UK
and of Boydell & Brewer Inc.
668 Mt Hope Avenue, Rochester, NY 14620, USA
website: www.boydellandbrewer.com

A CIP catalogue record for this book is available
from the British Library

The publisher has no responsibility for the continued existence or accuracy
of URLs for external or third-party internet websites referred to in this book,
and does not guarantee that any content on such websites is, or will remain,
accurate or appropriate

This publication is printed on acid-free paper

Typeset by Pru Harrison, Hacheston, Suffolk
Printed in Great Britain by
CPI Antony Rowe Ltd, Chippenham and Eastbourne

Studies in Medievalism

| Founding Editor | †Leslie J. Workman |
| Editor | Karl Fugelso |

Advisory Board

Martin Arnold (Hull)
Geraldine Barnes (Sydney)
Rolf H. Bremmer, Jr. (Leiden)
William Calin (Florida)
A. E. Christa Canitz (New Brunswick, Canada)
Philip Cardew (University of Winchester)
Elizabeth Emery (Montclair State)
David Matthews (Newcastle, Australia)
Gwendolyn Morgan (Montana State)
Ulrich Müller (Salzburg)
Nils Holger Petersen (Copenhagen)
Tom Shippey (Saint Louis)
Clare A. Simmons (Ohio State)
John Simons (Lincoln)
Paul Szarmach (Western Michigan)
Toshiyuki Takamiya (Keio)
Jane Toswell (Western Ontario)
Richard Utz (Western Michigan)
Kathleen Verduin (Hope College, Michigan)
Andrew Wawn (Leeds)

Studies in Medievalism provides an interdisciplinary medium of exchange for scholars in all fields, including the visual and other arts, concerned with any aspect of the post-medieval idea and study of the Middle Ages and the influence, both scholarly and popular, of this study on Western society after 1500.

Studies in Medievalism is published by Boydell & Brewer, Ltd., P.O. Box 9, Woodbridge, Suffolk IP12 3DF, UK; Boydell & Brewer, Inc., 668 Mt. Hope Avenue, Rochester, NY 14620, USA. Orders and inquiries about back issues should be addressed to Boydell & Brewer at the appropriate office.

For a copy of the style sheet and for inquiries about **Studies in Medievalism**, please contact the editor, Karl Fugelso, at the Dept. of Art and Art History, Towson University, 8000 York Rd, Towson, MD 21252–0001, USA, tel. 410–704–2805, fax 410–704–2810 ATTN: Fugelso, e-mail <kfugelso@towson.edu>. All submissions should be sent to him as e-mail attachments in Word.

Acknowledgments

The device on the title page comes from the title page of *Des Knaben Wunderhorn: Alte deutsche Lieder*, edited by L. Achim von Arnim and Clemens Brentano (Heidelberg and Frankfurt, 1806).

The epigraph is from an unpublished paper by Lord Acton, written about 1859 and printed in Herbert Butterfield, *Man on His Past* (Cambridge University Press, 1955), 212.

Studies in Medievalism

Editorial Note   Karl Fugelso   xi

I: Defining Neomedievalism(s): Some Perspective(s)

Medieval Unmoored   Amy S. Kaufman   1

Neomedievalism, Hyperrealism,   Brent Moberly and Kevin Moberly   12
and Simulation

A Short Essay about Neomedievalism   Lesley Coote   25

Neomedievalism: An Eleventh Little   Cory Lowell Grewell   34
Middle Ages?

The Simulacrum of Neomedievalism   M. J. Toswell   44

Sandworms, Bodices, and Undergrounds: E. L. Risden   58
The Transformative Mélange of Neomedievalism

Dark Matters and Slippery Words: Lauryn S. Mayer   68
Grappling with Neomedievalism(s)

II: (Neo-)Medievalist Interpretations

Utopia and Heterotopia: Byzantine Modernisms   Glenn Peers   77
in America

Queer Crusading, Military Masculinity, and Allegories   Tison Pugh   114
of Vietnam in Richard Lester's *Robin and Marian*

Getting Reel with Grendel's Mother: David W. Marshall   135
The Abject Maternal and Social Critique

The Colony Writes Back: Richard Utz   160
F. N. Robinson's *Complete Works of Geoffrey Chaucer*
and the *Translatio* of Chaucer Studies to the United States

False Memories: The Dream of Chaucer   †Richard H. Osberg   204
and Chaucer's Dream in the Medieval Revival

Notes on Contributors   227

Volume XIX 2010

Two great principles divide the world, and contend for the mastery, antiquity and the middle ages. These are the two civilizations that have preceded us, the two elements of which ours is composed. All political as well as religious questions reduce themselves practically to this. This is the great dualism that runs through our society.

Lord Acton

Editorial Note

In the previous volume of this series, one of the essays defining medievalism dwells on the relationship of that field to a budding new area of interest – neomedievalism.[1] The authors, Carol L. Robinson and Pamela Clements, claim that much of what is often categorized as medievalism is in fact part of a new field related to the latter but characterized by a "complexity of ideologies" that is "further independent" and "further detached" from the Middle Ages. Indeed, according to Robinson and Clements, this new field is "consciously, purposefully, and perhaps even laughingly reshaping itself into an alternate universe of medievalisms, a fantasy of medievalisms, a meta-medievalism."

It is also expanding faster than perhaps any other area of academia. Many recent or forthcoming publications are completely devoted to it, most notably Robinson and Clements' anthology *The Medieval in Motion: Neomedievalism in Film, Television and Electronic Games*; an increasing number of sessions at the Annual International Congress on Medieval Studies in Kalamazoo, Michigan, have revolved around it, as in the panels last May on "Neomedievalist Communities" and "Gaming Neomedievally"; in 2007 it was the official focus of the entire 22nd Annual International Conference on Medievalism, "Neomedievalisms"; and it has been increasingly referenced by our contributors, particularly in the definitions of medievalism for the last two volumes of *SiM*.[2]

Moreover, as has been evident in all of those venues, it has inspired extraordinary passion. Indeed, in my five years of editing *SiM* and many more years of studying (neo)medievalism, I have rarely seen the degree of emotion that was on display during the 2007 conference, in and around the Kalamazoo sessions, and from the readers of Robinson and Clements' essay. Whether for or against the latter, virtually every one of our reviewers expressed themselves in unusually colorful language wrapped around an exceptionally polar position.

Which naturally spurred us to invite some of those scholars, as well as others who have weighed in on the debate, to define neomedievalism, particularly with regard to medievalism and in light of Robinson and Clements' remarks. Since the respondents did not have any official or, apparently, unofficial contact with each other, there is some overlap in their positions. But perhaps for that very reason, there is also much originality and diversity among them. Amy S. Kaufman celebrates aspects of Robinson and

Clements' definition, while insisting that, as neomedievalism treats the Middle Ages as "an ahistorical historical state to which it is possible to return," it is characterized by repetition, refraction, and a tendency to look forward. Brent and Kevin Moberly build on Baudrillard as they argue that neomedievalism "ultimately functions as a 'deterrence machine set up to rejuvenate the fiction of the real in the opposite camp.'" Lesley Coote sees parallels between medievalism and neomedievalism in their historiographic impulse, as well as in their presentation and re-presentation of the Middle Ages to deliver at least the feel of history, but she also insists that neomedievalism is distinct in its unending efforts "to escape from the parameters that '-isms' impose." Cory Lowell Grewell claims that neomedievalism is developing along the early lines of medievalism and is not (yet) so different from the latter or so strong that it should risk disassociating itself from the field that gave birth to it. M. J. Toswell proposes that neomedievalism invokes a simulacrum of, rather than a "genuine link" to, the medieval. E. L. Risden claims that neomedievalism "does not so much contribute new matter to the growing body of creative and scholarly endeavor of medievalism as it borrows creatively from the old matter; almost inevitably [reshaping] the metaphors and conventions of medievalism for new means of conveyance and for audiences more savvy with and interested in alternative media than in the Middle Ages and its more scholarly offshoots." And Lauryn S. Mayer suggests we should shift our discussions of neomedievalism from what it is to what it is doing, for she sees it as so nascent and dynamic as to resist classification at this point in time.

Of course, none of these contributions is the final word on its particular subject or on (neo)medievalism in general. But they have hopefully refined our discussion and perhaps even opened new approaches to such issues as the manner in which medium and format affect history and historiography, the role of self-referentiality, or at least self-consciousness, in our field(s), and the degree to which we can in fact define what we as academics think, do, and feel.

We also hope our readers will consider the essays in light of the articles in the second section of this volume, even as the essays provide new perspectives on one or more of those articles. Though none of the latter fulfills every criterion our essayists apply to neomedievalism, many of the articles qualify in at least one regard for this new area, and even those that do not may serve as informative foils to it. In "Utopia and Heterotopia: Byzantine Modernisms in America," Glenn Peers refracts modern echoes of the Eastern Roman Empire through Michel Foucault's contrast of utopia as a perfected form of society that does not exist and heterotopia as a counter-site "simultaneously represented, contested and inverted." In "Queer Crusading, Military Masculinity, and Allegories of Vietnam in Richard Lester's *Robin and Marian*,"

Tison Pugh examines how recent American foreign policy is critiqued by a 1976 film that expands and supplements non-heterosexual implications in a landmark of Anglo-American literature. In "Getting Reel with Grendel's Mother: The Abject Maternal and Social Critique," David W. Marshall argues that some recent film adaptations of *Beowulf* resonate with Julia Kristeva's notion of *abjection*, as they interpret Grendel's mother to be a threat to masculine social structures. In "False Memories: The Dream of Chaucer and Chaucer's Dream in the Medieval Revival," Richard H. Osberg looks at nineteenth-century distillations of a national(ist) myth. And in "The Colony Writes Back: F. N. Robinson's *Complete Works of Geoffrey Chaucer* and the *Translatio* of Chaucer Studies to the United States," Richard Utz looks at nationalist reactions to twentieth-century scholarship about the works behind that myth.

In other words, even as our authors demonstrate the extraordinary range and vivacity of medievalism as it has been traditionally defined, they challenge its boundaries, particularly with regard to neomedievalism. Though they completed their papers before seeing our essays on the latter, they build on much of the work that led to those essays, and they provide important tests for them. They join the essayists in an extraordinarily fruitful debate that is only beginning and will keep pressing us to refine our identities as (neo)medievalists.

NOTES

1. Carol L. Robinson and Pamela Clements, "Living with Neomedievalism," *Studies in Medievalism* 18 (2009): 55–75.
2. *The Medieval in Motion* is forthcoming from the Edwin Mellen Press.

Medieval Unmoored

Amy S. Kaufman

At the end of a fruitful conference on Neomedievalisms in London, Ontario, in October 2007, I found myself in the audience of a Dante panel in which participants launched into an unexpected debate over the title of the conference itself. Why, some wondered, do we even need the word neomedievalism? After all, we have a perfectly sound word, medievalism, that encompasses all manner of interaction with the Middle Ages. Strong arguments have been raised before, during, and after the conference against the use of the new term, including the objections of Leslie Workman, the founder of medievalism as a field of study.[1]

Defenses of neomedievalism at the 2007 conference revolved tentatively around technology, refraction, theory, postmodernism, and Umberto Eco, but more compelling cases for distinguishing medievalism from neomedievalism have been evolving since then.[2] Carol L. Robinson and Pamela Clements deliver the most comprehensive explanation in their 2009 essay "Living with Neomedievalism," in which they argue that "neomedievalism is further independent, further detached, and thus consciously, purposefully, and perhaps even laughingly reshaping itself into an alternate universe of medievalisms, a fantasy of medievalisms, a meta-medievalism."[3] This corresponds to the definition posted on the website for the Medieval Electronic Multimedia Organization (MEMO), which adds that "this vision lacks the nostalgia of earlier medievalisms in that it denies history."[4]

Robinson, Clements, and MEMO provide a definition of neomedievalism that is giddy and joyful, one that implies growth and progress along with the wisdom of self-conscious irony. As a result, it is an extremely attractive definition, although perhaps not to everyone. The implicit progress narrative that seems to lurk in such an account, one in which neomedievalism abandons its stodgy old parent, is sure to raise eyebrows, for though neomedievalism may do a fine job of abandoning the Middle Ages as a historical period, it fails to leave medievalism itself entirely behind. In other words, neomedievalists may deny history, but that certainly does not stop them from repeating it.

It is what continues to link neomedievalism to medievalism that concerns this essay, not with the intention of conflating the two, but with the hopes of complicating the notion of neomedievalism as progress while still relying on the diligent and, on the whole, I think, valid definition provided by Robinson and Clements. Workman's primary objection to the term, according to Kathleen Verduin, is that neomedievalism "tacitly limited the broader range of implications on which he insisted."[5] This might be remedied if neomedievalism is conceived of as functioning within particular limitations, not as a companion to or evolution of medievalism, but a functional subset of it, one of the multiple medievalisms argued for by Tom Shippey, Nils Holger Petersen, and Elizabeth Emery in the first of two *Defining Medievalism(s)* volumes of *Studies in Medievalism*.[6] Neomedievalism is one way of doing medievalism, one that requires certain philosophical and technological shifts in order to exist at all. Yet while medievalism can exist perfectly independently at any point in time, neo-medievalism, despite its seeming ahistoricity, is historically contingent upon both medievalism itself and the postmodern condition.

Neomedievalism is new because it is vexed in new ways. If medievalism can be said to work within a framework of distance (reverential or otherwise), then neomedievalism obliterates distance in an intensified combination of love and loathing, its desire for the past torn asunder between the denial of history and a longing for return. Kathleen Biddick has provocatively suggested that medieval studies is traumatized by its artificial separation from "non-academic" medievalism in the nineteenth century, at which time academic medievalism insisted on the radical alterity of the Middle Ages, one that would make them impossible to "know" through non-academic means. She thus calls for a new medieval studies that can do "the work of mourning."[7] While neomedievalism might seem to fit the bill at first, given that the mourning Biddick calls for "[...] does not find the lost object; it acknowledges its loss, thus suffering the lost object to be lost while maintaining a narrative connection to it," it ultimately fails at the goal of mourning: to "unfuse past, present, and future" and "return to the narrative relation of temporality."[8] Neomedievalism's denial of history, its anachronisms, distortions, and fragmentation, sound less like "mourning" and more like what Biddick describes as the manifestations of trauma:

> Since its content is not grasped when it occurs, a traumatic loss has no present and therefore resists conventional contextualization based on either diachrony or synchrony. Trauma also resists representation since its traces recur *fragmentarily* in flashbacks, nightmares, and other repetitious phenomena. *Past and present symbolically fuse in such repetition*, and, in so doing, the possibility of futurity – change – is foreclosed. Such fusing is typical of melancholy.[9]

Biddick's account of melancholy relies on remarkably similar descriptors to the definition of neomedievalism offered by Robinson, Clements, and MEMO, in which "Histories are purposely *fragmented*" and in which history itself is denied. If the schism between medievalism and medieval studies resulted in trauma, then neomedievalism may be a new symptom, one that appeared when postmodernism further separated medievalism from its desired object. The medieval past as an object, in other words, has been lost twice: first, when nineteenth-century medieval studies insisted on the radical alterity of the Middle Ages, and then again, when we all learned that history was relative and were asked to reject the very positivism that caused the traumatic split. Neomedievalism finds a way of clinging to the past by rejecting the "history," the alterity, the time and space that separated it from its desired object and bringing it into the present. But what initially appears to be neomedievalism's denial of history may, instead, be a desire for history alongside the uncomfortable suspicion that there is no such thing. Neomedievalism consumes the Middle Ages in fragmented, repetitive tropes as a way of ensuring against loss. And as we shall see, in many of neomedievalism's manifestations, futurity is foreclosed, for the future leads only to the past.

Through a (Cracked) Glass, Darkly

Repetition and refraction are generally acknowledged to be key facets of neomedievalism.[10] The neomedieval idea of the Middle Ages is gained not through contact with the Middle Ages, but through a medievalist intermediary: Tolkien's *Lord of the Rings* series, T. H. White's *Once and Future King*, or even books by medieval scholars, such as Linda Malcor and C. Scott Littleton's *From Scythia to Camelot*, which heavily influenced the 2004 film *King Arthur*. Neomedievalism is thus not a dream of the Middle Ages, but a dream of someone else's medievalism. It is medievalism doubled up upon itself.

Refraction, however, is inadequate for categorizing a "new" medievalism. First, the prefix of the term, *neo*, implies that there is something specifically new, specifically different, about this brand of medievalism, and there is nothing new about accusations that medievalism in any of its forms is a distortion. Secondly, such a definition too closely echoes the academic's "medievalism as error" fallacy.[11] But as Robinson and Clements argue, "it is not just the distortion of the medieval that makes a work neomedieval *but the nature of that distortion*."[12] The distortion is not error, but choice, owing in part to a postmodern vision of malleable and impermanent history in which error is simultaneously impossible and inevitable.

Live Action Role Players, colloquially "LARPers," are a fine example of this facet of neomedievalism. LARPers deck themselves in homemade leather leggings and chainmail, arm themselves with foam-padded weapons and bags of birdseed meant to represent magic spells, and venture together into the wooded areas surrounding such unlikely locales as Atlanta, Georgia, in order to collectively suspend disbelief in modernity. Despite the homemade chainmail and their otherwise vivid imaginations, they are not really trying to replicate the Middle Ages, and few of them imagine that they are.[13] LARPers, instead, immerse themselves in the products of medievalism: games like the wildly popular *Dungeons & Dragons* world, both the pen-and-paper version and its many virtual offshoots, as well as the fantasy environs of Tolkien's *Lord of the Rings*. Thus, when the stockbroker hits the trial lawyer over the head with a well-padded steel pipe, she imagines herself in Lothlórien or Waterdeep rather than Tintagel or Brocéliande.

Here, suspended in the image of a leather-clad stockbroker and her foam pipe, is where my definition of neomedievalism deviates slightly from "Living with Neomedievalism." In their definition of neomedievalism, Robinson and Clements argue that "'medieval' equals simply 'other.'"[14] Yet it seems likely that to our stockbroker, this refracted version of the Middle Ages is not necessarily other, but self. In her created world, the Middle Ages as she imagines them both belong to her and include her. However she acquired it, this is the only medieval that matters. Neomedievalism is not as interested in creating or recreating the Middle Ages as it is in assimilating and consuming it. The danger of assimilation, of course, is that the essence and the beauty of difference can be lost.

Before we fall back on familiar accusations of anachronism, however, we must consider for a moment how medieval scholars are complicit in this rendering. Most of us teach within a system that is increasingly insistent on both the practical application of classroom knowledge and on making sure students can "relate" to material. Such an environment makes professors of medieval studies eager to enlist the aid of popular medievalisms, which enable us to drag students into the past without hearing any complaints against its uselessness and its distance. What medieval studies professor these days has not put Arthurian films on the syllabus (or even designed a whole course around them), passed around a medieval-themed graphic novel, or let students do their homework on the Xbox in order to make their classes more timely, more relevant, or more exciting? This has served us well as teachers and even given some of us a surprising cachet among colleagues who, just a few short years ago, probably felt sorry for us most of the time. Do our classrooms aggravate the suspension of time, the irreverence for history, by manipulating popular neomedievalisms, or are they merely the products of them? Either way, they are exemplary of an increased tendency both academically and culturally to drag the Middle Ages *out* of the past and transport it to the present. Possessing the Middle Ages in this way is one solution to overcoming the double trauma of what some scholars have called the "hard-edged alterity" of the past, one that renders it unknowable, as well as the loss of the past instigated by postmodernism, which renders it disparate and imagined.[15] One of neomedievalism's defining features is therefore its exceptional, sometimes insufferable presentism. Despite its desire to erase time, neomedievalism is situated in time: it just happens to be our time. Neomedievalism's dreams, however, extend far beyond the present.

Back to the Future

The prefix *neo* has a second implication that I take to refer to its vision: it suggests looking forward rather than backward. Neomedievalism dreams of an impending, inevitable new Middle Ages in the future. The most obvious manifestations of this dream appear in the post-apocalyptic neomedievalisms of science fiction and fantasy. For instance, Robert Jordan's *Wheel of Time* series seems from all early appearances to take place in a thoroughly medievalist universe; it even contains characters with names like *Nynaeve* al'Meara and Thom *Merrilin*. And yet, in the fourth book, *The Shadow Rising*, the reader learns with some alarm that the castles, forests, and sword-and-sorcery state of affairs is, in fact, a reversion: Once there were cars. Once there were airplanes. The past even held skyscrapers, democracy, and feminism, all of which ended with the explosion of a mysterious weapon that wiped out everything, including an entire species of tree.[16] The "new" Middle Ages of the *Wheel of Time* is the logical conclusion of an excess of progress. A similar neomedievalism is the premise of S. M. Stirling's *Dies the Fire*, in which a mysterious event wipes out all technological innovations, and before you know it, hyper-masculine airplane pilots are building crossbows while self-styled warlords lead lingerie-clad women around in chains.[17] In both texts, the fantasy of the medieval, though full of pain, fear, suffering, evil, and self-indulgent gender discrimination (even Jordan's feistiest female characters exhibit an incongruous fondness for being spanked), is clearly a preferable state of affairs to the dangerous indeterminacy of the present. If we are reconciled to the idea that we can never "have" the past, even in the past, then we shall make due by transporting it forward, either to the here and now, or better yet, into the future.

Neomedievalism sees the possibility of the Middle Ages as a cycle, an ahistorical historical state to which it is possible to return. The fantasy of return also brings us to the dismal neomedieval forecasts of scholars in political science, economics, and international relations, which warn that, in the words of Stephen J. Kobrin, "The modern era may be a window which is about to slam shut."[18] Surveys of such approaches and their implications from a humanist's perspective have been treated elsewhere; my concern here is the neomedievalist praxis of the theorists themselves.[19] They, too, assimilate a particular set of "medieval" tropes, refracted through medievalism, into the present, and thus read everything from gated communities, private security, and the European Union to Bill Gates (whom one imaginative writer labels a "postmodern Medici") as neomedieval.[20] That such readings are exercises in neomedievalism as much as studies of them is clear both from their free-play of symbolism and from accounts such as Stephen J. Kobrin's article "Back to the Future: Neomedievalism and the Postmodern Digital World Economy," which argues that increasingly globalized trade and the disappearing nation state represent a "detour" toward a new Middle Ages.[21] In order to help us imagine what this looks like, Kobrin proceeds down what at first seems like a logical path, until it takes a rather startling turn:

> A closer look at medieval Europe, the "immediate" past, can help us imagine our postmodern global future. In the *Star Wars Trilogy*, Darth Vader is clad in the armor of the traditional villain of medieval epics – the Black Knight – and he and Luke Skywalker duel with laser sabers in a fight that, but for the weapons, would be at home in *Henry IV*. Similarly, the costumes in the futuristic *Waterworld* have been described as neomedieval iron and kelp. In politics and economics, as in science fiction movies, it may help to attempt to visualize the unknown future in terms of the known past.[22]

The easy leap from medieval Europe to battle scenes on the Death Star is especially telling: Kobrin's examples are not thoughtful examinations of the Middle Ages that help us to understand our past and future, but indiscriminate assimilations of medieval tropes into neomedieval, futuristic settings. Hence, Kobrin's essay on neomedievalism is, perhaps, one of the best examples *of* neomedievalism that a humanities scholar could hope to find. It is, like its cinematic analogues, an exercise in consumption.

The consumable Middle Ages are themselves deeply limited. When social scientists wring their hands and warn of return, they imagine one kind of Middle Age: the Western European one. The specter of "return" denies the reality that there have always been Middle Ages in the plural. Medievalism and neomedievalism in the humanities are no different. M. J. Toswell notes that, "Incidentally, the Middle Ages under discussion by way of the term 'medievalism' denote only the Western, more specifically the European and North American, approach to the years 500–1500."[23] But why, one wonders, should this be the case with neomedievalism, which has an irreverence for convention and a spirit of free play, not to mention the postmodern recognition that Western culture was not isolated, autonomous, or uninfluenced by the civilizations thriving around it?

Despite its scattered and inclusive surface, neomedievalism tends to be homogenizing in what it selects from the past. If neomedievalism wants to erase the unknowable, erase distance, then it must also erase difference. Its rejection of history, its spirit of integrating past and present, often cause *all* of the Middle Ages to be absorbed completely into a Western notion of the medieval: knights, European castles, court ladies, Christian spirituality. The dark side of neomedievalism's lingering attachment to medievalism is that it inherited a school of thought that developed at the height of Eurocentricism and cultural oppression, along with its tendencies to ignore, to demonize, or to assimilate the "other." Thus, neomedievalism sometimes borrows tropes from feudal Japan, the landscape of *One Thousand and One Nights*, or Native American spirituality, but it tends to absorb and redefine these symbols, stripping them of their cultural baggage and leaving only essentialized incarnations of the Western imagination. A minor case in point is virtual *Dungeons & Dragons* games in which a wide array of weapons is available for the player to purchase or loot, including the katana, the kukri, and the shuriken. These three are labeled "exotic" weapons and hence require special proficiencies. Nor are these weapons attached in any way to the cultures that formed them. Instead, characters wield such "exotic" weapons while wearing "traditional" Western armor and prancing through remarkably proto-European landscapes.[24] Non-European game worlds are rare, and when they do exist (such as the jungles of Chult in *Storm of Zehir*, an expansion game for *Neverwinter Nights 2*), the locals and the landscape are markedly prehistoric, not medieval. Chult, for instance, is even plagued by dinosaurs.[25] Thus non-Western cultures, if not absorbed into the European Middle Ages, are generally excluded from the cultural fantasy of the medieval. Neomedievalism, despite its lofty promises, is in danger of colonizing the past as effectively as Renaissance, Restoration, and Victorian Europe colonized the rest of the world.

MEMO's website optimistically notes that neomedievalism is dominated by contemporary values, which "rewrite the traditional perceptions of the European Middle Ages, even infusing other medieval cultures, such as that of Japan."[26] If infusion is on the way to transforming into recognition, then neomedievalism may eventually recognize a multiplicity of Middle Ages. This, too, would take it down the path of healing trauma, of unfusing past, present, and future, for acknowledging history is essential to imagining true diversity. Perhaps we might even dream of multiple, global Middle Ages interacting within an inclusive, dynamic cultural fantasy. Now *that* would be a new medievalism.

NOTES

1. As Kathleen Verduin writes of Leslie Workman, "'neo-medievalism,' suggestive of intentional (and hence usually fatuous) efforts at regeneration, was a coinage he abhorred, since it tacitly limited the broader range of implications on which he insisted. [...] Instead, medievalism involved any engagement with the Middle Ages, conscious or unconscious, from the lunatic fringe of medievalist kitsch to the most solemn scholarship and from approximately 1500 to the present and beyond." Kathleen Verduin, "The Founding and the Founder," *Studies in Medievalism* 17 (2009): 23–24.

2. Umberto Eco coins the term "neomedievalism" in "Dreaming of the Middle Ages," *Travels in Hyperreality*, trans. William Weaver (San Diego, CA: Harcourt, 1986). He does so in such a way, however, as to make it difficult to distinguish from Leslie Workman's definition. For further discussion of the similarities between the two terms, see Elizabeth Emery, "Medievalism and the Middle Ages," *Studies in Medievalism* 17 (2009): 68–76 (83); and Carol L. Robinson and Pamela Clements, "Living with Neomedievalism," *Studies in Medievalism* 18 (2009): 55–75 (59).

3. Robinson and Clements, "Living with Neomedievalism," 56. Additional definitions include M. J. Toswell's, who argues that "new medievalism(s) [...] appears to mean new approaches to the study of the medieval period (and particularly approaches using new theoretical paradigms)," in "The Tropes of Medievalism," *Studies in Medievalism* 17 (2009): 68–76 (68–69). Emery also argues that Eco's term might be useful to define a sub-category of medievalism of "those who create a vision filtered through previous examples of medievalism" ("Medievalism and the Middle Ages," 83).

4. <http://medievalelectronicmultimedia.org/definitions.html>.

5. Verduin, "The Founding and the Founder," 23.

6. Tom Shippey, "Medievalisms and Why They Matter," *Studies in Medievalism* 17 (2009): 45–54 (48); Nils Holger Peterson, "Medievalism and Medieval Reception: A Terminological Question," *Studies in Medievalism* 17 (2009): 36–44; Emery, "Medievalism and the Middle Ages," 83–84.

7. Kathleen Biddick, *The Shock of Medievalism* (Durham, NC: Duke University Press, 1998), 1–15. Biddick explains that "In order to separate and elevate themselves from popular studies of medieval culture, the new academic medievalists of the nineteenth century designated their practices, influenced by positivism, as scientific and eschewed what they regarded as less-positivist, 'nonscientific' practices, labeling them *medievalism*" (1).

8. Biddick, *The Shock of Medievalism*, 10.

9. Biddick, *The Shock of Medievalism*, 10 (emphasis mine).

10. For instance, Robinson and Clements argue that neomedievalism "does not look to the Middle Ages to use, to study, to copy, or even to learn; the perception of the Middle Ages is more filtered, perceptions of perceptions (and of distortions), done without a concern for facts of reality, such as the fact that The Knights Who Say 'Ni' never existed," "Living with Neomedievalism," 62. See also Emery, "Medievalism and the Middle Ages," 83–84; and Verduin, "The Founding and the Founder," 23.

11. See Gwendolyn A. Morgan, "Medievalism, Authority, and the Academy," *Studies in Medievalism* 17 (2009): 55–67 (56); and Biddick, *The Shock of Medievalism*, 4.

12. Robinson and Clements, "Living with Neomedievalism," 64.

13. As a result, academic analyses of Live Action Role Playing rarely even mention the word "medieval," and LARPers tend to emphasize the fantasy dimensions of their created universe when they are interviewed; they do not consider themselves historical re-enactors. See, for instance, Marinka Copier, "Connecting Worlds. Fantasy Role-Playing Games, Ritual Acts and the Magic Circle," *Proceedings of DiGRA 2005 Conference: Changing Views – Worlds in Play*, <http://www.digra.org/dl/db/06278.50594.pdf> and an interview with LARPers at <http://people.howstuffworks.com/larp.htm>.

14. Robinson and Clements, "Living with Neomedievalism," 63.

15. For the phrase "hard-edged alterity," see *The New Medievalism*, ed. Marina S. Brownlee, Kevin Brownlee, and Stephen G. Nichols (Baltimore, MD: Johns Hopkins University Press, 1991), 12; and Stephen G. Nichols, "Modernism and the Politics of Medieval Studies," in *Medievalism and the Modernist Temper*, ed. R. Howard Bloch and Stephen G. Nichols (Baltimore, MD: Johns Hopkins University Press, 1996), 25–56 (49). However, see Biddick, *The Shock of Medievalism*, 4, for the deconstruction of this term.

16. See Robert Jordan, *The Shadow Rising* (New York: Tor Books,

1993). Cars and airplanes are coyly referred to as "jo-cars" and "sho-wings," respectively, and skyscrapers as "silvery buildings that touched the sky." People also call one another "Citizen," a marked distinction from the feudal system in the rest of the novels, and the male narrator is considering repeated and insistent formal marriage proposals from a woman (435–36).

17. S. M. Stirling, *Dies the Fire: A Novel of the Change* (New York: Penguin [ROC], 2004).

18. Stephen J. Kobrin, "Back to the Future: Neomedievalism and the Postmodern Digital World Economy," *Journal of International Affairs* 51.2 (1998): 361–86 (364).

19. See especially Bruce Holsinger, *Neomedievalism, Neoconservatism, and The War on Terror* (Chicago: Prickly Paradigm Press, 2007); and Emily Apter, "Mobile Citizens, Media States," *PMLA* 117.1 (January 2002): 79–83.

20. Parag Khanna, "Neomedievalism," *Foreign Policy* (May/June 2009): 91. See also Robert Kaplan, "The Coming Anarchy," *Atlantic Monthly* (February 1994): 44; and Kobrin, "Back to the Future," 366.

21. Kobrin, "Back to the Future," 364.

22. Kobrin, "Back to the Future," 364.

23. M. J. Toswell, "The Tropes of Medievalism," *Studies in Medievalism* 17 (2009): 68–76 (69).

24. The *Dungeons & Dragons* role-playing universe made some attempts to create non-Western realms (such as Kara-tur, which represents Asia, and Anaurauch, a desert in the style of the Middle East). Descriptions of these realms, which reinforce their distance from the "real" Middle Ages, can be found in *D&D* handbooks with such titles as *Unapproachable East* by Richard Baker, Matt Forbeck, and Sean K. Reynolds (Renton, WA: Wizards of the Coast, 2003). These did not translate well to virtual-gaming formats, which suggests that the realms may be outside the imaginative limits of designers, at least for now.

25. Chult is described in the most recent *Forgotten Realms Campaign Guide* as "a savage land of fearsome jungles plagued by carnivorous monsters. Human civilization is virtually nonexistent here." Bruce R. Cordell, et. al, *Forgotten Realms Campaign Guide* (Renton, WA: Wizards of the Coast, 2008), 102.

26. <http://medievalelectronicmultimedia.org/definitions.html>.

Neomedievalism, Hyperrealism, and Simulation

Brent Moberly and Kevin Moberly

"Everything is metamorphosed into its opposite to perpetuate itself in expurgated form."
Jean Baudrillard, Simulacra and Simulation[1]

Although most definitions of the neomedieval begin with Umberto Eco's "Return of the Middle Ages," we feel that it is more appropriate to begin with his "Travels in Hyperreality," as it is here that Eco describes the interplay between the authentic and the inauthentic, the historical, mythical, and the technological that constitutes neo-medievalism as a representational strategy.[2] Searching for instances "where the American imagination demands the real thing and, to attain it, must fabricate the absolute fake," Eco's essay invariably leads him to the Movieland Wax Museum and the Palace of the Living Arts in Buena Park, California. Standing beside each other, these museums present visitors with what, to Eco, is the contemporary equivalent of the *Wunderkammern* that were popular in Renaissance Europe – collections of curiosities in which a "unicorn's horn would be found next to a copy of a Greek statue, and later, among mechanical crèches and wondrous automata, cocks of precious metal that sang, clocks with a procession of little figures that paraded at noon."[3] As in these Renaissance collections, Movieland and the Palace of the Living Arts mix the historical and the fictional for maximum effect. Movieland restages famous moments from feature films, dressing wax statues of notable actors and famous movie characters in period clothing and posing them among period furniture and other artifacts. The Palace of

Living Arts employs similar techniques to recreate famous works of art. The result, as Eco writes, is not simply that "the 'completely real' becomes identified with the 'completely fake',", but that the two function to validate each other.[4] The period props, furniture, and clothing displayed in the exhibits make the wax statues of the film stars appear more realistic, more authentic, and more true-to-life, while the statues themselves, which are promoted as authentic copies of their originals, make the furniture, clothing, and other objects appear to be more than simply antiques requisitioned for the exhibits.

A similar interplay takes place amongst the exhibits themselves. Movieland visitors, for example, discover Mozart and Tom Sawyer standing within feet of each other, and, as Eco relates, "enter the cave of The Planet of the Apes after having witnessed the Sermon on the Mount with Jesus and the Apostles."[5] Not content only to reproduce individual works of art, the Palace of the Living Arts presents visitors with a full-size reproduction of Leonardo da Vinci painting the *Mona Lisa* in his workshop and, in the next moment, with the "Aristotle of Rembrandt, contemplating the bust of Homer."[6] Visitors to the museums also often discover that they have become part of the exhibits. As Eco explains:

> The scenes unfold in full continuum, in total darkness, so that there are no gaps between the niches occupied by the waxworks, but rather a kind of connective décor that enhances the sensation. As a rule there are mirrors, so that on your right you see Dracula raising the lid of a tomb, and on the left your own face reflected next to Dracula's, while at times there is a glimmering figure of Jack the Ripper, or of Jesus, duplicated by an astute play of corners, curves, and perspective until it is hard to decide which side is reality and which is illusion.[7]

To Eco, Movieland and the Palace of the Living Arts are emblematic of hyperreality. Designed to sell visitors an experience that is simultaneously more realistic and more fantastic than anything they have yet encountered, the museums do not simply seek to reproduce or copy their subjects. They offer visitors versions of the originals that are somehow better or more complete, even if the original was fictional or never existed. As Eco writes, the "philosophy is not, 'We are giving you the reproduction so that you will not want the original,' but rather, 'We are giving you the reproduction so that you will no longer feel the need for the original.'"[8]

Although Eco draws his examples of hyperrealism from the museums, theme parks, and roadside attractions that dot the American landscape, he could have easily described many of the works of cultural production that are characterized as neomedieval. As the primary producer and custodian of many of the works of "fantastic neomedievalism" that Eco cites in his "The Return of the Middle Ages," popular culture expresses its fascination with the medieval through many of the techniques that Eco encounters in his search for hyperreality.[9] Take Peter Jackson's cinematic adaptations of Tolkien's *The Lord of the Rings*, for example.[10] Mixing the historical, mythical, and the technological, Jackson's films blend computer-generated characters and scenery with live actors, props, and real-world sets and locations. In doing so, the films recreate Tolkien's Middle Earth with an absolute realism that is apparent even in minor details such as the half-timbered framing of the houses in Hobbiton, the Celtic tracings on various bits and pieces of armor, and the figures meticulously carved into many of the heavy wooden doors of the films' sets. Yet, as is the case with Movieland and the Palace of the Living Arts, these films do not simply aim to copy or reproduce Tolkien's novels, but rather (if the text overlays in the *Fellowship of the Ring* trailer can be believed) to bring the novels "to life" just in time for the 2001 Christmas shopping season.[11]

Peter Jackson's films seek, in other words, to produce a version of Tolkien that is more Tolkien than Tolkien – a total audience experience that, supplemented through computer games, toys, and endless DVD extras, promises the same sort of privileged access to the site of production as the *Mona Lisa* exhibit in the Palace of the Living Arts. The irony, of course, is that Tolkien employs many of the same techniques in his fiction, though perhaps with less commercial zeal. Following the formula he outlines in his essay "On Fairy Stories," Tolkien creates Middle Earth by mixing the authentic, the inauthentic, the historical, and the mythical. He not only appropriates names and folk elements from Old Norse, Anglo-Saxon, Germanic, and other European traditions, but composes languages, legends, and music, all of which he maps onto a landscape that, according to Paul Kocher, often seems more mundane than magical.[12] Moreover, Tolkien presents *The Lord of the Rings* as part of a larger philological project, constructing the narrator of the work as a scholar who has pieced together the details of Frodo's journey during the War of the

Ring from a variety of primary and secondary sources.[13] Playing with the distinction between author, scholar, and narrator, Tolkien offers readers a version of himself that is genuinely fake, but which nevertheless employs an academic prose that, in the prologue and appendixes, appears as authentic (and therefore as fictional) as any of the languages that he composes for the elves or the dwarves.[14] Like the period decoration of the wax statues Eco encounters in Movieland, these elements are amplified and accentuated by the presence of the inauthentic, and function, in turn, to amplify and accentuate the inauthentic. As Baudrillard writes in *Simulacra and Simulation*, the effect is that the "whole system becomes weightless, it is no longer itself anything but a gigantic simulacrum – not unreal, but a simulacrum, that is to say never exchanged for the real, but exchanged for itself, in an uninterrupted circuit without reference or circumference."[15]

Neomedieval works, in this sense, do not simply seek to describe, reproduce, or otherwise recover the medieval, but instead employ contemporary techniques and technologies to simulate the medieval – that is, to produce a version of the medieval that is more medieval than the medieval, a version of the medieval that can be seen and touched, bought and sold, and therefore owned. Neomedieval works thus abolish what, to Baudrillard, is the sovereign difference between the real and the representational – between the territory and the map. In doing so, they produce a version of the medieval that, as Baudrillard writes about simulation in general, "is no longer really the real" in the sense that its point of origin is not a historical epoch or event, but a conglomeration of models and data in which the medieval and all of the traits traditionally associated with it (nobility, chivalry, feudalism, etc.) become indistinguishable from and equivalent to any number of other historical, fictional, and mythical elements.[16] The result is a hyperreal medievalism – a neomedievalism that, as Baudrillard points out, is not only reproduced ad-infinitum "from miniaturized cells, matrices, and memory banks, models of control," but that, as a consequence, also "no longer needs to be rational, because it no longer measures itself against either an ideal or negative instance."[17]

If the neomedieval has a privileged mode of performance, it is not the epic, the romance, the novel, or any of the other medieval or modern genres it simulates, but what Guy Debord understands as the spectacle. As Debord argues in his 1974 work, *The Society of the*

Spectacle, the "spectacle is not a collection of images; rather, it is a social relationship between people that is mediated by images."[18] The spectacle, as such, is "capital accumulated to the point where it becomes image."[19] At once symbolic and material, it is a demonstration of the power of capitalism and its underlying social relationships to produce, commodify, and therefore control the lived experience of its subjects. As Debord explains:

> The world the spectacle holds up to view is at once here and elsewhere; it is the world of the commodity ruling over all lived experience. The commodity world is thus shown as it really is, for its logic is one with men's estrangement from one another and from the sum total of what they produce.[20]

Debord's point is immediately obvious in the wax museums Eco tours and in Peter Jackson's *Lord of the Rings* trilogy. Although these works seek to reproduce unreality rather than reality "as it really is," they nevertheless embody what, to Debord, is one of the fundamental symptoms of late-capitalist society in which "all effective 'having' must derive its immediate prestige and its ultimate raison d'être from appearances."[21] Proof positive of the power of capitalism to produce and package the real, these works testify to the fetishized status of the image in a society whose representations appear (as Marx writes about commodities in general) to possess lives of their own that are independent of and superior to those of the people who produce them.[22]

The neomedieval achieves its fullest articulation as spectacle in Massively-Multiplayer Online Role-playing Games (MMORPGs) such as *World of Warcraft*.[23] Like many contemporary computer games that invoke the medieval, *World of Warcraft* presents players with a fully realized neomedieval world that is constructed entirely from images. Organized around a topography that recalls the medieval romance, the game's landscape constitutes a number of imperiled settlements that serve as centers of commerce and quest hubs, and which are perpetually threatened by vast tracts of ever-encroaching wilderness.[24] As players travel between these settlements, they encounter the usual "authentic" Tolkienesque menagerie of dwarves, elves, orcs, goblins, and dragons, along with other recognizably medieval or pseudo-medieval elements.[25] Players also discover, however, some unsettling allusions to mass culture. In Stranglethorn Vale, an immense marble statue of a goblin with its arms outstretched like those of Rio de Janeiro's *O Cristo Redentor* overlooks the pirate town of Booty Bay. In Netherstorm, a rocket ship that looks very much like the one that Marvin the Martian used in the Bugs Bunny cartoons stands at the center of an outpost named "Area 52." The gnomes and goblins that populate the outpost at the center of the Shimmering Flats regularly stage races between homemade contraptions that look suspiciously like the pod racers from *Star Wars*. Not to be outdone, the inhabitants of Toshley's Station (another gratuitous *Star Wars* reference) reprise a well-known scene from the film *Starship Troopers* as they fight for their lives against an onslaught of insect-like ravagers.[26]

World of Warcraft interpolates players into this world as images. Promising a "living, breathing, online world […] of myth, magic and limitless adventure" in which an "infinity of experiences await," the game requires players to construct avatars for themselves by selecting and combining a number of predefined images that correspond to social variables such as race, age, gender, and class, and which function to represent these choices in the game to other players.[27] When players enter the world of the game proper, they discover that everything in the world is accomplished through images. To travel from place to place, for example, players must maneuver their avatars among, around, and through the images that constitute the game's landscape, architecture, and inhabitants. To interact with one of these inhabitants, players must first select its image, and then select the icon that represents the appropriate response in the menus that subsequently appear. Combat is likewise accomplished through an icon-driven system that translates the offensive or defensive choices that players make into a series of animations that are played out in real-time on the screen. Even interaction with other players is facilitated through images – through the game's system of animated emotes and the endless lines of text communication that, color-coded, fill the chat windows superimposed over the three-dimensional landscape.

As with the mirrors and other technological tricks that the Movieland Wax museum employs to integrate visitors (as images) into the space of the exhibits, the result is that players in MMORPGs invariably become spectacles themselves. As they advance in the game, completing quests, vanquishing creatures, and venturing further and further into its wilderness, players are not only exposed to more and more images, but accumulate more and more images – weapons, armor, mounts, currency, and various other items. Represented as icons in their characters' inventories, and as three-dimensional models in the space of the game, these items function as visual emblems that display the prowess of individual characters both for the players who control (own) them and for other players who come into contact with them. Understood in this sense, *World of Warcraft* presents players with a panoptic world of surveillance and counter-surveillance that is not only manifested, as Debord writes about contemporary society in general, "as an immense accumulation of spectacles," but that structures participation as an essentially alienated series of actions that is never performed by the players themselves, but by avatars that represent and constrain the players that control them.[28] The result, as Debord explains, is that the player is ultimately alienated by his or her in-game representation:

> The spectator's alienation from and submission to the contemplated object [...] works like this: the more he contemplates, the less he lives; the more readily he recognizes his own needs in the images of need proposed by the dominant system, the less he understands his own existence and desires. The spectacle's externality with respect to the acting subject is demonstrated by the fact that the individual's gestures are no longer his own, but rather those of someone else who represents him.[29]

This recursive, hall-of-mirrors-like effect produces a version of the medieval that is wholly subsumed by its own spectacle. A testament to the power of third-stage capitalism to produce and commodity the real, the neomedieval spectacle not only demonstrates the power and the prowess of the society that produces it, but in doing so, involves its audience in an idealized version of the social hierarchy.

Neomedieval works are, in this sense, very different from the works that define late-nineteenth- and early-to-mid-twentieth-century medievalism. These works were a reaction to burgeoning technologies of capitalism, most notably industrialization. As was the case with medievalesque pageants, celebrations, and spectacles, along with works such as Arthur Conan Doyle's *The White Company* and the various volumes of the Victoria County History Series, they allowed the elite and aspiring elite to imagine the origins of their authority in localized, historical precedent.[30] Neomedievalism, by contrast, deconstructs the historical and heraldic claims of medievalism with apparent irreverence. Noble birth, as such, no longer becomes a matter of historical or genealogical precedent, but merely "a detail" – as William Thatcher, the peasant protagonist of Brian Helgeland's 2001 film, *A Knight's Tale*, puts it.[31] The neomedieval, however, does not entirely abandon the medievalist fervor for such concepts as knighthood, chivalry, romance, or quests; instead it commodifies them, extending these privileges to anyone who can afford them. The result is an egalitarian, consumerist version of the medieval in which nobility is measured by one's purchasing power.

Many neomedievalist works make this point explicitly. In *A Knight's Tale*, for instance, Thatcher only comes into his own as Sir Ulrich von Lichtenstein from Gelderland after acquiring the latest in armor technology, prominently embossed with a Nike swoosh.[32] Likewise, a recent Mountain Dew campaign invites players to "choose your side" in the fight between the Alliance and the Horde for the control of Azeroth by buying *World of Warcraft*-themed versions of the drink. In one ad for the campaign, two shoppers transform into an orc and a night elf and turn the checkout aisle of their local supermarket into an impromptu battlefield.[33] Nobility, in this sense, does not simply mean being able to participate in *World of Warcraft* – that is, possessing the leisure time and the capital to afford the game and the minimum of technology that it requires. Measured in terms of conspicuous consumption, nobility means possessing a degree of capital that affords players a significant advantage over others – a fast computer, a fast internet connection, and enough surplus leisure time to access content that is too resource intensive for less fortunate players. Nobility, however, also means being able to afford the soda, t-shirts, collector's editions, novelizations, playing-card games, figurines, and all of the other material manifestations of an otherwise digital gaming experience.

Designed to demonstrate the power of democratic capitalism to provide something for everyone, neomedievalism thus reproduces the Middle Ages with conspicuous plurality, producing version after version of the medieval, each of which promises an experience that is more authentic than the last. At the same time, however, the neomedieval also works to reproduce the very notion that social privilege in capitalism is dependent on – the notion that there is something that not everyone can have, something that can be owned only by the wealthy, and against which the value of everything else is determined.

Caught in this double-imperative, many neomedievalist texts insist on the real even as they deconstruct it. Works like C. S. Lewis's *Chronicles of Narnia* and J. K. Rowling's *Harry Potter* series, for example, propose medievalesque realms that do not proceed, but exist in tandem with contemporary reality. In these works, the transition between the actual and the medieval is often traumatic.[34] Accomplished through various boundaries that divide the fantastic from the actual – Lewis's wardrobe or Rowling's Diagon Alley or Platform 9¾– the transition to the medieval is invariably constructed so that it becomes synonymous with (and representative of) the trauma of the protagonists as they struggle to make the transition from adolescence to adulthood. These works thus foreground a trope that is implicit even in novels such as Tolkien's, which present the medieval as a precursor to the actual. They construct the medieval as an accessory to the real, a ready-made and authentic experience that, as in Victor Fleming's 1939 *Wizard of Oz*, offers the consumer privileged, Technicolor access to a fetishized world of adolescent wish-fulfillment in which the anxieties and struggles of the mundane play out through a relentless succession of ever more improbable and fantastic creatures.

As Baudrillard writes about Disneyland, the neomedieval is thus implicated in a larger strategy of deterrence that functions to "rejuvenate the fiction of the real in the opposite camp."[35] Indeed, the neomedieval does not simply propose worlds that, self-contained, are free from the constraints and complications of the actual. As with Gandalf driving his wagon-load of fireworks into the shire, it raises the possibility that the boundaries between the real and the unreal, the historical, the fantastic, and the fictional are not as well defined or as well policed as one would like. In doing so, the neomedieval stages its own death, calling attention at every turn to the fact that it is not real – that despite the conspicuous realism of its spectacles, it is constructed and consumerist, an exercise in adolescent wish-fulfillment. The neomedieval thus presents itself, as Baudrillard writes about Disneyland, "as imaginary in order to make us believe that the rest is real."[36] Openly promoting itself as only offering a simulation, via displacement, of the medieval, it presents itself as "childish in order to make us believe that the adults are elsewhere, in the 'real' world, and to conceal the fact that true childishness is everywhere – that is that of the adults themselves who come here to act the child in order to foster illusions as to their real childishness."[37] The neomedieval, in this sense, is implicated in what, to Baudrillard, is the "only solution-alibi of every power, of every institution attempting to break the vicious circle of its irresponsibility and of its fundamental nonexistence, of its already seen and of its already dead."[38] As with other contemporary manifestations of simulation and hyperreality, the neomedieval presents itself as a product, and in doing so, reaffirms, through the negative, the belief that there is something out there that has not yet been commodified – the belief, perhaps, that it is still possible to speak about, write about, study, or otherwise recover a real middle ages.

NOTES

1. Jean Baudrillard, *Simulacra and Simulation*, trans. Sheila Faria Glaser (Ann Arbor: University of Michigan Press, 2002), 19.

2. Umberto Eco, "Travels in Hyperreality," in *Travels in Hyperreality*, trans. William Weaver (San Diego, CA: Harcourt Brace Jovanovich, 1986), 3–56. Recent discussions of neomedievalism that invoke Eco's "Living in the Middle Ages" include Emily Apter's "Mobile Citizens, Media States: A Panel at the 2000 MLA Convention," *PMLA* 117:1 (2002): 79–83 (80); and Carol L. Robinson and Pamela Clements' "Living with Neomedievalism," *Studies in Medievalism* 18 (2010): 56–75.

3. Eco, "Travels in Hyperreality," 5.

4. Eco, "Travels in Hyperreality," 7.

5. Eco, "Travels in Hyperreality," 14.

6. Eco, "Travels in Hyperreality," 18.

7. Eco, "Travels in Hyperreality," 13.

8. Eco, "Travels in Hyperreality," 19.

9. Eco, "The Return of the Middle Ages," in *Travels in Hyperreality*, 63.

10. *The Lord of the Rings: The Fellowship of the Ring*, dir. Peter Jackson (New Line Cinema, 2001); *The Lord of the Rings: The Two Towers*, dir. Peter Jackson (New Line Cinema, 2002); *The Lord of the Rings: The Return of the King*, dir. Peter Jackson (New Line Cinema, 2003).

11. "Theatrical Trailer," *The Lord of The Rings: The Fellowship of the Ring*, 2001, <http://www.youtube.com/watch?v=Pki6jbSbXIY>, accessed 1 September 2009.

12. J. R. R. Tolkien, "On Fairy Stories," in *Tree and Leaf* (Boston: Houghton Mifflin Company, 1965), 147.

13. Paul Kocher, "Middle Earth: An Imaginary World," in *Understanding the Lord of the Rings: The Best of Tolkien Criticism*, ed. Rose A. Zimbardo and Neil D. Isaacs (Boston: Houghton Mifflin, 2004), 148.

14. Tolkien also offers readers two versions of the hero, which he juxtaposes. As Verlyn Flieger argues, Tolkien constructs Aragorn in the image of the heroes of the medieval romance – the knightly, noble youth who emerges from obscurity to restore order to the kingdom (125). By contrast, Tolkien constructs Frodo as the son of solidly middle-class parents, an everyman figure who, as Flieger notes, "reacts to being thrust into epic events with the cry of the common man – 'Why me?'" (134). Frodo thus emerges as a curious combination of the old and the new, "a character who conforms to mythic patterns and yet invokes the identification and the empathy that the modern reader has come to expect from fiction" (135). One can argue, however, that the same is true of Aragorn, or, for that matter, any of the elements of the trilogy that appear genuinely medieval. Just as Aragorn's status as a common epic hero is affirmed in part through his essential difference from Frodo (and just as Frodo's status as uncommon commoner depends, in large part, on his essential difference from Aragorn), the elements of the trilogy that recall the medieval are not diminished by the presence of the obviously fake or constructed. See "Frodo and Aragon: The Concept of the Hero," in *Understanding the Lord of the Rings*, 122–45.

15. Baudrillard, *Simulacra and Simulation*, 5–6.

16. Baudrillard, *Simulacra and Simulation*, 2.

17. Baudrillard, *Simulacra and Simulation*, 2.

18. Guy Debord, *The Society of the Spectacle*, trans. Donald Nicholson-Smith (New York: Zone Books, 1994), 12.

19. Debord, *The Society of the Spectacle*, 24.

20. Debord, *The Society of the Spectacle*, 26.

21. Debord, *The Society of the Spectacle,* 16.

22. Karl Marx, *Das Kapital: A Critique of Political Economy*, ed. Frederich Engels (Washington, DC: Regnery Publishing, Inc., 2000). Marx writes that "the relation of the producers to the sum total of their own labour is presented to them as a social relation, existing not between themselves, but between the products of their labour" (52).

23. *World of Warcraft* (PC Version), Blizzard Entertainment, 2004.

24. We explore *World of Warcraft*'s appropriation of romance and medieval tropes of landscape and labor more fully in our article " 'For Your Labor I Will Give You Treasure Enough': Labor and the Third-Estate in Medieval-Themed Role-Playing and Massively-Multiplayer Role-Playing Games," forthcoming in *The Medieval in Motion: Neomedievalism in Film, Television, and Video Games*, ed. Carol Robinson and Daniel Kline.

25. For an overview of the use of the medievalesque in contemporary role-playing computer games, see Oliver M. Traxel's "Medieval and Pseudo-Medieval Elements in Computer Role-Playing Games: Use and Interactivity," *Studies in Medievalism* 16 (2007): 125–42.

26. For a detailed list of the various allusions at play at Toshley's Station, see "Toshley's Station," *WowWiki*, <http://www.wowwiki.com/Toshley's_Station>, accessed 1 September 2009.

27. "Game Overview," *World of Warcraft*, <https://signup.worldofwarcraft.com/trial/overview.html>, para. 1 of 3, accessed 1 September 2009. For a more detailed study of avatar-creation and identity in games such as *World of Warcraft*, see Lauryn S. Mayer's "Promises of Monsters: The Rethinking of Gender in MMORPGs," *Studies in Medievalism* 16 (2007): 125–42.

28. Debord, *The Society of the Spectacle*, 12.

29. Debord, *The Society of the Spectacle*, 23. Debord's point has not been lost upon media observers. A recent parody produced by *The Onion* announced that the next sequel to *World of Warcraft*, the "World Of World Of Warcraft," will let players play players playing *World of Warcraft*. The tag to the *YouTube* version of the parody reads "World Of World Of Warcraft's amazing level of detail makes players feel like they are actually in a cramped, dark apartment playing World Of Warcraft." See "Warcraft Sequel Lets You Play a Character Playing Warcraft," *The Onion*, <http://www.youtube.com/watch?v=Rw8gE3lnpLQ>, accessed 1 September 2009.

30. Paul Readman, "The Place of the Past in English Culture c.1890–1914," *Past and Present* 186 (2005): 147–99. According to Readman, the Victoria County History Series "aimed to appeal to the local patriotism (and self-importance) of county notables interested in the history of their 'own individual ancestors,' while simultaneously providing 'a National Survey [...] tracing [...] the story of England's growth from its prehistoric condition, through the barbarous age, the settlement of alien peoples, and the gradual welding of many races into a nation which is now the greatest on the globe' " (180).

31. *A Knight's Tale*, dir. Brian Helgeland (Columbia Pictures, 2001). Built around a sports-movie frame, *A Knight's Tale* is essentially the spectacle of a spectacle.

32. Kathleen Forni writes that "William lives by the motto that 'we can change our stars,' the presumably medieval version of Renaissance self-fashioning or the modern myth of consumerist *carpe diem* brilliantly commodified by the Nike slogan 'Just do it' (modified for film promos as 'Joust do it')." See "Reinventing Chaucer: Helgeland's *A Knight's Tale*," *Chaucer Review* 37:3 (2003): 256. For other treatments of *A Knight's Tale* as capitalist narrative, see Nickolas Haydock's "Arthurian Melodrama, Chaucerian Spectacle, and the Waywardness of Cinematic Pastiche in *First Knight* and *A Knight's Tale*," *Studies in Medievalism* 12 (2002): 5–38; and Caroline Jewers' "Hard Day's Knights: *First Knight*, *A Knight's Tale* and *Black Knight*," in *The Medieval Hero on Screen: Representations from Beowulf to Buffy*, ed.

Martha W. Driver and Sid Ray (Jefferson: McFarland, 2004), 192–210. Helen Dell, however, argues that the film's overt capitalist narrative is complicated (and at times undermined) by courtly narratives of desire. See "Past, Present, Future Perfect: Paradigms of History in Medievalism Studies," *Parergon* 25.2 (2008): 58–79.

33. "Choose Your Side," *Mountain Dew*, 2009, <http://www.youtube.com/watch?v=iioJ0UY4JHM>, accessed 1 September 2009.

34. To an extent, the emphasis of neomedievalism upon the traumas inherent in the intersections of the medievalesque and the "real" parallels the move in recent American academic historiography away from accounts of the medieval as more or less continuous with contemporary experience to accounts of the medieval as, in the words of Paul Freedman and Gabrielle M. Spiegel, "the West's quintessential other." See "Medievalisms Old and New: The Rediscovery of Alterity in North American Medieval Studies," *American Historical Review* 103:3 (1998): 677–704 (677).

35. Baudrillard, *Simulacra and Simulation*, 13.
36. Baudrillard, *Simulacra and Simulation*, 12.
37. Baudrillard, *Simulacra and Simulation*, 13.
38. Baudrillard, *Simulacra and Simulation*, 19.

A Short Essay about Neomedievalism

Lesley Coote

In this essay, I shall concentrate on an examination of the *neo* element of neomedievalism, not to the exclusion of *medievalism*, but in acknowledgement of the many contributions that have already been made to defining and exploring this concept in the past fifty years or so – many of them in the pages of *Studies in Medievalism*.[1] Whether one or many, medievalisms manifest themselves in one of two ways. First, there is the presentation and re-presentation of (essentially, the European) Middle Ages in art, literary text, and on screen, in order to deliver what Anthony Mann, one of the most gifted and effective auteurs of the historical epic film, termed "the feel of history." This is the "nominative" meaning of medievalism, in that it centers on the production, or reproduction, of some kind of object, whether book, picture, film, television program, video game, or some other resource in any available medium. In its other form, medievalism describes the intellectual process of examining the way in which both producers (in the general not the cinematic or commercial sense, although they may be this as well) and audiences, or "readers," of medievalist objects construct their meanings. In other words, medievalism also functions as an examination of the epistemology by which the "medieval" is presented, re-presented, received, and understood.[2] In this sense, medievalism is a branch of historiography. In both of these manifestations, *neo*medievalism may be said to be a part of medievalism (maybe one of Tom Shippey's "many medievalisms"), in that it does precisely this – in the same way that "postmodern medievalism" can also be identified as a form of medievalism.[3] On the other hand, I shall argue that *neo*medievalism, by its nature, cannot be fully contained within "medievalism," or any other, similar, terminology, as it seeks always to escape from the parameters that "-isms" impose.

Studies in Medievalism XIX, 2010

Theories of representation, in particular the ideas of Jean
Baudrillard, developed from the deconstruction theories of Roland
Barthes, form the basis of much contemporary media and cultural
theory.[4] Applying Barthes' theories of deferral in a cultural context,
Baudrillard maintained that "reality" is actually a representation, or a
series of representations, of that which already claims to be a cultural
representation of the "real." Given that this represented "real" is itself a
representation, we are left with no reality at all, but a series of representations of representations. Postmodern medievalism takes this
reductive stance, which is particularly well suited to satire. The 1974
film *Monty Python and the Holy Grail* offers such an epistemological
analysis of classical representations and adaptations of the medieval, in
a film that is actually a series of independent, but interlinked, or
"medievally interlaced" sketches on a theme.[5] The film is part of a
postmodern debate concerning the nature of authenticity, akin to that
reflected in the work of postmodern historiographers. This approach
leads to the conclusion that "history," being a construct made up of
other constructed accounts, never existed at all, except as representations of representations. Later scholars, following the lead of theorists
such as Frederic Jameson, would leave open the possibility that
constructed accounts do, ultimately, lead back to events that "really"
happened once. Neomedievalism embraces both the postmodern
emphasis on epistemology, *and* the possibility of some form of
"reality" that exists behind the construct. In *Monty Python and the
Holy Grail*, this is represented by the cartoons of Terry Gilliam (the
importance of which in the film is often overlooked). They reproduce
– but not exactly, as they have been re-drawn and re-colored in a late
1960s/early 1970s idiom akin to that of the *Sergeant Pepper's Lonely
Hearts Club Band* artwork – elements of medieval manuscript illustration. Gilliam introduces some items from later illustrative material,
and then animates the whole in what is a humorous comment on this
text (i.e., the film), and the texts that the film is itself critiquing.
Although seemingly anarchic, this attempt to seek a different basis for
mastery of the chaos that is the whole film from within the film's own
margins is a work of neomedievalism within a postmodern text. The
film itself recognizes, even foregrounds, its own unfinished nature
(with the well-known final "tape-cutting" sequence), revealing
postmodernity's acknowledgement of its own status as a work-in-
progress, rather than any kind of "finished article."[6] *Neo* is not content

with reduction and deconstruction only; although decentered and localized, it seeks positively to build up from what it happily accepts as having been broken down.

In a literary context, something similar can be seen in Umberto Eco's novel *The Name of the Rose*. Seeking the identity of a murderer who has been killing the monks, William of Baskerville and his teenage disciple Adso "discover" that the abbey's librarian has been murdering in order to keep the monks from reading a book in praise of the comedic, of the scatological and marginal. The resulting chaos culminates in the burning down of the library and the destruction of centuries of philosophy and learning; the destruction of that which makes sense of the symbolic: "I behaved stubbornly, pursuing a semblance of order, when I should have known that there is no order in the universe."[7] The novel itself defies the detective's, and the detective/audience's, attempts to read significance into objects or events – it is a postmodern work. The concluding lines, in Latin (a "dead" language unknown to many of the book's readers), imply that history, the medieval past, is unknowable to its future, even to those who were there, as their remembrances are like Baudrillard's representations: "I [Adso] leave this manuscript I do not know for whom; I no longer know what it is about: *stat rosa pristine nomine, nomina nuda tenemus.*"[8] At the center of the library is a labyrinth, which the two have to negotiate with the help of a list of clues. The clues, like William's belief in signs, fail, and the pair are forced to rely upon the marginal, the local and the individual (i.e., the *neo*): in the novel, the novice's naive interventions; in Jean-Jacques Annaud's 1986 film, the thread from Adso's habit. William's final remark to Adso is not the end-game … from his marginal position as teenage acolyte Adso has emerged to assert both identity and mastery in the form of a narrative, the book that we are reading.

The re-presentation of symbols until they are emptied of meaning is a feature of postmodern cultural theory; it is seen to lie behind the commercial exploitation of "heritage" in late twentieth- and early twenty-first-century culture. The use of cultural "labelling" by tourist boards, museums, theme parks, and heritage attractions, and the sale of such symbols in the form of consumable artifacts, are examples of this, along with the planning, cleansing, and ordering of heritage spaces in order to make them "visitable."[9] In a postmodern sense, the "visitable" heritage space is a representation of representations of what such a space should be, and Baudrillard's theory appears to hold true: "it's like being in a movie!" is a common response to extraordinary events. Neomedievalism challenges what Jameson has identified as "the cultural logic of late capitalism."[10]

"[...] as the model of the integrated private self of the author fades, the rights of the author as a persistent self-identity also become more evanescent."[11]

The mastery, the point of view of the singular subject, which lies at the heart of "classical" texts such as the classical Hollywood narrative or the classic novel, has been revealed by postmodernity to be an illusion; the subject has become decentered to the point at which, as Barthes put it, the author is "dead." *Neo*, however, asserts that although THE AUTHOR is no more, there are in fact many authors, decentered and marginalized from the main text, but still very much alive, and capable of reasserting mastery. These many authors do not seek control in the manner of the dominant subject of modernity, but from localized communities within the margin. Neomedievalism draws its energy from the margins of the manuscript where, as Michael Camille put it, "the offshoots of the Word have begun to form free-floating and uncircumscribed pockets of independent life."[12] This margin is inhabited by the babewyns, grotesque creatures sometimes monster, sometimes human, sometimes part-human and part-monster. They inhabit the place of the gloss, both affirming and challenging the authority of the central, hegemonic text, both comforting and dangerous. They urge the reader to think about meanings and understanding, about his/her own perceptions. The players of Massive Multi-Player Online Role Playing Games (MMORPGs) tend to create babewyn-like creatures. With these they then invent their own narratives to affirm and to challenge the socially accepted/acceptable "texts" from which they have, however, sprung. Such narratives may work from scratch, as in *World of Warcraft*, or from within historical/legendary narratives, such as *Civilization* and *Quest for Camelot*, where the paradigms of past histories and legends must be observed, but can be manipulated to create fresh scenarios, new characters, and varied conclusions. By means of social-networking software and digital production, these marginal narratives can be released from the parameters of the game and taken out into the wider world. Such marginal narratives are, like the chaotic and the unplanned disliked and cleared away by "heritage" planners, potentially dangerous to the hegemonic meaning of the text, or of the cultural space. In terms of cultural heritage, this is now evidenced in the efforts of minority groups, such as native peoples, or workers in defunct or near-defunct crafts or industries, to introduce their own narratives into the heritage spaces where they are on display for the heritage tourist.[13] This form of exhibition, which Darley calls "*neo display*" (my italics) can affirm or trouble accepted historical narratives.

Neomedievalism frequently adopts the apparently unpredictable playfulness characteristic of the medieval margin. The game, according to Victor Turner, uses the rules to create unprecedented performances.[14] This destabilizing power of the game structure is integral to the challenge offered by medieval Robin Hood narratives to established social and political ideologies. The rules are, however, followed, and this is a contradiction inherent in the world of the neomedieval. The margin does reference the center, and the parameters of the game, including the elements of which the babewyn-like body or the "second self" may be made, are pre-set by the programmer. Although neomedieval representations assert their own (multiple) subjectivities, the game's rules cannot be entirely divorced from those of the dominant culture. As Silvio Gaggi puts it, the game offers "access to otherness in conditions of sameness."[15] The neomedieval takes its inspiration and its materials from what is hegemonically accepted as "the medieval," thus affirming the central narrative. However, it then deploys these elements in ways unacceptable to "traditional" medievalists, in order to create playful narratives that trouble and challenge the central "medievalist text." In this way, the neomedieval is adopting a very *medieval* form of behavior.

In epistemological terms, neomedievalism brings understandings gained from the theory and use of new technologies to bear on our understanding of the medieval, and of medievalist representations. The "classical" narrative is predicated upon the idea of history as linear progression. This has been shattered by postmodern medievalism, and is denied by neomedievalism. With many competing narratives constructed by decentered subjects, neomedievalism cheerfully embraces the idea that history is not necessarily linear or progressive. By this means it opens up possibilities for fresh appreciations of medieval ideologies, philosophies, and understandings. Medieval people, for example, also saw history as a circular, rather than a linear, motion.

The neomedieval does not necessarily see paradigmatic legends, objects, characters, and time-frames as "given," but selects from them and mixes them up, in order to create new histories and new significations. Medieval subjects took a similar attitude to their own historical materials and legendary icons, using them to create new meanings in a way akin to that made possible by new technologies and the advent of hypertext. In digitized form, the text is not only open to manipulation, but is also porous: it is possible to drop through the word on the page in order to reach other levels, alternative texts, new meanings and significations. Deconstructing the text is postmodern, but cutting and pasting it to make something new is neomedieval – and it brings the cut-and-paster surprisingly, dangerously, close to medieval reading practices. Medieval readers were also expected to read on many levels.

> A writer ... y'know, I *write*, with ink and parchment ... probably read my book – *Book of the Duchess*? (they shake their heads)
>
> Fine ... well, it *was* allegorical ....[16]

Brian Helgeland's character "Geoffrey Chaucer" highlights both the opportunities and the problems with neomedievalism. The film *A Knight's Tale*, which offers images from the Middle Ages in the setting of contemporary (western) ideologies and icons, does bring the medieval to a wider audience, and offers scholars a variety of new insights into the world of medieval chivalry. On the other hand, it can also be accused of "dumbing down": it offers an invitation to smugness in a small amount of knowledge. The director/screenwriter implies that he knows the contents of the book, but there is no evidence in the rest of the film that he actually does. Chaucer's words (spoken to a group of illiterate pages/squires) imply that it really is not important that people should have read *The Book of the Duchess*, or any of Chaucer's other works; they should just be able to give the impression that they have. The representation of knowledge can take the place of "real" knowledge – although at the same time "Chaucer" implies that "real" knowledge can, and does, exist.

The film, the main theme of which is the rise to status and wealth of a poor craftsman's son, also demonstrates the neomedieval tendency towards democratization of medieval studies. Those previously excluded from identification with the medieval, by not being members of academe or of the intelligentsia, can now "possess" the

Middle Ages. Groups previously excluded by their lack of facility with the written word-on-the-page, such as those with learning difficulties, have been significantly enabled by digital culture and new technologies. In addition to this, neomedievalism globalizes the Middle Ages, making it accessible to multi-racial, multi-ethnic communities. The term "neomedieval" is, like the currently well-used term "medieval film," oxymoronic – being in the past and therefore completed, the Middle Ages cannot be "new" any more than the modern medium of film can "be" medieval. *Neo*, like *film*, is a term associated with both European and non-European (in particular the North American) world, rather than just the European world to which the Middle Ages historically belongs. *Neo* goes even further than this, erasing "real" geographical space, ethnicity, and race. In MMORPGs such as *World of Warcraft*, it is possible for a character to have a medievalist setting, clothing, speech patterns, and gestures, together with non-white, non-European, non-Caucasian racial characteristics. Spirituality and ethnicity associated with non-Christian traditions and literatures may also be included as part of the gameworld. This is also true of neomedieval drama such as the BBC's *Robin Hood* and *Merlin* series, which playfully mix medieval, fantasy, and contemporary elements. In *Merlin* Guinevere is both a servant and a girl of color, and in Robin Hood this is true of the male character Friar Tuck, whilst one of the "merry men" was an Asian girl. The "normative rules" seem to apply, however, in that the male heroes still follow the central, normative text for epic heroes in western European (and North American) cultures. This view is, however, partial. Neomedievalism can also be seen as elitist, in that its opportunities and understandings require access to the digital world. This excludes individuals and groups (for example, the elderly) who are less than familiar with the skills required to operate hardware and software. It also excludes those who cannot afford hardware, software, or subscriptions, a category that includes very large numbers in the developing world. Neomedievalism (or any other "neo" space) has the ability to function as a "third space" in which alternative identities can be forged, whilst sensitive and potentially dangerous political and philosophical subjects may be negotiated in relative safety. *Neo* is, however, dangerous … the voices of the margin may be contained, but they have the potential to escape (like medieval sin) and contaminate the main text/the rest of the world.

Writing of the historical novel, Jerome de Groot notes that it is

"in gaps of history, in the spaces between knowledges ... that historical novelists work, and it is the very insubstantiality of the past that
allows them to introduce their version of events."[17] Similarly,
neomedievalism has developed in the gaps between the shattered
mirror-shards of postmodernism. At one end of the spectrum, the
neomedieval encourages the substitution of superficial understanding,
the "gist" gathering of cultural bits and pieces, for real knowledge and
understanding of the Middle Ages. On the other, it offers the insights
of a space in which the medieval can "speak back" from the margins to
which *it* has been confined by the domination of the modern. This is
dangerous historiography, which may upset accepted understandings
of the Middle Ages in future.

NOTES

1. The title of this essay is unashamedly adapted from Krzysztof
Kieslowski's *A Short Film About Killing* (1988), also a short essay (but cinematic) on a theme.
2. By "medieval" in this sense, I mean artifacts, settings, mannerisms,
dress, characters, historical events, literary tropes, and other "signifiers" of
the Middle Ages.
3. Tom Shippey's article, "Medievalisms and Why they Matter," is one
of a series of important articles on the subject in *Studies in Medievalism* 17
(2009); the topic of postmodern medievalism is covered in *Studies in Medievalism* 13 (2004).
4. Jean Baudrillard, *Simulacra and Simulations*, trans. Paul Foss, Paul
Patton, and Philip Beitchman (New York: Sémiotext[e], 1983); *Selected
Writings*, ed. and intro. Mark Poster (Stanford, CA: Stanford University
Press, 1988); Frederic Jameson, *Postmodernism, or the Cultural Logic of Late
Capitalism* (Durham, NC: Duke University Press, 1991).
5. Ellen Bishop, "Bakhtin, carnival and comedy: the new grotesque in
Monty Python and the Holy Grail", *Film Criticism* 15 (Fall 1990): 49–64;
David D. Day, "Monty Python and the medieval Other," in Kevin J. Harty,
Cinema Arthuriana: Twenty Essays (orig. publ. as *Cinema Arthuriana: Essays
on Arthurian Film* [New York: Garland, 1991]; rev. ed. Jefferson, NC:
McFarland, 2009): 83–92; M. Burde, "Monty Python's Medieval Master-
piece," *Arthurian Yearbook* 3 (1993): 3–20.
6. Lesley Coote and Brian J. Levy, "The Subversion of Medievalism in
Lancelot du Lac and *Monty Python and the Holy Grail*," *Studies in Medievalism* 13 (2004): 99–126.

7. Umberto Eco, *The Name of the Rose* (London: Vintage, 1998), 492

8. Eco, *The Name of the Rose*, 502: "of the rose which originally existed, we have the name only" (a word-for-word translation is impossible in English).

9. Bella Dicks refers to this labeling as "image tags": "culture is displayed as unique and special, yet in forms which are market-produced." Bella Dicks, *Culture on Display: The Production of Contemporary Visibility* (Maidenhead: Open University Press, 2003), 33.

10. Jameson, *Postmodernism*; also Silvio Gaggi, *From Text to Hypertext: Decentering the Subject in Fiction, Film, the Visual Arts and Electronic Media* (Philadelphia: University of Pennsylvania Press, 1997), 98.

11. Michael Heim, *Electrical Language: A Philosophical Study of Word Processing* (New Haven, CT: Yale University Press, 1987), 221.

12. Michael Camille, *Image on the Edge: The Margins of Medieval Art* (London: Reaktion Books, 1992), 20.

13. Andrew Darley, *Visual Digital Culture: Surface Play and Spectacle in New Media Genres* (London: Routledge, 2000), 124.

14. Victor Turner, quoted by Camille, *Image on the Edge*, 41.

15. Gaggi, *From Text to Hypertext*, 172.

16. Brian Helgeland, *A Knight's Tale* (Columbia Pictures, 2001).

17. Jerome de Groot, *The Historical Novel* (London: Routledge, 2010), 182.

Neomedievalism:
An Eleventh Little Middle Ages?

Cory Lowell Grewell

In many ways, the scholars working on establishing "neomedievalism" as a legitimate field within the academy are taking what seems to be a very parallel path to that followed in years past by the scholars who established medievalism as a legitimate field of study, distinct from Romanticism and medieval studies. That is to say, neomedievalist scholarship is establishing itself by mapping contemporary cultural phenomena that re-imagine the Middle Ages in a way that is distinctively "neomedieval" and analyzing those phenomena's relation to culture at large, the historic Middle Ages, and previous forms of medievalism.

Among those at the forefront of the attempt to define and establish neomedievalism within the academy is the online intellectual community known as the Medieval Electronic Multimedia Organization, or MEMO, a community maintained by, among others, Carol L. Robinson, who is, herself, one of the scholars most actively engaged in neomedievalist work. Through facilitating online discussion of neomedievalism, through sponsorship of conference panels devoted to the new subject at the annual International Congress of Medieval Studies at Kalamazoo and the International Conference on Medievalism, and more recently through publications such as the forthcoming book *The Medieval in Motion: Neomedievalism in Film, Television and Electronic Games*, Robinson and other contributors to MEMO have initiated a dynamic and vital scholarly discussion devoted to outlining the parameters of neomedievalism and to analyzing its relationship to contemporary culture, to past medievalisms, and, of course, to the Middle Ages. The collection of essays attempting to define neomedievalism in this present volume of *Studies in Medievalism* is testament to the early success neomedievalist scholars have had in securing the interest of medievalist scholarship at large, and it suggests the need for further inquiry into the field and exploration of its implications for culture and for medievalist studies.

Given the relative youth of neomedievalism, however, its scholars must answer several questions regarding its nature and parameters as a specific field of academic inquiry. First, of course, is what exactly is *neo*medievalism? What cultural phenomena are included in the neomedieval? Second, and related, is the question, why "neo"? That is to say, how is neomedievalism distinct from medievalism, and is the distinction enough to warrant its existence as a separate field of study, or is neomedievalism simply one more manifestation of medievalism, an eleventh little Middle Ages, as Umberto Eco might call it? The answers to these questions will, of course, have important ramifications for how scholars approach neomedievalism, including whether there should be conferences and other institutional resources devoted exclusively to its study or whether inquiry into neomedievalism should be carried on under the broader umbrella of medievalism in general.

The task of defining what exactly constitutes neomedievalism is a very difficult one, as the field is very broad and contains within its purview a substantial number of specific cultural manifestations, ranging in fields from politics to literature to digital media. One is tempted to pluralize the term when discussing the many forms taken by neomedievalism, as Tom Shippey does with "medievalisms," in order to give a more accurate sense of the multi-faceted nature of the cultural trend.[1] The difficulty, as, Robinson and fellow MEMO contributor Pamela Clements describe it, is that neomedievalism "crosses definitions nearly as much as it crosses disciplines – from aesthetics to pop-culture, to economics, to government, to perhaps beyond."[2] MEMO, however, has provided a tentative definition of the term on its website in a "Definitions" page that also attempts to elucidate neomedievalism's distinction from various forms of medievalism.[3] Though these definitions are of necessity rather abridged, they do clearly imply a sort of progressive development: that neomedievalism grows out of a progression of medievalisms, emerging as its own particular re-imagination of the Middle Ages. The key aspect of neomedievalism, according to MEMO's definition, that distinguishes

it from prior medievalisms, is its marked lack of nostalgia for the
Middle Ages and its self-conscious denial of history. Though a helpful
starting point, the definitions provided as references by MEMO are
not developed enough to answer fully the questions posed above
regarding the proper place of neomedievalism in academic study, nor
do they purport to be so.

Luckily, Robinson and Clements have significantly expanded the
definition of neomedievalism provided on the MEMO website in
their *Studies in Medievalism* 18 essay "Living with Neomedievalism,"
which gives an extended description of neomedievalism and more
extensively distinguishes it from previous forms of medievalism. The
essay begins by citing Umberto Eco's coinage of the term in *Travels in
Hyperreality*. Robinson and Clements note that "Eco's definition of
neomedievalism is not much different from Leslie Workman's definition of medievalism."[4] In fact, it seems to me that Eco uses the terms
"neomedievalism" and "medievalism" more or less interchangeably,
with the possible exception that the former occasionally carries connotations that are less academic and more popular, as when he sets
"fantastic neomedievalism" against "responsible philological examination" in "Dreaming of the Middle Ages."[5]

According to Robinson and Clements, Eco's apparent working
definition of the term is not what they have in mind in forging their
definition of neomedievalism.[6] However, there is a certain resonance
apparent between the descriptions of the neomedieval that follow in
their essay and Eco's reference to "fantastic neomedievalism." The
similarity is not that the neomedievalism of Robinson and Clements is
somehow less seriously academic. Rather, the resonance is found in
the senses of fantasy and popular culture that Eco attaches to
neomedievalism (at least in this particular usage), for neomedievalism,
as Robinson and Clements define it, is entirely fantastical in its
creation of alternate universes from quasi-medieval contexts and
tropes, and utterly unmoored from "responsible philological examination" in its "anti-historical" nature.[7] It is this fantastical and anti-
historical aspect of neomedievalism – the "denial of history," as the
MEMO website calls it[8] – that they contend distinguishes it in large
part from medievalism. They write that, in comparison with "its 'parent' medievalism," which, of course, re-imagines and recreates the
Middle Ages in particular ways for various ends, "neomedievalism is
further independent [of the historic Middle Ages], further detached,

and thus consciously, purposefully, and perhaps even laughingly reshaping itself into an alternate universe of medievalisms, a fantasy of medievalisms, a meta-medievalism."[9]

The fantastic "alternate universes" of neomedievalism take many forms, but it seems that electronic media are the most conducive locales for the neomedieval, as the key role taken by the Medieval *Electronic Multimedia* Organization in advancing neomedievalist studies might imply (emphasis added). In fact, if the number of panels devoted to the subject at recent medievalist conferences is any indication, electronic games – and particularly the virtual universes of Massive Multi-player Online Role Playing Games (MMORPGs) – seem to be the quintessential instantiations of neomedievalism. After all, a description of the game-worlds of typical quasi-medieval MMORPGs like *World of Warcraft* or *Everquest* fits hand in glove with the central characteristics of neomedievalist universes as defined by Robinson and Clements. Such worlds liberally employ medieval tropes and images with very little, if any, concern for the actual, historical Middle Ages. Rather than re-imagining the Middle Ages per se, fantasy MMORPGs tend to re-imagine previous medievalist re-creations, invoking, for instance, the medievalism of J. R. R. Tolkien. This added level of remove from history is typical of neomedievalism as described by Robinson and Clements.[10]

Perhaps what makes electronic gaming the most quintessentially neomedieval genre, though, is that the game-playing experience in a neomedievalist MMORPG setting is heavily constructed and, at the same time, acutely aware of its constructed nature. The player-character quite literally fashions his or her own persona and then sallies forth with it into a universe that is just as self-consciously imaginary and constructed. The player is very aware that this persona is removed from the real world, and the medievalist tropes employed by game-designers in building the world only reinforce this distance from the current and real.

This self-consciously constructed nature of neomedievalism, as evidenced most clearly in the gaming experience of MMORPGs, reflects the influence of postmodern theory on neomedievalism as a scholarly ideology, an influence that Robinson and Clements explicitly acknowledge later in their essay:

For our purposes, neomedievalism is a post-postmodern ideology
of medievalism that has perhaps taken its cue from French theorists and other postmodernist thinkers (Eco included) [...]. For
better or for worse, neomedievalism draws from the Middle Ages
(European, but more recently also from non-European sources,
such as Japanese). Unlike in postmodernism, however, neomedievalism does not look to the Middle Ages to use, to study, to
copy, or even to learn; the perception of the Middle Ages is more
filtered, perceptions of perceptions (and of distortions), done
without a concern for fact or reality [...]. This lack of concern for
historical accuracy, however, is not the same as that held in more
traditional fantasy works: the difference is a degree of self-
awareness and self-reflexivity. Nor is it the same as what we
conceive to be medievalism.[11]

The description of neomedievalism as a "post-postmodern ideology" is
an interesting one to consider in that it is possible to see
neomedievalism as something of a reaction to postmodernism. One of
the more prominent themes of neomedievalist forms of art and entertainment – including literature, film, and, most notably, video games
– is a staging of a struggle between good and evil wherein the
viewer/player is often encouraged to identify with the good and, in the
case of neomedievalist gaming, take an active role in defeating evil,
which is often visibly and constitutively "other" than the forces of
good. These polarized moral contexts that are so often established in
constructed neomedievalist worlds provide an escapist alternative
from a postmodern cultural climate dominated by a popularly
perceived relativism, in which the monikers "good" and "evil" tend to
lose much of their sense of universal approbation or condemnation.

The imagined neomedievalist universes that are the settings for
these struggles between good and evil, however, in spite of their
employment of quasi-medieval tropes and images, do not generally
invoke the "historical" morally rigid climate that is so often ascribed
to the Middle Ages in the popular imagination, at least not directly.
Again, Robinson and Clements note that one of the most defining
features of neomedievalism is its fantastic alterity and its unapologetic
anti-historicism. Therefore, the battle between good and evil in
neomedievalist fantasy is not usually carried out in a context that
reflects the dogma of medieval Christendom, as it would be, for
instance, in an actual medieval morality play. Rather, where ethical

issues do come to the fore within the narrative of neomedievalist fantasy, they are almost always more reflective of contemporary moral culture than they are of anything remotely medieval. For instance, in the popular neomedievalist *Dungeons & Dragons* trilogy for PC gamers, *Baldur's Gate*, issues of contemporary race relations are brought to the fore in the player-character's interactions with the dark-skinned Drow Elves.[12] As I have noted above, the complete and self-aware alterity of the neomedievalist universe puts the moral struggle at a theoretically safe remove from either real history (the Middle Ages) or the real world. (It, of course, goes without saying that the "safety" of the fantastic, unreal others of neomedieval narrative needs to be interrogated to determine just how safe it really is.[13])

Moreover, the "evil" of neomedievalist narrative is not only usually substantially different from evil as defined by medieval Christian dogma, it is often not even systematic or thoroughly ideologically developed within the bounds of its own narrative universe. Rather, in much neomedievalist narrative, evil is as evil does and exists almost solely for the purpose of being vanquished. The obvious example of this is any one of the innumerable orcs, goblins, or other beasts that roam the landscapes of neomedievalist electronic games simply for the purpose of falling to the player-character's sword, bow, magic spell, or what have you. The monsters are not evil because of what they believe or represent; they just are evil, and their evil nature is signified, usually, by their visible otherness, as well as the fact that they will attack the player-character on sight.[14] This aggressive nature of neomedievalist instantiations of evil seems to hold across the board. The ultimate evil in many neomedievalist narratives is usually represented by a character or entity that is actively attempting to destroy or enslave the peaceful inhabitants of his universe. In the third installment of the neomedievalist *Underworld* film series, *Rise of the Lycans*, for example, what distinguishes the vampires from the lycans (werewolves) as the "bad guys" is the vampires' enslavement of the lycan race and their extortion from and oppression of their human vassals. Of course, both races are traditionally perceived as evil and visibly other (from normative humans).[15] Other behaviors traditionally encoded as evil, such as living in pervasive darkness and engaging in sensual decadence, characterize the vampires, but it is their oppressive nature that clearly marks them as evil in the film. *Rise of the Lycans*, as a typical neomedievalist narrative, illustrates the tendency of

neomedievalist rehearsals of good versus evil to be rather reductive and
to conform to an ideology that Shippey criticizes in medievalist films
such as *First Knight* (1995) and *King Arthur* (2004) as a belief that
"the troubles of this world are caused by oppressors: remove the
oppressors, liberate the people, and all will be well."[16]

The preceding comments on the recurring struggles between
good and evil in neomedievalism are, of course, cursory and only
suggest an area for further exploration in neomedievalist academic
inquiry. There is not sufficient space within the bounds of this essay to
give such an exploration the development that it deserves. I include
these comments here, though, because they seem to naturally rise
from the definition for neomedievalism provided by Robinson and
Clements, which identifies it as a "post-postmodern" phenomenon.
The way that neomedievalism reacts to postmodernism by intermin-
gling postmodern concerns like multi-culturalism and contemporary
socio-political issues (such as matters of gender and race) with
quasi-medieval fantasy universes characterized by the struggle between
good and evil seems to me one of its strikingly definitive facets and
one worthy of scholarly exploration. Such exploration, moreover,
might go a long way towards detailing some of the particular ways
that neomedievalism responds to our contemporary cultural moment.
Domenico Pietropaolo asserts that an expression of medievalism
"always presupposes that in contemporary culture there is a need that
it can meet."[17] The provision of a fantastical location in which to
rehearse our age-old fascination with the struggle between good and
evil and of assumed "safe," anti-historical "others" on which to project
an evil to vanquish may be one way in which neomedievalism meets
certain psychological desires of our culture.

To return, then, to the questions posed above as to what
neomedievalism is and how it is distinct – if at all – from medievalism,
it seems safe to say, as Robinson and Clements do, that neomedievalism is a form of medievalism that is intrinsically influenced
by postmodern ideology, that it is integrally linked to late twentieth-
and twenty-first-century advances in technology, and that it is distinguished from previous forms of medievalism by its multi-culturalism,
its lack of concern for history, and its habit of imagining the medieval
through the lens of previous medievalisms. I would add that it constitutes a particular response – or responses – to postmodernism, the
construction of fantastic universes of good and evil being perhaps only

one among many. I would disagree, however, with Robinson and Clements when they assert that neomedievalism is something other than medievalism.[18] While neomedievalism is constituted from a variety of its own forms and while those forms are markedly distinct from previous forms of medievalism, insofar as these forms are essentially an employment of medieval tropes and images in a series of aesthetic and ideological responses to contemporary culture, they seem to conform to the artistic and intellectual processes definitive of other forms of medievalism, in spite, perhaps, of the anti-historical way in which these forms approach the Middle Ages itself. Then again, the anti-historical handling of the medieval, itself, might be argued to constitute an ideological stance toward history. Tom Shippey's definition of medievalism(s), which I referenced at the outset of this essay, is as follows: "Any post-medieval attempt to re-imagine the Middle Ages, or *some aspect* of the Middle Ages, for the modern world, in any of many different media; especially in academic usage, the study of the development and significance of such attempts [emphasis added]."[19] There seems ample room for inclusion of neomedievalism within the bounds of this working definition of "medievalisms." In sum, I would argue that it is more beneficial to theorize neomedievalism in terms of a new and multi-faceted instantiation of medievalism rather than something else entirely. Neomedievalism, to once again borrow Eco's phrasing, might best be explored as an eleventh little Middle Ages.

Moreover, it seems rather obvious that the benefits of intellectually treating neomedievalism as a branch of medievalism outweigh benefits that would result from neomedievalism's declaration of academic independence from its parent, which declaration, by the way, I do not take from Robinson and Clements' essay, but which one might infer. There is doubtless, for instance, much to be gained from an intellectual interchange between, on the one hand, scholars devoting their studies to neomedievalism and, on the other hand, scholars of more traditional medievalisms. Additionally, given popular consciousness's unfortunate perception of academic study as being overly esoteric and irrelevant, there seems to me to be a possible danger that neomedievalist study, rooted as it is in the analysis of alternative, "meta" universes of fantasy, will be perceived in the public eye as completely esoteric and offering nothing of "real" cultural benefit. This danger is exacerbated by the widely held popular opinion of

MMORPGs, one of the quintessential forms of neomedievalism, as being largely irrelevant and somewhat silly, as illustrated by a recent parody of online medievalist gaming on the animated series *South Park*, in which the boys must, in mock-epic fashion, "save the world [...] of *Warcraft*."[20] Keeping neomedievalist scholarship moored to medievalism, which has gained academic legitimacy, would do much to prevent any possible negative public (and perhaps institutional) perception of irrelevance.

These are only a few of what must be many practical scholarly benefits that would result from academically treating neomedievalism as a branch of medievalism. As I have noted above, I think that there are also ideological benefits to theorizing neomedievalism as a form of medievalism rather than as something else. It may be that as more attention is given specifically to academic inquiry into neo-medievalism, that its purview will grow too large to be contained under the umbrella of medievalism, but for now it seems that medi-evalist journals and conferences are the best academic home for inquiry into the field.

NOTES

1. Tom Shippey, "Medievalisms and Why They Matter," *Studies in Medievalism* 17 (2009): 46.
2. Carol L. Robinson and Pamela Clements, "Living with Medi-evalism," *Studies in Medievalism* 18 (2009): 58.
3. <http://medievalelectronicmultimedia.org/definitions.html>.
4. Robinson and Clements, "Living with Medievalism," 59.
5. Umberto Eco, "Dreaming of the Middle Ages," in *Travels in Hyperreality*, trans. William Weaver (San Diego, New York, and London: Harcourt Brace Jovanovich, 1973, 1976, 1983), 63.
6. Robinson and Clements, "Living with Neomedievalism," 61.
7. Robinson and Clements, "Living with Neomedievalism," 56.
8. <http://medievalelectronicmultimedia.org/definitions.html>.
9. Robinson and Clements, "Living with Neomedievalism," 56.
10. Robinson and Clements, "Living with Neomedievalism," 67–68.
11. Robinson and Clements, "Living with Neomedievalism," 61–62.
12. Amy Kaufman and I have written an analysis of the interplay between race and the "othering" of evil in the essay "Blood Will Out: Gene-alogy as Destiny in Medieval(ist) Gaming," forthcoming in *The Medieval in Motion: Neomedievalism in Film, Television, and Electronic Games*.

13. In the aforementioned essay, "Blood Will Out," Kaufman and I argue that the projection of visible evil onto the "othered" Drow elves in the *Baldur's Gate* trilogy becomes problematic in the context of historical race relations.

14. Of course in most neomedievalist game modules, a player can choose to construct for him- or herself an "evil" character. The ethical behavior of the player-character is then expected to conform to that choice, meaning that, though the player can ostensibly identify with the cause of evil, it does not truly muddy the moral waters of the game world. The actions of the player-character are still clearly defined in the game world as evil.

15. *Underworld: Rise of the Lycans*, dir. Patrick Tatopoulos, perf. Michael Sheen, Bill Nighy, and Rhona Mitra (Sony Pictures Home Entertainment, 2009).

16. Shippey, "Medievalisms and Why They Matter," 52.

17. Domenico Pietropaolo, "Eco on Medievalism," *Studies in Medievalism* 5 (1993): 135–36.

18. Robinson and Clements, "Living with Neomedievalism," 62.

19. Shippey, "Medievalisms and Why They Matter," 45.

20. "Make Love, not Warcraft," *South Park*, Comedy Central, 4 October 2006.

The Simulacrum of Neomedievalism

M. J. Toswell

I would like to propose a genuine distinction between medievalism and neomedievalism, a distinction that can be used going forward but also one that, I believe, is already in place in the way in which individuals construct their approach to the medieval – whether consciously or unconsciously. The difference between the two terms as they are used in the English-speaking world is that medievalism implies a genuine link – sometimes direct, sometimes somewhat indirect – to the Middle Ages, whereas neomedievalism invokes a simulacrum of the medieval. I do not impute any higher value to the one than the other, but simply want to find a way to distinguish between the two terms as they are currently being used in North America. The general distinction that the one involves modern digital technology and new media as opposed to the other using the rather stodgy old-style approaches of books and pictures does not seem to me to adequately describe the way in which "medievalism" and "neomedievalism" function in use. Thus, neomedievalism is not well explained by its media, and it is quite possible to identify a neomedievalist book. Similarly, it is equally possible to find a movie that is an example of medievalism, and not simply neomedievalist. For example, one recent screen-treatment of the story of Beowulf and Grendel is a clear example of medievalism, in that the director, Sturla Gunnarsson, researched deeply into Anglo-Saxon and Icelandic legend, worked out an interpretation of the Old English poem depending on the theme of fathers and sons, and reworked the material to present a movie profoundly tied to a medieval place and time. *Beowulf and Grendel* turns the action from the marvelous to the thoroughly explicable; it postulates that monstrous behavior is passed from generation to generation as humans and the giants who are Grendel and his kin mutually hate and destroy each other. In order to make this argument, the film intro-duces one rather startling character, a witch who has prophetic powers, but otherwise the film works very hard to recreate the Anglo-Saxon story as a medieval storyteller might provide it in the modern age.[1] If a film can be a good example of medievalism, so too can a novel be a good example of neomedievalism: to wit, Peter S. Beagle's classic fantasy story, *The Last Unicorn*.[2] Here a patently absurd pseudo-medieval world – with castles, a king, a prince, a unicorn, and various medievalizing monsters and servants – includes a quest narrative that is patently modern, about finding and under-standing the existential self. The text's engagement with the medieval is solely to play with the notion of the medieval, to pretend to authority that the author profoundly rejects, and to present the trap-pings of a fairy tale while forcing the reader to subvert that narrative. Thus, although a very traditional-looking novel, Beagle's work is a good example of neomedievalism, given that the characters and even the plot explicitly and implicitly do not offer representation or any link to reality, whereas Gunnarsson's modern-looking movie reaches for specific sources and ideas, and constitutes medievalism. The simulacrum that is neomedievalism functions no matter what the medium or the postmodernity of the text, whereas medievalism requires engagement with the medieval text.

The notion of the simulacrum was first developed by Jean Baudrillard as a way of engaging with the alienated texts of postmodernism, but it applies here to the peculiarly a-medieval qualities of neomedievalism, to the construction of an "other" that is putatively medieval but whose connection to a medieval source or medievalizing idea is insubstantial, flimsy, even chimerical. A simulacrum is a copy of a copy of a nonexistent original, an original that never had tangible existence, a posited will-o-the-wisp. Neo-medievalism depends upon a simulacrum of the medieval; medi-evalism refers to an existing medieval text, even if seen through the transcendent light of nineteenth-century constructions of the medi-eval. Baudrillard's construction of the simulacrum carries significant interpretive force in literary and theoretical studies, such that the concept of the simulacrum is now approaching the status of a truism. Its interpretive power, nonetheless, remains formidable, since it allows for a range of four possible options for constructing the whole edifice of representation itself, as Baudrillard would have it:

Such would be the successive phases of the image:

> it is the reflection of a profound reality;
> it masks and denatures a profound reality;
> it masks the *absence* of a profound reality;
> it has no relation to any reality whatsoever: it is its own
>   pure simulacrum.[3]

Baudrillard argues that his first two options have to do with appearance, and while the first offers a good or genuine, even a sacred, appearance, the second offers a maleficent one. In my terms, both of these appearances, since both engage with a reality principle (the first to present it and the second to question or parody it), would be medievalism as it is currently understood. Baudrillard's third and fourth options, masking the fact that a profound reality does not exist (which he calls sorcery) and having no real relation to any reality – the true simulacrum – would be neomedievalism as it is currently constructed. Thus, texts that have but the trappings of the medieval without any genuine effort at particularity or which use the medieval as a way of reaching for nostalgia are neomedievalist. Baudrillard himself develops the concept of the simulacrum as a way of commenting on society, and particularly on media. He proposes, for example, that "[h]istory is our lost referential, our myth" and suggests that "[m]yth, chased from the real by the violence of history, finds refuge in cinema."[4] As a result, Baudrillard focuses particularly on cinema and on mass-media and the modern consumer for his more detailed analyses, which tread into social anthropology, sociology of the consumer, and cultural studies. Baudrillard seems to be suggesting that modern humanity has lost its access to myth, and with that its access to meaning.[5] I think that Baudrillard would argue that neomedievalism disengages itself from the semiotic, from the meaningfulness of the sign. This is neither a strength nor a weakness, neither a sign of free-floating uncertainty nor a parodic play on a nonexistent source. Simply, a neomedievalist text is one that is presented as a copy of an absent original, a sign that no longer speaks to a semiotic. Medievalism, on the other hand, attempts to ground itself not just in a generalized myth or history, but in specific representations, in particular constructions. These may be medieval, or they may involve the lens provided by the great era of medievalizing, the nineteenth century; in any case, they reach for a sense of the real.

Two texts involving Neil Gaiman offer a good pair of examples to demonstrate the difference I am positing between medievalism and neomedievalism, or between what Baudrillard would term the first or second stage of reproduction or image-making – either a basic reflection of reality or a perversion of reality – as opposed to the third and fourth stages, the simulacrum that offers a pretense of reality where there is no model or that bears no relation to any reality whatsoever. Neil Gaiman produces medievalism in his novel *American Gods* [6] and neomedievalism in his co-written screenplay for the 2007 movie version of *Beowulf.* [7] *American Gods*, a novel that garnered Gaiman a clutch of awards, might be his most well-known mainstream publication before the screenplay of the Robert Zemeckis CGI (computer-generated imagery) production of *Beowulf*, although Gaiman is perhaps most revered for his work on the graphic novel *The Sandman*. [8] The novel opens with a just-released prisoner named Shadow Moon (two archetypes in one) meeting a man in an airplane. Gaiman describes the man:

> His hair was a reddish gray; his beard, little more than stubble, was grayish red. A craggy, square face with pale gray eyes. The suit looked expensive, and was the color of melted vanilla ice cream. His tie was dark gray silk, and the tie pin was a tree, worked in silver: trunk, branches, and deep roots. [9]

The stranger invites Shadow to call him "Mister Wednesday." Later in the novel he describes his favorite grift, the Bishop Game, a two-man con in which a bishop buys a necklace, only to be hauled back into the store by a supposed cop who declares him a counterfeiter, and writes out a receipt for both the necklace and the money used to pay for it. [10] As always, the grifters play upon human greed and gullibility. Shadow notices that both the Bishop Game and the Violin Game, as previously described by Wednesday, are two-man scams, and Odin in response agrees that he once "had a partner. A junior partner. But, alas, those days are gone." [11] By the end of the novel it becomes clear that Woden (Mister Wednesday) and Loki (Low Key) are engaged in a gigantic version of the Bishop Game, and one whose purpose is to bring about a battle of the gods. Thus, Norse gods that they are, they will feed on the battle.

The premise of the novel, then, is an unreal element – that the gods live only so long as people believe in them [12] – but it figures itself

in a very realistic world of America at the millennium. The corollary is
that the gods come to the New World when that belief carries over in
the soul and heart of someone who emigrates, and new avatars of old
gods develop. Gaiman creates a conflict among the gods by developing a cadre of "new gods," the gods of television, radio, the media,
and popular culture; that is, the gods in whom we believe in the
modern day. When the new gods and the old gods come together to
battle in a new Ragnarök, or "Twilight of the Gods," they believe that
they are battling to the death over their rights to the hearts and souls
of humankind. The protagonist Shadow, however, goes along with all
the preparatory travels and meetings, then recognizes the deceit,
prevents the battle, destroys both Odin and Loki, and kills another
god before resuming his journey – he engages in the classic road trip
of American realist novels. Neither the new gods nor the old ones die
to feed the Norse gods, who thrive on strife and hatred. Shadow saves
the day, the son of a god who as a human hero turns back the gods.

A plot summary, however, does little to explain this novel.
Replete with carefully delineated vignettes depicting the arrival and
behavior of gods from all over the world, the novel focuses more
particularly on the *Bildungsroman* of Shadow, the protagonist who
travels with and works for Odin for the first half of the novel, then as
the god's servant accepts the nine-day watch tied to Yggdrasil to see
Odin safely to the afterworld. In the final stages of his ordeal, Shadow
dies but is brought back to serve a higher purpose and to rethink the
premises upon which he has so far lived his life. His debt to Odin is
discharged as he has honorably died, and he can start again. He does
so by catching out Odin and Loki, the two deceiving and conniving
gods of the Norse pantheon, and they are beaten honorably at their
own game. The novel thus presents the gods, and in particular the
Norse gods, in ways that are wholly faithful to the medieval constructions of those gods and their behavior.[13] Modern or even postmodern
figures, the gods retain all their medieval characteristics; more, they
are recreated and re-vivified in *American Gods*. Gaiman thus meditates
on the role of gods in modern America, but does so with a profound
and detailed understanding of their Norse heritage and its complications.

More, *American Gods* serves as an excellent example of
medievalism that functions by way both of direct sources, from the
Middle Ages, and indirect medievalizing through nineteenth-century

recreations of medieval materials. Thus Gaiman uses the *Poetic Edda*, the *Prose Edda*, and the invocations of the Norse gods in various Icelandic sagas, presenting their fundamental characteristics and invoking their legends with tremendous care. The relationship between Odin and Loki reflects the trickster and poet roles that both pursue in the *Edda*, although it also reflects the nineteenth- and twentieth-century retellings by Kevin Crossley-Holland and Roger Lancelyn Green (among others, but Gaiman himself cites these two) of Norse mythology, which create – as much as is possible – a single homogeneous version of their existence, their stories, and especially their expectation of Ragnarök, the end of existence. Secondly, reflecting the first great swell of medievalism in the nineteenth and early twentieth centuries, *American Gods* is also a rollicking adventure novel, a picaresque adventure in which a son of the gods mediates his relationship with his father and with humanity. It plays with the plot-driven novels of the nineteenth century, with its twists and turns, with its stock of grotesque characters and themes that are larger than life. Gaiman's structural models for the novel are Dickens and Collins, Tolkien, Dunsany, and – perhaps especially – E. R. Eddison. By his own account he wanted to write about American myth, or myth as it would be altered and changed in America in the twenty-first century. At one point, Shadow and his boss Wednesday stop at a purely modern American tourist attraction, the House on the Rock, where they ride the carousel and Shadow encounters the gods. Gaiman, who had himself only recently relocated from England to Minnesota, clearly wanted to embed the novel as part of modern America, especially modern rural America, with a roadside attraction in Wisconsin as the location for a pivotal scene about the role of the gods. Gaiman thus has three layers (at least) to the novel: the mythic Old Norse material available from the Middle Ages, the nationalist rediscovery of the Middle Ages in nineteenth-century Europe and America and its tendency towards long and convoluted narratives, and the modern or postmodern eye of the narrator and audience. Gaiman here blends medievalism with his own sense of American myth and the construction of American identity, offering very specific and particularized images both of the Norse gods and of America at the second millennium.

In a later work, although Gaiman himself felt that in the screen-play he co-wrote he was being "faithful" to the original poem, the resulting text, Robert Zemeckis' production of *Beowulf*, is a kind of animated film of the hyperreal variety only (to use Baudrillard's term). The film, first appearing in 2007, brought with it a great range of ancillary productions. Caitlín Kiernan wrote a novelization of the screenplay by Neil Gaiman and Roger Avary that was published as a paperback.[14] Also available before the movie appeared was a "the-making-of" book described on the jacket as a "deluxe volume" with "the best and most formative pieces of *Beowulf* production art, including sketches, sculpts, 3-D renders, and digital paintings."[15] The movie itself is a quite remarkable piece. In order to establish dramatic unity, the screenplay has Beowulf remain at the Danish court and become king after Hrothgar (who rather oddly announces his heir then walks to the balcony and flings himself into the abyss); more significantly for the coherence of the plot, Gaiman and Avary have Grendel's mother (Angelina Jolie) seduce Beowulf (Ray Winstone) and offer him riches and power. Her son with Hrothgar was Grendel; her son with Beowulf is the dragon, who is a shapeshifting man-dragon.[16] Because Beowulf remains at Heorot with his men (including Wiglaf, who is Beowulf's closest retainer from the beginning of the film), this retelling has a significantly clearer and simpler story.

More important than the changes to the plot, however, is the decision made by the director to film the story in performance capture. Having earlier completed a well-received CGI film, *The Polar Express*, Zemeckis chose to use the same technology here in order to be able to create particularly striking monsters and, especially, action sequences. The result is that the movie as watched is an as-yet-strange mix between animation and live human acting, with the voices and movements of the actors captured and translated through the magic of digital animation (easily quadruple the number of people worked on the animation than on the acting) into a strangely stilted but impressive visual effect. The result is unreal, non-real (Baudrillard would say "hyperreal"), inhuman, but oddly convincing. Crispin Glover as Grendel rips apart three-foot puppets on the set; this is captured and built into a twelve-foot Grendel ripping apart six-foot warriors in the hall. Beowulf vanquishes him by wrapping a chain around his arm, getting the chain around one fulcrum (or perhaps two – it gets difficult to tell) and using the door through which Grendel is exiting (apparently not the door that he blasted to smithereens on his entrance) to offer the final bit of power with which to rip off the monster's arm. Thus, the actual fight with Grendel is "realistic" by modern standards since the hero simply could not just grasp the monster by the hand and wrestle him about in the hall in the twenty-first century, but the monster is the more monstrous in that its base is a human actor – the movement of Grendel may be awkward and obviously weird, but it remains fundamentally human. Represented as a version of the duel between Grendel and Beowulf in the poem, the film sequence is not anything like its original; in fact, it is a copy of an original that does not exist, a simulacrum.

The producer and the screenwriters have a lot to say about their approach to the text in the ancillary matter provided in the director's cut of the movie. Zemeckis is very clear about his attitude; just before the filming on the set begins, he says:

> This is *Beowulf* and the true story of what goes on here on the stage. It's gonna be no bullshit and it's gonna be just the way it is. In the process it'll evolve as we figure out what the movie is. Right now I can only say that this has nothing to do with the *Beowulf* you were forced to read in junior high school. It's all about eating, drinking, killing and fornicating. [He turns towards the stage/ image capture centre.] I can't wait. I can't wait.[17]

Zemeckis clearly considers the movie he is about to make as a truer image than the poem *Beowulf*, as having its own deeply felt integrity, as being a more honest and more genuine version of the text. Later, in another of the ancillary clips, he says:

> As far as the classic *Beowulf* story, nothing about the original poem ever appealed to me. I remember being assigned to read it in junior high school and not being able to understand it, but then when I read the screenplay that Neil Gaiman and Roger Avary did, I thought it was really intriguing; and so I said, "So what is it about this screenplay that is so interesting when the story is so boring?" And their answer was, "well, the story was written somewhere between the seventh and the twelfth century – it's the first thing ever written in the English language – but the story had been told for centuries before that, and the only people who knew how to write were monks, so […]."[18]

Here Zemeckis makes it clear that the translation that he read of the poem while in junior high school was not the *real* text, whereas the screenplay by Gaiman and Avary reflects a deeper reality, one that takes into account the editing and changing that monks must have done to the text when they reworked it and wrote it down. The errors of fact in his comments, that the poem could have been written as late as the twelfth century when the only extant manuscript dates to no later than 1025 and probably around 1000 and that this was the first thing written in English, can be ignored given that this is not his field, but his argument that he has produced a somehow better and more correct version of the text by using the Gaiman and Avary screenplay is interesting. Gaiman is more circumspect in his comments, simply suggesting that *Beowulf* is one of the "oldest kinds of stories"[19] but elsewhere maintaining that:

> [...] in the case with *Beowulf*, I'm the one doing the damage to the original thing. I'm the one saying, this is how you turn it into this other thing. Let's turn it into a movie while being faithful, but without hesitating to do damage to the poem if it makes a better film.[20]

Gaiman sees the screenplay as a more complex interaction with the original poem than does Zemeckis. He clearly reaches towards an ideal of fidelity, while explicitly acknowledging that he and Avary have done "damage" to the originary text. He wants this to be a version of the text that is medievalist, even if it seems to be a kind of parody or reinterpretation of the original. However, the movie is without question neomedievalist, even if only because performance capture (having actors perform in a blank space while hooked up to a surreal quantity of electrodes, with minimal props and sometimes no other actors at work, even in a crowd scene) is an extraordinarily perfect example of Baudrillard's concept of the simulacrum at work. The purpose of the performance is to generate a digitized cartoon for the animators to manipulate. The other issues – the fact that Hrothgar lives in a late-medieval castle with outbuildings and a bridge over a deep abyss as the only entry, the high-medieval robes that the characters seem to prefer (except Beowulf, who seems to prefer a loincloth or going naked with bits of furniture hiding his genitalia), the golden horn that looks not unlike a Wagner tuba and has the same dire function as the ring of the Nibelungs, the rhyming doggerel in praise of Hrothgar at the beginning of the poem, the question of why Beowulf as king seems to need both a wife (Robin Wright Penn as Wealthow) and a mistress (Alison Lohman as Ursula) who luckily serve as a focus for the dragon's rage – these issues simply confirm that the film is neomedievalism. Zemeckis is perfectly honest; he wants to tell his story of Beowulf, not the one that he was forced to read – the one that he can create based on another story that is based on a combination of a DC comic version, the Christopher Lambert version, and other versions that Gaiman and Avary enjoyed. The movie copies an original that does not exist.

It is certainly possible – even perhaps required – to complicate this argument. The House on the Rock in *American Gods* serves the same function as Disneyland and the other "imaginary stations that feed reality"[21]; it is a "perfect model of all the entangled orders of simulacra."[22] By being so perfectly unreal, the House points to the ways in which the real is located in the novel. Baudrillard would argue that this kind of childish and infantile play-world demonstrates the ways in which supposed adults are turning away from the real and towards "a sinking reality principle."[23] However, this neomedievalist episode in *American Gods* actually serves as the mythic turning-point for Shadow as he realizes that, like Gylfi in the Old Norse *Gylfaginning*, he is embroiled with the gods and their plots and must figure out the grift. It does not have Baudrillard's chaotic and even entropic function, but forces the central character into an epiphany, an understanding of the real as it exists in the novel. Similarly, at several points in Zemeckis' *Beowulf* there are irruptions of Old English, one as Grendel lies dying and speaks to his mother, and another as Beowulf celebrates the fiftieth anniversary of his kingship and as his courtiers re-enact the battle with Grendel using the relevant passage from the poem to describe Grendel's delight in his feeding (lines 739–47).[24] They offer a kind of realism, a distant echo of the poem. The screenwriters in the ancillary clips profess themselves delighted that Zemeckis chose these distant echoes of the poem. When Grendel's mother asks him what he has been up to at Heorot, he replies "Mordor" or perhaps "Morðor." He has indeed been up to murder, but the blurring of the "d"/"th" sound causes a neomedievalist rupture as the watcher tracks to Tolkien's Mordor, and back to this movie. Even when a gesture towards medievalism occurs, it doubles back upon itself into neomedievalism.

A definition has to have some explanatory power in order to be

functional, but at the same time definitions are circumscribed by the
exceptions that clarify their limits. Here I have attempted to offer a
way of perceiving medievalism as engaged with history and with what
Baudrillard calls "the imagery of representation," while neomedievalism is engaged with simulation and what Baudrillard calls
"the neoreal and the hyperreal."[25] Elements of the one can certainly be
at play in the other, but if my definition works, the two are mutually
separable. Perhaps the most intriguing fact of all is the sheer extent to
which we find ourselves making these negotiations as the medieval
and the neomedieval pervade modernity. Baudrillard calls history "our
lost referential" and implies that we are trying to find that reference.[26]
That search might explain the massive thirst for the Middle Ages that
inheres in the modern day, perhaps a thirst for roots and origins,
perhaps simply a thirst for simplicity and a clear sense of the order of
things, perhaps a search for myth and apocalyptic explanation,
perhaps a more complex engagement with the concepts of tradition
and modernity (as Brian Stock would have it) as competing impulses
in the postmodern world.[27]

At the same time, Baudrillard's own construction of the
simulacrum can itself be questioned. He refers throughout to history,
yet his detailed examples come from geography, and though
Baudrillard clearly wants to make a chronological argument, his
primary approach seems to be anthropological. Victor Li points out
that Baudrillard's critique is on one level "neo-primitivist in that it
reinscribes an all-too-familiar binary model of a debased modern West
and an idealized primitive Other," an ironic reversal.[28] Nonetheless, Li
concludes more moderately that Baudrillard's neo-primitivism is not
fatal to his argument about the simulacrum as an historical construct,
in that Baudrillard "may use historical and ethnographic accounts to
illustrate his theory of radical otherness, his theory does not require
the actual, living presence of the primitive Other since the Other is
needed only as a *discursive* element of rupture, a *structural* antithesis to
Western thought."[29] Baudrillard uses the simulacrum to posit a discursive Other, to set up a binary. The Other that Baudrillard invokes can
never be fully simulated. The simulacrum thus turns in upon itself,
having opened a rupture in order to establish a way of critiquing
postmodernity. Replacing the term "primitive" in these passages –
appropriate since Baudrillard uses as his examples of the Other
geographically distant peoples such as the Cashinahua in South

America or the Tadasay in the Philippines – with "medieval" to imply chronological rather than topographical distance, results in an uneasy recognition that the use of the simulacrum as a method of definition is a simulation in and of itself. Nonetheless, perhaps it is a useful simulation, even if it is as slippery as Grendel in Zemeckis' *Beowulf* or Odin in Gaiman's *American Gods*.

NOTES

1. *Beowulf and Grendel*, screenplay by Andrew Rai Berzins, dir. Sturla Gunnarsson, perf. Gerard Butler, Stellan Skarsgärd, Ingvar Eggert Sigurdsson, and Sarah Polley (Warner Brothers, 2006). The credits include Andy Orchard, University of Toronto, as a consultant on Old English and Old Norse, and the ancillary material includes several episodes in which actors and members of the production staff discuss the urge towards realism and fidelity that grounds their production.

2. Peter S. Beagle, *The Last Unicorn* (1968; Harmondsworth: Penguin, 1991).

3. Jean Baudrillard, "The Precession of Simulacra," in *Simulacra and Simulation*, trans. Sheila Faria Glaser (Ann Arbor: University of Michigan Press, 1994), 1–42 (6).

4. Baudrillard, "History: A Retro Scenario," in *Simulacra and Simulation*, 43–48 (43).

5. See, for example, his *The Consumer Society: Myths & Structures* (London: SAGE Publications, 1998), which ends with an analysis of a silent film from the 1930s, *The Student of Prague*, in which there is a pact with the Devil, analyzing its processes of alienation and commenting on the mythic theme whose absence is at the heart of contemporary alienation.

6. Neil Gaiman, *American Gods* (New York: HarperTorch, 2001).

7. *Beowulf, Director's Cut*, A Robert Zemeckis film, screenplay by Neil Gaiman and Roger Avary, dir. Robert Zemeckis, perf. Ray Winstone, Anthony Hopkins, John Malkovich, Robin Wright Penn, Brendan Gleeson, Crispin Glover, Alison Lohman, and Angelina Jolie (Paramount, 2007).

8. *American Gods* won both the Hugo and Nebula Awards in 2002 (the two most notable science-fiction and fantasy awards), as well as a handful of other lesser-known awards and nomination for the World Fantasy Award. *The Sandman* was a serial comic that appeared in the early 1990s and garnered high critical acclaim, and a World Fantasy Award, to date the only one awarded to a graphic novel. It is now available in ten trade paperback collections, beginning with *Preludes and Nocturnes* (New York: DC Comics, 1991).

9. Gaiman, *American Gods*, 22.
10. Gaiman, *American Gods*, 239–41.
11. Gaiman, *American Gods*, 243.
12. For a similar premise, and a not dissimilar treatment, though the Greek gods are the focus, see Tom Robbins, *Jitterbug Perfume* (Toronto: Bantam, 1985).
13. In the "Acknowledgements" at the end of the novel (589–92), Gaiman does not provide information as to where he derived his understanding of the Norse gods; however, on his website he offers several texts as possible sources, while also somewhat vaguely gesturing at translations of the *Poetic* and *Prose Edda*. The text he acknowledges as his greatest source is Kevin Crossley-Holland, *The Norse Myths* (New York: Pantheon, 1980). Of it he says, "My copy is dog-eared, coffee-stained, has many paper bookmarks in it, and has been read more times than I can say. Really good, clear writing, which can send a shiver up my back. Notes and bibliography, and this was the book I based all the Norse stuff on in *Sandman*." He also cites the less scholarly Roger Lancelyn Green, *Tales of the Norsemen* (London: Puffin, 1960) as his childhood reading on the topic. See <http://www.neilgaiman.com/works/Books/American+Gods/in/183/>, accessed 8 September 2009. For translations of the eddaic material that seem likely to have influenced Gaiman, see Snorri Sturluson, *The Prose Edda: Tales from Norse Mythology*, trans. Jean I. Young (Berkeley: University of California Press, 1966); and *Poems of the Elder Edda*, trans. Patricia Terry (Philadelphia: University of Pennsylvania Press, 1990).
14. Caitlín R. Kiernan, *Beowulf. Based on the screenplay by Neil Gaiman & Roger Avary* (New York: HarperEntertainment, 2007). Neil Gaiman provides an introduction to the text, in which he offers the information that his first encounter with the poem was a news clipping in his classroom, and the second was the comic-book version in which the hero "wore a metal jockstrap and a helmet, with horns so big he could not have made it through a door" (viii). Later, he acquired the Penguin translation when he began to work on the screenplay with Roger Avary.
15. Mark Cotta Vaz and Steve Starkey, *The Art of Beowulf*, preface by Robert Zemeckis, foreword by Neil Gaiman (San Francisco: Chronicle Books, 2007).
16. The decision to make the dramatic structure much tighter by having fathers create their sons with the monstrous Grendel's mother, done here rather differently than in the 2006 Icelandic version of *Beowulf* mentioned above, does seem likely to owe something to an earlier movie version. Gaiman in his introduction to Kiernan's novelization mentions that there "have been numerous accounts of *Beowulf* on the screen already, ranging from a science fiction version to a retelling in which Grendel is a

tribe of surviving neanderthals" (viii). The science-fiction version he refers to is *Beowulf*, screenplay by Mark Leahy and David Chappe, dir. Graham Baker, perf. Christopher Lambert, Oliver Cotton, Gotz Otto, and Layla Roberts (Buena Vista, 1999). In that version Grendel's mother is a seductress, and Grendel is her child with Hrothgar. The movie stops after Christopher Lambert as Beowulf has used *Mortal Kombat* moves to kill both Grendel and Grendel's mother (a shapeshifter from a beautiful woman, who mouths lines from the poem about her delight in eating humans, into a strange spider-like being). Her monster is incidentally not unlike Shelob; Crispin Glover's Grendel in Zemeckis' film is not unlike Gollum in the *Lord of the Rings*, especially the Peter Jackson version produced by performance capture.

17. "A Hero's Journey: The Making of *Beowulf*," in *Beowulf*, dir. Zemeckis. Title 5, chapter 1, 00:14–00:44.

18. "The Origins of *Beowulf*," in *Beowulf*, dir. Zemeckis, Title 8, chapter 1, 1:02–1:40.

19. "The Origins of *Beowulf*," Title 8, chapter 1, 00:15–00:20.

20. "An Interview with Neil Gaiman," Bookslut (October 2006), 10 pages, p. 8, <http://www.bookslut.com/features/2006_10_010057.php>, accessed 8 September 2009.

21. Baudrillard, "The Precession of Simulacra," 13.

22. Baudrillard, "The Precession of Simulacra," 12.

23. Baudrillard, "The Precession of Simulacra," 15.

24. See *Klaeber's Beowulf*, ed. R. D. Fulk, Robert E. Bjork, and John D. Niles (Toronto: University of Toronto Press, 2008), 27. The lines, rather interestingly, coincide with the lines that Grendel's mother speaks in the 1999 *Beowulf*, dir. Baker.

25. Baudrillard, "The Precession of Simulacra," 7.

26. Baudrillard, "History: A Retro Scenario," 43.

27. The idea of the desperate thirst for the medieval I have borrowed from Veronica Ortenberg, *In Search of The Holy Grail* (London: Hambledon Continuum, 2006), 246. See also Brian Stock, *Listening for the Text: On the Uses of the Past* (Philadelphia: University of Pennsylvania Press, 1990).

28. Victor Li, "The Premodern Condition: Neo-Primitivism in Baudrillard and Lyotard," in *After Poststructuralism: Writing the Intellectual History of Theory*, ed. Tilottama Rajan (Toronto: University of Toronto Press, 2002), 88–109 (91).

29. Li, "The Premodern Condition," 94. Emphasis his.

Sandworms, Bodices, and Undergrounds: The Transformative Mélange of Neomedievalism

E. L. Risden

"Who put the bop in the bop-shoo-bop-shoo-bop? Who put the ram in the ram-a-lam-a-ding-dong?" asks the famous pop song.[1] Well, then, who put the *neo* in neomedievalism? Some usages, many of them Continental – Eco's for instance – imply essentially the same thing that most American and British scholars mean by *medievalism*: the matter of the Middle Ages renewed in more modern works of literature and art.[2] Other academic volleys have suggested the *new* move appears in shifting the old matter of medievalism to new technologies: high-tech, effects-heavy films, personal video games, multiple-player online role-playing games.[3] That usage seems to me both near the common mark and a useful deployment of the term. *New* may also imply a new audience rather than new approaches or subject matters: medievalism tuned to the tastes of readers enamored of Harry Potter or steampunk rather than *Beowulf* and Dante, who dress goth whether or not they read Stoker, who enjoy alternative-world films and computer games full of "barbaric," whiz-bang violence and highly visualized adventure quests, and who take *Dungeons & Dragons*-type role-playing games into other media such as highly competitive card games.

To acquire and disseminate its dominant metaphors neo-medievalism exploits not only technology, but also urban fantasy and dark science fiction more than it does traditional medievalism or anything a medievalist would recognize as authentically of the Middle Ages. Neomedievalism does not so much contribute new matter to the growing body of creative and scholarly endeavor of medievalism as it borrows creatively from the old matter; almost inevitably it reshapes the metaphors and conventions of medievalism for new means of conveyance and for audiences more savvy with and interested in alternative media than in the Middle Ages and its more scholarly offshoots. Medieval elements seed alternative neomedieval worlds, functioning, as Tolkien would say, mythopoeically, to provide atmosphere and variety and add completeness and verisimilitude to stories, but those worlds bear little resemblance to the Middle Ages or to "first generation" medievalism.[4] Lots of novels and movies that ride the post-wave of medievalism, that fall within what I feel comfortable distinguishing as *neo*medieval, have, for instance, an "underground"; they explore the "heart of darkness," their own peculiar universes or multiverses of gothic inferni; they tend to truncate the "heart of light," the celestial element, which often in medieval aesthetic embodies the end or goal of adventure quests. So perhaps neomedievalism dispenses with the need for medieval or medieval-like setting in favor of borrowing and transforming its elements for a more "hip" audience, one that finds its aesthetic more in Neo-Gothic, the Dark Romantic, in recent rather than classic film noir, in heavy metal and hip-hop rather than in the costume and ornament of Baroque, the towering landscape of the natural Romantic, or the fresh-air high fantasy of Tolkien.

In some respects Tolkien was already leaning toward neo-medievalism: he created not an alternative medieval world, but a world of his own making with a smattering of medieval elements such as dragons, traveling wizards, wise elves, and battles dominated largely by swordplay. But Tolkien's work has fully integrated itself into our conceptions of medievalism – it has even shaped them as much as has any other single source. However, it came too early for postmodern, technological, and neo-neo-gothic movements that so fully inform and shape neomedievalism, which, while it admires his status, often rejects him as socially conventional. Peter Jackson has brought Tolkien's work back into the neomedieval mix, but more because of his own influence on technical aspects of filmmaking and on visualized imagination than for anything explicitly Tolkienian.

The shadowy realm of the Byronic hero – male, female, or gender-neutral – and the neo-gothic palette of the Romantics, plus a measure of science fiction (animated or otherwise), especially where it

indulges in grotesque figures and frightening creatures, and a dollop
of pop-culture kung-fu,[5] accompanied by the sense of participation in
something at once aesthetically counterculture and ludically cutting-
edge, contribute most significantly to the draw of the neomedieval.
And the movement is not exclusively Western: the sword-and-sorcery
or sword-and-spaceship *anime*, borrowing generously from the
samurai traditions, evolved a similar taste, though from and amidst a
culture that began with a different set of values and metaphors. From
what I can tell, *anime* continues to grow in popularity in the West as
audiences gain exposure to it. Even comics, from the early Batman to
graphic novels, borrow their noirish underworlds and violent encounters as much from medieval or medievalismic sources as from
twentieth-century hard-boiled fiction and film. Their alternative
worlds tend to feature danger and moral ambiguity and to develop
their Dick Tracy-ish grotesque villains equally with semi-grotesque
protagonists.

The novel, though in some instances it appears as a secondary
rather than primary development, remains an important means of
conveyance for neomedievalism. And not all the neo-novels are
shiny-new. While I would situate Larry Niven and Jerry Pournelle's
Inferno,[6] a modern version of the first book of Dante's *Commedia*,
safely within the realm of traditional medievalism for its use of the
medieval hell, *The Legacy of Heorot*, by Niven, Pournelle, and Steven
Barnes,[7] falls more within the fuzzy boundaries of neomedievalism.
The story occurs far from earth on another planet where a colony,
unwary of its insufficient defenses, faces attack from a brutal indige-
nous beast. While the book derives inspiration obviously from
Beowulf, the borrowings represent a minimal and interesting but
unnecessary dipping into medieval matter to enhance a science-fiction
plot and world. James Blaylock's *The Elfin Ship* (1982)[8] and its sequels
combine elves, castles, and flying machines. Holly Black's *Tithe*
(2004)[9] begins in Philadelphia, then shifts across a liminal boundary
to a Faerie of magic and knights. Perhaps most interesting for their
minimal mix of medieval elements – despite their inspiration in medievalism – are Neil Gaiman's *Neverwhere* and China Miéville's *Perdido
Street Station*.[10] The former began as a BBC television special series in
1996, with the novelized version first appearing the same year. It
makes particularly powerful use of its parallel-city "Lower London"
Underworld, at once a criminal underworld of violent chases and a

medieval Underworld of magic and metamorphosis. The latter also depends on a parallel "underworld" of garbage dumps and tunnels, of Boschian-hybrid grotesques: the grotesque as neighbor, mate, lover. *Perdido* in its Latin root implies the Dantesque, something lost or ruined. The city in which the narrative takes place lies beneath the body of a dead monster, but the world itself is in no way Dark Ages; one enters instead, as in Gaiman's work, the dark science of contemporary urban fantasy. Miéville combines magic with steampunk with Ovidian metamorphosis, invasive criminal underworlds, alchemy, and the ravages of modern racism with a Gormenghastian, Victorian, post-gothic, noirish city of trains and towers.

The key *neo* element in this important touchstone work is the removal and recasting of medieval elements into an alternative world that combines modern and postmodern problems. While it may dispense with traditional didacticism, it can hardly help raising the authors' own concerns about, say, socio-political brutality or political economics. Even an author's statements against didacticism represent a kind of didacticism: "one shouldn't teach – unless of course I have something I want you to know and do." And as with all fads, hip literary topics rise and fall. In our own time we expect authors to stand ahead of the social curve, to advocate those issues we find most important, even if their own time hardly allows for the possibility. Who can say that a generation from now a critic will not look back on *Perdido Street Station* and bemoan its unfortunate inattention to the nuances of quantae-politicae textuo-entomological ephemerism?

While the *Batman* series notably brings the neo-gothic aesthetic into film as well as comics, the *Underworld* trilogy (2003–09) best exemplifies film's narrative and visual exploitation of neomedievalism. Vampires face werewolves in a steely underworld of black-leather corsets, *Matrix*-style weapons accompanied by Asian-style hand-to-hand combat, and ancient family vendettas. On the lighter side *A Knight's Tale* (2001) combines the modern motif of teamwork and working-class-boy-makes-good with Geoffrey Chaucer as fight-night emcee, violent jousts, and misplaced rock anthems, but without the punk-ish irreverence typical of neomedievalism. While John Gardner in *Grendel* successfully hazarded a Freudian fictional remake of *Beowulf*, no one has done a better film version of the epic than the neomedieval *No Such Thing* (2002), which takes large neo steps.[11] An American cub reporter goes to a remote rock in Iceland to find the monster who killed her boyfriend. She does, develops a sympathy and even affection for his jaded, drunken immortality, returns with him to New York and her ruthless, exploitative editor, and finally helps him find the scientist who has the knowledge and technology to un-make him – the end of the movie hints that in eliminating the monster, we also eliminate ourselves, the real source of the monstrous. A smart, satirical, as yet underappreciated film, *No Such Thing* combines pop culture with carefully selected medieval elements severed from their source and context – traits typical of neomedievalism – but it does not shy away from addressing the ills of our flash-and-dash, insensitive, ethics-free culture.

Robert Zemeckis' *Beowulf* (2007) sits on the border between medievalism and neomedievalism: it draws its subject from a medieval text and keeps the original name for its public recognition, but only to refigure it in a postmodern way with little concern for the original beyond the name. It focuses more on its medium through the visual possibilities of performance-capture technology and 3D to deliver its fantastic elements, and it feels more like an attempt to upgrade (via video-game look and feel) the viewing experience from the graphic-novel quality look and violence of *300* to something even quirkier and more viscerally roller-coasterish. The moral point of the epic dims, and it shifts from one's need for steadfast courage and composure in the face of monstrous enemies to the evil of male libido and the willingness of the monstrous, if curvaceous, female to exploit that failing. The medium becomes the message, along with the film-makers' attitudes toward the original subject: *Beowulf* does not receive the respect that Peter Jackson gave Tolkien throughout the *Lord of the Rings* series.

The medium most typical of neomedievalism may be none of those we now think of as traditional: not novel, film, or even personal video game. Neo may have found its most definitive incarnation in MMORPGs and competitive trading card games such as *Magic: The Gathering*. Massively-multiplayer online role-playing games, a billion-dollar industry, draw devoted players from all over the world who enjoy the adventures, character development, unfolding worlds, and social organization that they find in online games. Early games from the late 1990s include *Mazewar* and *Neverwinter Nights*, while the most popular games currently include *World of Warcraft* and *Rohan: Blood Feud*. Most games draw elements from both medievalistic fantasy and science fiction, but not all highlight battle; they do, though, apparently tend to inspire addictive behavior as players get more and more caught up in the intricacy of the fantasy worlds. The most recent trend involves greater amounts of player-created content: one can help create the game and the world as one goes.[12] Through the 1990s, *Magic* (published by Wizards of the Coast), an adventure card game that requires large decks the content of which the player may partly control, gained a considerable following (millions world-wide) and this led to tournaments with the potential for players to win substantial sums of money. Each player takes the role of a "planes-walker," a wizard. Each deck has a color designator that indicates the kind of land in which the action takes place and the type of character and magic one chooses (e.g., order and equality, intellect and trickery, power and amorality, creativity and fury). Individual cards in the decks represent, for instance, spells, artifacts, monsters, warrior allies that one attempts to play in such a way as to gain energy and "life" or to inhibit or damage an opponent. The cards themselves blend materials from many different sources, some of them from the medieval world or from medievalism: knights, gargoyles, codices of spells, magic stones, enchanted shields, plagues, elves, druids, orcs, gnomes, and trolls.[13] Players may willingly select "evil" characters: the game involves no special quest for wisdom or courage or some other virtue. One wins by destroying the opponent – amorality often characterizes neo texts. The creation of a new "text" with each deck and each match lends an element of variety and creativity to the game: the cards themselves represent the tastes of neo artwork in their blend of contemporary comic illustration with the grotesque, the wild, imaginative landscape, and an alchemical attention to color and transformation. Multiplicity and the ability within a controlled realm to gain and display power contribute to the appeal of the experience.

The "ideal" neomedieval text would comprise multiple texts in multiple media, with no particular medium privileged: it would begin as a role-playing computer game but quickly extend to novels, a 3D, semi-animated movie series, trading cards, and a specialty video game available on cell phones. Set in an alternative reality, the story would follow a band of multi-racial, multi-gender samurai dedicated to the katana and horsemanship as they battle a Euro-ursine race who sport plate mail and two-handed claymores – no one can remember exactly why. The asiatics would maintain continual negotiations with a merchant class who travel by steam-powered trains and yachts and who indulge their tastes for gambling and fancy Victorian clothing, especially tight-fitting silk corsets; the euros would show a taste for meat bordering on cannibalism, and they would idealize the image of a muscular vampire king who prefers but need not restrict himself to nighttime travel. They would acquire their wealth through harrying by sea. In deep, reinforced caverns beneath their respective capital cities would dwell – unknown to all but the secret societies who worship them – the real powers behind the two cultures: a white, catlike sorceress and a dark-pelted, snake-eyed, transgender warlock. Cousins, they play out an ancient family feud through their influence on their peoples (deploying mass hypnosis and psychotropic drugs): they feel from afar at once an intense sexual attraction and a driving desire to cause each other's violent death. Both seek the holy ritual-cup of their Ancient Mother, the presence of which, tradition holds, can free peoples from the influence of violence and barbarism – they want it to supply it, without the knowledge of the military classes, to the other side, so that it will lose the power to resist invasion. Common folk have a deep, subconscious desire for the cup without knowing exactly what it is and have no idea how to get it; many of them spend nearly all their incomes in therapy trying to understand their strange dreams about and obsessions with simple drinking cups.

The story would do all that, but in an especially and self-consciously irreverent way. Movie or video-game scores would use hip-hop, heavy metal, or non-harmonic folk fusion. The prose or music or images would stray as far as they could economically safely stray from convention, aiming for extreme reactions from arousal to titillation to disgust – the more one can claim counterculture, the better, since the neo move implies not a step, but a leap away from lingering oppressive forms.

The products related to the alternative world would make a few entrepreneurs extremely rich, and a number of offshoot companies would arise, providing employment for directionless college graduates for several years until the fashion and technology changed. Twelve-year-olds would make their parents wait in queues overnight outside of specialty gaming shops for the latest e-book or game enhancement disks. The entrepreneurs would appear at gaming conferences wearing multiple earrings in each ear and designer clothing mimicking that of their favorite characters from the series, and when sales had peaked and faded, they would take up academic jobs in pop-culture departments at second-tier universities and reminisce over pints of dark beer with admiring students who wanted to pull off the same magic in their own time. Essential: one must maintain the *punk* attitude, the willingness to fight authority and resist pressures from mainline society to conform – to anything.

Neomedievalism, barely a generation old, has yet fully to stake its own course, and practitioners will resist and even deride limitations: they will follow Jean Valjean and the Phantom and Selene the beautiful vampire warrior through sewers and steam-drenched tunnels and beyond. They will select the details that appeal to them from medieval, Victorian, and science-fiction worlds and refigure them as they please.[14] They will explore alternative fashion, gothic subculture, independent media, and "Dark Aesthetics."[15] While my attempts to define and exemplify it in this essay are fraught with idiosyncratic readings and observations – as any will be during the time that we sort out what it means and what it does – we may at this stage of our study of an emerging mode speculate without undue fear; how much can we err in defining the nascent child when we have not yet fully defined the parent? And our current discussions may even contribute to how the child grows toward adulthood.

NOTES

1. Barry Mann put them in, in 1961. The song was sung by the Platters.
2. See "Dreaming in the Middle Ages," in *Travels in Hyperreality*, trans. William Weaver (San Diego, CA: Harcourt Brace, 1986), 61–72. In their *Studies in Medievalism* 18 essay "Living with Neomedievalism," Carol Robinson and Pam Clements describe Eco's point as "neomedievalism is an intentional rewriting of medieval social codes and ethics into contemporary aesthetics" (59) – in that sense it is a "more pop-culture coinage" (59). In this essay I will not be using the term as it appears in some recent journalism and Neoconservative jargon in reference to aggressive international political agendas and their means of influence.
3. Prof. Jane Toswell, who hosted the 2007 Studies in Medievalism conference at Western Ontario University, gave the conference a theme of neomedievalism. She said that, at least up to that time, in North America the term has been used by a relatively small group of persons interested in how

ideas, images, and motifs of the Middle Ages were appearing in video games and other technologies (personal communication). Robinson and Clements conclude that "Neomedievalism works from a postmodernist stance of multiplicity in our thinking about medievalism [...] [a] significant change in process, clearly a self-reflexive and often humorous twist upon medievalism" (70). They note, humorously but not joking, I think, that "A neomedievalist academe would consciously and unabashedly play a re-created video game of an alternative medieval university on her office computer!" (70). The combination of play and technology goes far toward defining neomedievalism in practice.

4. They take a greater interest in the facets and effects of the "reel Middle Ages" than in the real Middle Ages, as Kevin Harty might say.

5. Increasingly popular since the film *The Matrix*, with its cyberpunk mix of circuits, martial arts, and a dark, conspiratorial underworld subconscious.

6. Larry Niven and Jerry Pournelle, *Inferno* (New York: Pocket Books, 1976). A sequel, *Escape from Hell* (New York: Tor), appeared in early 2009.

7. Larry Niven, Jerry Pournelle, and Steven Barnes, *The Legacy of Heorot* (New York: Pocket Books, 1987).

8. James Blaylock, *The Elfin Ship* (New York: Del Rey, 1982).

9. Holly Black, *Tithe* (New York: McElderry Books, 2004).

10. Neil Gaiman, *Neverwhere* (New York: HarperCollins, 1998). Readers may also call to mind Mervyn Peake's Gormenghast trilogy of 1946–59, made into a television series by the BBC in 2000. While it builds a more Victorian world, it features a similarly strong coloring of the neogothic, along with swords, castles, and poisonings. China Miéville, *Perdido Street Station* (New York: Ballantine, 2000). While Miéville acknowledges that anyone writing fantasy cannot escape Tolkien's influence, he reportedly has referred to Tolkien as the "wen on the arse of fantasy literature." I found that quotation incompletely attributed on a couple of websites and hope it inaccurate or fictional. I mention it here only because, regardless of its source and despite its unfortunate descent into silly insult, its association with the author suggests neomedievalism's discomfort with more traditional medievalism, a perception of it as diseased and oppressive. Much of neomedievalism seems to know its debt while hurrying from it with an insistence that exhibits conscious distaste for its popular parent – a point Harold Bloom makes more generally in *The Anxiety of Influence* (1973; 2nd ed. Oxford: Oxford University Press, 1997).

11. *Underworld*, dir. Len Wiseman (Lakeshore Entertainment); *A Knight's Tale*, dir. Brian Helgeland (Columbia Pictures); *No Such Thing*, dir. Hal Hartley (American Zoetrope); *Beowulf*, dir. Robert Zemeckis (Paramount Pictures).

12. For games and information, see <www.mmorpg.com> and <www.wizards.com>. The latter, the site for Wizards of the Coast, provides material for purchase in many different media and has been a major source of fantasy novels as well as *Dungeons & Dragons* and related products for more than thirty years.

13. One will also find distinctly unmedieval entities: sandworms, gorillas, muses, and mechanized creatures.

14. The key to neomedievalism is that its truest medievalism appears not in the text, but in the footnotes.

15. A student at the college where I teach uses that term to describe his *neo* subculture, which includes interest in postmodern philosophy, themed nightclubs, neo-gothic tastes such as contemporary and sometimes subversive *noir* film, and alternative, often gender-transgressive dress.

Dark Matters and Slippery Words: Grappling with Neomedievalism(s)

Lauryn S. Mayer

> *Uncle Julian rubbed his hands together. "I am going to begin the chapter with a slight fabrication, and then proceed to an outright lie."*[1]

In Passus Eight of William Langland's *Piers Plowman*, Will sets off to discover Dowel, convinced that he is on a quest for a single correct answer. Many years, paths, and interpretive mires later, he (and the reader) finally grasp the hard truth: Dowel is a reflexive and reflective process that must be continually repeated in a postlapsarian world. If there is one aspect of neomedievalism that critics can agree upon, it is that it resists any easy definition, and the problem may lie in the questions we are asking. To ask "what is neomedievalism?" or even "what are neomedievalisms?" is to treat a continuously unfolding and changing phenomenon as if it were a finished and static entity; any answer given will by default be "a slight fabrication." With this in mind, I want to explore four patterns within the "continuing process of creating the Middle Ages" with the aim of providing interpretive models while avoiding the problems of strict taxonomy.

The Neo/medieval

The Neo/medieval model I would like to propose builds on the foundation that Carol Robinson, Pam Clements, and MEMO offer: "a medievalism that seems to be a direct and unromantic response to the general matrix of medievalisms from which people are partially 'unplugged'."[2] The reference here is from the 1999 movie *The Matrix*, in which the hacker Neo learns that his destiny is to free a populace enslaved by their belief in and dependence upon projections of "reality" from an enormously complex computer system, the matrix of the title. However, the programming is not foolproof, and the system itself betrays its constructed nature at times:

> Cypher: What happened?
> Neo: A black cat went past us, and then another that looked just like it.
> Trinity: How much like it? Was it the same cat?
> Neo: It might have been. I'm not sure.
> [...]
> Neo: What is it?
> Trinity: A déjà vu is usually a glitch in the Matrix. It happens when they change something.[3]

The Neo/medieval text occurs when its creators play Morpheus, deliberately disrupting medievalist programming by the insertion of "red pills," blatantly anachronistic elements. In the process, the text offers some inherent commentary on the phenomenon of medievalisms themselves. Moreover, it must do so in a way that is obvious to the intended audience. A medievalist might take exception to the portrayal of Guinevere in Antoine Fuqua's *King Arthur*, but the film is serious in its attempt to show the "historical" beginnings of Camelot. As Fuqua comments in one interview:

> The truth is, the Pics [sic], the people, were warriors. Back in those days, and a lot of people haven't made movies about female warriors yet and I don't know why, there were a lot of female warriors. A lot of Scandinavian women would cut, I think it was their left, breasts off so that they could fire the bow and arrow. Yeah. They were pretty hard core. [Laughs] The females were quite tough. And the Pics [sic], the people, they actually used to fight naked. They used to fight in the nude. And they used to paint themselves, with blue paint. They did it because it was a spiritual thing. The wode [sic] is a plant they used to use to paint their bodies blue. And they fought naked to scare their enemies, to disrespect them, show 'em they had no fear. So that stuff is real.[4]

Brian Helgeland's *A Knight's Tale*, by contrast, is Neo/medieval in that its audience is expected to know that the music of Queen or Bowie and the Nike logo do not date to the fourteenth century. The pleasure for the audience comes from the deliberately disjointed nature of Neo/medievalism: the kind of connections it makes between medieval aristocrats and sports superstars, courtly favors and corporate sponsorships, and the bread and circuses nature of public spectacle in the fourteenth and twenty-first centuries. More importantly, the film invites us to examine the agendas governing our constructions of the past: the false origin of the Nike logo points out the fragility of any genealogical project; the sly jab at nostalgia present in the "Golden Years" dance scene uncovers the dissatisfaction with the present that often motivates recreations of past, and the character of Chaucer constantly reminds the viewer that representation is power: "I will eviscerate you in fiction. Every pimple, every character flaw. I was naked for a day; you will be naked for eternity," promises an enraged Chaucer after literally losing his shirt to Simon the Summoner and Peter the Pardoner.[5] Similarly, Graham Baker's *Beowulf*, which opens with a shot of Hrothgrar brandishing a broadsword/chainsaw hybrid, conflates postindustrial dystopianism and the "life is filthy, brutish, and short" view of the Middle Ages to critique progressive or providential histories, replacing them with Adorno's grim "slingshot to atom bomb" narrative.[6] There are, however, relatively few texts that fit this definition, perhaps because of the very investment cultures have in retaining the medieval matrix as an epistemological and emotional resource. Much more common are medievalist texts that engage in light subversion, usually poking fun at certain elements within the medieval matrix while keeping its larger structure(s) and purpose(s) intact. Texts that mix the "medieval" and the "modern" perform some of these connecting and interrogating functions in some areas – Twain's *A Connecticut Yankee in King Arthur's Court* deliberately deflates the romance of chivalry, as does Stephen Weeks' *Sword of the Valiant*,[7] but does not question the possibility of accessing "the medieval" itself; indeed, all instances of time-travel narratives depend on the ontological stability of periodization and most privilege an evolutionary history of continual progress. While *Timeline*'s junior historian Chris notes the relatively advanced hygiene practiced among the nobility, this is more than balanced by the amount of horror Kate feels at the "casual violence" and abysmal technology at Castlegard. Andre Marek, the Yale academic, becomes more and more animal with each day spent in the past.[8] In Gil Junger's *Black Knight*, the time-travelling Jamal tries to persuade the fourteenth-century Nicole to come back with him, contrasting her life of "eating slop" to an Edenic vision of "drinkin' Mai Tais, gettin' your legs waxed."[9] These last two examples, instead, participate in one of the multiple *neomedievalisms* (particular visions or practices that have emerged or become more prevalent in the last decade) noted by Robinson and Clements. In the next section, I expand upon three of these that I consider the most important threads running through Neo medievalism.

Neomedievalisms

Medievalism as a stance towards the Middle Ages

Whether positive or negative, the implicit argument is that the Middle Ages can be understood, usually within a fairly limited set of terms that can then be used for a variety of agendas. Medievalism in this sense is the process of locating a particular set of phenomena as an anachronism or a return of the past. In the process, the idea of historical progress is reaffirmed as a pattern, even if elements of the present are seen as "returns" from the past. In its most egregious form, medievalism takes phenomena present in the Middle Ages, generalizes that presence as a hallmark of the Middle Ages (with the implicit assumption that its existence was bounded by that period), and then treats the presence of similar phenomena in other periods, with concomitant anticipation or dread, as irruptions of the medieval. The Middle Ages envisioned in this process does not admit of historical change within the period nor recognize geographic or cultural particularity. Cullen Murphy's article in the October 2003 issue of the *Atlantic* is a nice synecdoche of this phenomenon. Beginning with a very loosely spun tissue of correspondences (a group of men talking on cell phones while standing at urinals is an "iconic" image that "stands as a contemporary analogue, perhaps, to the chanted refrains of ancient monks in their stalls at Westminster or Chartres."),[10] Murphy quickly moves from these "frankly trivial" instances to the real problem:

> In the West the path away from the Middle Ages was marked by the evolution of governments and nation-states with a sense of responsibility for the public interest rather than merely private interests. Power was no longer a form of property. Social services

and protections became a consequence of citizenship, not a private deal between a lord and his vassals, or between a private entity and its clients [...] But at some point in the late twentieth century evolution's arrow began changing direction – toward the reprivatization of everything.[11]

Privatization is conflated with feudalism, and, for Cullen, a return to feudalism poses a threat to the entire narrative of progress: "To be sure, the self-perception of people in the developed world has very little of the medieval about it. We inhabit the Information Age. We proclaim the Era of Globalization. We consider ourselves postmodern, maybe even posthuman. But it is also true that elements of a prior *regime* were never quite *eradicated* and in some cases are *growing back* (emphasis mine)."[12] Evidently the Middle Ages is equal in its noxious persistence to dandelions or crabgrass. The double move of this kind of neomedievalism is that it allows both fears about contemporary culture to be voiced as fears of invasion from an "alternate world" rather than endemic elements and dreams for the future to be seen as available from past practice(s).

Medievalism as texts that work with the dynamic "matter"
of the Middle Ages

"Matter" here is used in the medieval sense of the term: the accumulation of texts that make up the ever-growing body of a subject. The "matter" of the Middle Ages, then, includes not only texts and artifacts from the medieval period, but its every subsequent representation in any medium. In this sense, it operates as the procedural opposite of the previous instance of medievalism; rather than imposing a static definition of "the medieval" as a foundation for analysis, this medievalism defines itself as inherently contingent and hybrid in nature, creating a complex text by the interaction of elements within the matter, an interaction akin to the phenomenon of "emergence" in artificial-life theory. As Christopher Langton notes:

> Artificial life starts at the bottom, viewing an organism as a large population of simple machines, and works upwards synthetically from there – constructing large aggregates of simple, rule-governed objects which interact with one another nonlinearly in the support of life-like, global dynamics.[13]

We can think of the production of medievalist texts in a similar fashion, since the matter itself is composed of both content and generic matters. For example, within the larger matter of the medieval is the matter of Arthur, which contains places (Camelot, Rome), genres (romance, chronicle), events, characters, and so forth, each of which has particular coded features (the rule-governed objects) that may be expressed or suppressed when combined with other elements of the matter of the medieval. If the matter of Arthur combines with the elements of the Tolkien universe and *The Mists of Avalon*, it produces a world such as that found in the computer game *Dark Age of Camelot*. If it combines with the governing aesthetics of superhero comic books and science fiction, it can produce *Camelot 3000*. In each case, this cannot be called completely free play or anarchy, because each element of the matter, to remain coherent, must be governed by a certain set of rules: a culturally legible comic superhero must look and behave within certain parameters, for instance. However, the possibilities for recombination and mutation are nearly endless. The benefit of this approach is that it provides a more coherent structure for analysis while avoiding the problems inherent in strict taxonomic approaches to medievalist texts.

Neomedievalism as the process of compilation and collaborative production

This model posits medievalism as practice, not product. As Robinson and Clements have noted, "One additional aspect of neomedieval entertainments is the dissolution of single authorship."[14] I would like to expand upon this and argue that one important element of neomedievalism may have nothing to do with the content of a particular text, but with its forms of production, reproduction, and consumption. As Elizabeth Bryan points out, medieval textual communities operated on a set of assumptions that differ dramatically from those governing print culture:

> This set of attitudes did not, as in later scholastic theorizing or in modern print culture, center textual authority in human authors in the sense of devaluing the "transmitters", those who collaborated in the series of textual reproductions. Rather than prioritizing any one manuscript version of a text on the basis of a place in its chronological sequence, this set of assumptions

prioritized the continuance itself of a text. The emphasis of this particularly configured medieval scribal textual community is not only on the object of the text but on the process between text and reader, a process of collaboration among first authors, scribes, illuminators, correctors, annotators, and other readers. The continuance of such a scribal text did not mean exactly repeated "mechanical" reproduction, but instead a renegotiation among meaning and words of preceding models and current writers and readers each time a single codex was produced.[15]

The ease of contacting collaborators, producing content, and finding an audience online has led to an exponential rise in collaborative production, and in the kinds of texts being produced. To give one example, Make Literature Online is a site devoted to the collaborative production of fiction. To provide structural integrity, there are six project frameworks offered at any given time, one in each of the following genres: Science Fiction and Fantasy, Mystery and Horror, Crime and Thriller, Romance and Comedy, History and Adventure, and Children's and Social. Storylines are chosen based on popularity (how many hits a particular storyline receives), member rankings, and reviews. Once the storyline is chosen, members may submit selections in order to be chosen as collaborators in the creation of the text, which will then be made available for purchase. Dabbleboard and other virtual whiteboards permit the collaborative production of visual and written text, and are becoming increasingly popular. Even more common is the process of collaboration among first authors and subsequent users. Fanfiction.net, one of the largest fan-fiction sites on the Web, contains submissions in the hundreds of thousands (17,592 for *Pirates of the Caribbean* alone). The practices of fansub (user translation of a film from its original language into another and adding subtitles) and fandub (user dubbing or redubbing of a film in a way that usually changes its storyline, dialogue, and character personalities) gains more producers and a larger audience every month, and remixing is now standard musical practice. These kinds of recombinations gain another level of meaning when users then create their own compilations, incorporating their own and others' texts into neomiscellanies. A typical text of this kind may include, for example: the opening chapters of *Pride and Prejudice*; a favorite fan-fiction chapter providing backstory on Mr. Bennet's early courtship of Mrs. Bennet and his growing disillusionment; a clip of Colin Firth plunging into the pond in the BBC production; a soundtrack assembled by the user; and a Photoshopped "cover" with the user appearing next to Keira Knightley's Elizabeth. The single-author work is not eradicated in the process, nor is there an outright rejection of the terms "author" or "work"; rather, author and work become part of a continually growing text, a *compilatio* that retains and preserves the multiplicity of meaning it had for the Middle Ages: form, process, and principle.[16]

The neomedieval is a vast compilation in its own right, in which form, practice, and principle cannot and should not be separated. Perhaps the best approach is to worry less about what, precisely, it is and to spend more time thinking about what it does and why it does it. In Geraldine Heng's discussion of the equally protean nature of medieval romance, she argues that the romance "must be identified by the *structure of desire* which powers its narrative, and the transformational repetitions of that structure through innumerable variations, rather than by any intrinsic subject matter, plot, style, or other content."[17] If we adopt a similar model for the study of neomedievalism, we may be able to find a way to satisfy our own desire for a coherent rather than constricting structure.

NOTES

1. Shirley Jackson, *We Have Always Lived in the Castle* (New York: Popular Library, 1963), 46.
2. Carol Robinson and Pam Clements, "Living with Neomedievalism," *Studies in Medievalism* 18 (2009): 56.
3. *The Matrix*, dir. Andy Wachowski and Larry Wachowski, perf. Keanu Reeves, Laurence Fishburne, Carrie-Ann Moss, and Hugo Weaving (Warner Brothers, 1999).
4. Antoine Fuqua, interview with Jeff Otto, *IGN* 9 July 2004 <http://movies.ign.com/articles/529/529517p1.html>, accessed 2 August 2009.
5. *A Knight's Tale*, dir. Brian Helgeland, perf. Heath Ledger, Rufus Sewell, Shannon Sossaman, and Paul Bettany (Columbia Pictures, 2001).
6. *Beowulf*, dir. Graham Baker, perf. Christopher Lambert, Rhona Mitra, Oliver Cotton, Götz Otto, Roger Sloman, and Layla Roberts (Capitol Films, 1999).

7. *Sword of the Valiant*, dir. Stephen Weeks, perf. Thomas Heathcote, Miles O'Keefe, Leigh Lawson, Trevor Howard, and Sean Connery (The Cannon Group, 1984). Mark Twain, *A Connecticut Yankee in King Arthur's Court* (Oxford: Oxford Unversity Press, 2004).

8. Michael Crichton, *Timeline* (New York: Alfred A. Knopf, 1999).

9. Cullen Murphy, "Feudal Gestures," *Atlantic Monthly* 292 (October 2003): 135–37.

10. Murphy, "Feudal Gestures," 135.

11. Murphy, "Feudal Gestures," 136.

12. Murphy, "Feudal Gestures," 135.

13. Christopher Langton, "Artificial Life," in *Artificial Life*, ed. Christopher Langton, Santa Fe Institute Studies in the Sciences of Complexity, vol. 6 (Reading, MA: Addison-Wesley, 1989), 2.

14. Robinson and Clements, "Living with Neomedievalism," 68.

15. Elizabeth J. Bryan, *Collaborative Meaning in Medieval Scribal Culture: The Otho Layamon*, Editorial Theory and Literary Criticism 14 (Ann Arbor: University of Michigan Press, 1999), 45.

16. R. H. Rouse and M. A. Rouse, "*Ordinatio* and *Compilatio* Revisited," in *Ad litteram: Authoritative Texts and Their Medieval Readers*, Notre Dame Conferences in Medieval Studies 3 (South Bend, IN: University of Notre Dame Press, 1992), 116.

17. Geraldine Heng, *Empire of Magic: Medieval Romance and the Politics of Cultural Fantasy* (New York: Columbia University Press, 2003), 3.

Utopia and Heterotopia:
Byzantine Modernisms in America[1]

Glenn Peers

Dreams and visions of Byzantium traveled across the Atlantic Ocean many times over the course of the twentieth century, and they helped to determine the creation and understanding of modern art in America. Broadly speaking, the dreams were utopian desires on the parts of critics, historians, and artists for a world where unified humanity and essential art were possible; the visions were newly framed representations of Byzantium and no less historically wishful. Michel Foucault (1926–84) discussed this cultural dichotomy: he described one emplacement, on the one hand, as utopia, self-evidently no-place, a perfected form of society that does not exist; or, on the other hand, as heterotopia, a more difficult and interesting concept, that is a counter-site, "simultaneously represented, contested and inverted."[2] In broad terms, American engagement with Byzantium in the twentieth century takes either of these forms: when Willem de Kooning called New York City a "Byzantine city," he projected an idealized version of Constantinople on Manhattan, and when John and Dominique de Menil commissioned a Byzantine Fresco Chapel Museum in Houston, Texas, Foucault's emplacement finds vivid expression in a "new" Byzantium, an active suspension between urban America and rural Cyprus.[3]

   This article examines these Byzantium "places" in America. Versions of Byzantium circulating in their milieus have informed modernist American projects. Dreams of Byzantium fueled modernist utopias, traces of which are in American art of the late 1940s and 1950s, but all dreams have some residue in them of the world. And, so, Byzantine utopias also lead to emplacement in the world, places like Houston's Rothko Chapel and the Byzantine Fresco Chapel Museum, heterotopias where modern bodies and souls find themselves perfectly and strangely reflected. Those Byzantine "places" are threads of an intricate historical web, which cannot be fully analyzed within the scope of this article, but important changes took place in the sea voyage between Byzantium and America: in its new settings, Byzantium became both a forceful idea and a powerful reality, utopian and heterotopian, and always new.

Byzantine Utopias

An examination of Byzantine modernisms needs to begin in 1948 with the convergence of the ideals of an American master, Barnett Newman (1905–70), and of a French art historian and critic, Georges Duthuit (1891–1974).[4] One vector of that convergence is relatively minor in the history of post-war American culture, but its role in the development of Byzantine modernisms cannot be overestimated. In 1948, Duthuit used his considerable energy, erudition, and connections to initiate the publication of a journal, *Transition*.[5] The journal ran for six issues and finished publication in 1950, but in that space of time it attracted a very engaged readership. It published recent work of French intellectuals in English and thereby made those developments, which were so compelling to American intellectuals, more easily accessible to English speakers than they had been. The journal was read avidly, for instance, by the artist and connoisseur John Graham (1881–1961) and his circle. His strong affinity for the art scene in Paris made him a link between that city and New York, and his Francophile leanings, including the reading of *Transition*, informed the development of Willem de Kooning (1904–97).[6] de Kooning still remembered that journal in the 1970s.

The first three numbers of *Transition* from 1948 coincide with one of the heroic moments of American art, the creation of Newman's *Onement I* (Museum of Modern Art, New York City) (Fig. 1). Their convergence is likely more than coincidence, as Newman possessed the inaugural issue of the journal.[7] But first came the making of the painting. The creation story has something of the miraculous in it, for on his forty-third birthday, 29 January 1948, Newman was working through a painting, and in the process

Fig. 1 Barnett Newman, Onement I, 1948. Oil on Canvas, 69.2 41.3 cm.
The Museum of Modern Art/Licensed by Scala/Art Resource NY.
Barnett Newman Foundation/Artists Rights Society (ARS), New York.

of its unfolding, the canvas brought him up surprisingly short. He had applied a layer of brownish-red paint to the small canvas, which measures only 69.2 × 41.3 cm, and he had affixed a strip of narrow masking tape down the center to which he then applied an uneven and irregular coat of red-orange paint. He was brought up short because the painting then declared itself finished. Newman heard the declaration but did not understand its meaning, and he struggled, as only a highly principled intellectual would, to comprehend the implications of this breakthrough. And the painting did constitute a breakthrough – though of course it has organic connections to his previous painting – because it constitutes a perfect moment of abstract art: the symmetry of the two lateral fields bisected by a quivering, almost breathing "zip," as he called it, is a condensation of how humans organize their perceptions of their worlds.[8] It is like an inverted mirror. The scale of his work increased, and he experimented with the perceptual range of abstraction, but *Onement I* represented a revolutionary advance for American art. It did not participate in a western history of aesthetics, nor did it participate in a western history of art; it was itself and nothing else, and it was universal, a perfect concentration of modernist perception.[9]

The painting worked on Newman through most of 1948, and he only stepped back, in a sense, on Yom Kippur, the Jewish Day of Atonement. The span of Newman's contemplation was marked at one end by his own birthday and at the other by Yom Kippur, the high holiday of atonement and cleansing, in religious terms a day of re-birth. The title of the painting, *Onement I*, partook of the same heroicizing process as the making and comprehending of the painting itself. When Newman showed at the Betty Parsons Gallery in 1950–51, his work bore no titles at all, and his attitude toward titling was ambivalent at this time:

> In the beginning, I suppose, I was vague about titles [...]. But I realized that the issue was an important one for me, because the title could act as a metaphor to identify the emotional content or the emotional complex that I was in when I was doing the painting.[10]

The title came several years later, but its roots are in his experiences in and around 1948. The word "onement" is an archaism, seldom used in modern English, and it was evidently chosen for its resonances. The intersection with Yom Kippur points to a work marking new beginnings through cleansing, and the religious connotations of the word are manifested in its cognate, atonement. The title also refers to self-sufficiency, an integrity of perceptions by the individual, an important element to the anarchist Newman, as well as to a material integrity, a non-referentiality important also to figures like the critic Clement Greenberg (1909–94).[11]

But another cognate in currency in New York in 1948 was "at-one-ment," a neologism coined by Duthuit in the first number of *Transition*, published 15 February of that same year and soon after,

apparently, in Newman's library. While not a catalyst for the creation
of the painting, the journal was circulating among New York intellectuals in 1948, and the contents made an impact. Generated by
Georges Duthuit's ardent idealism, his foundational editorial made
the restitution of the fragments of post-war life its necessary goal.
Duthuit claimed that the contributors were:

> [...] united by a common will to be true to truth, and a common
> awareness of a new age already kicking in the womb. That age,
> they hold, will utter a simplification, an astonishing simplification:
> whereby science and divination, metaphysics and the arts, all the
> lusty incompatibles, will no longer seem apart or out of joint, but
> fused and re-minted into a wise wholeness. It is their aim, and the
> ambition of this paper, to recover somehow the virtue that has
> gone out of life: to unseal the spirit of festivity; to find again the
> adjustment, togetherness, at-one-ment of the tavern; to return to
> the sense of rapture.[12]

The prose is typical of Duthuit, whether he was writing in French or
in English, of modern art and society or of Byzantine, Coptic, or
Chinese art. It was always, in parts, poetic, impressionistic, sincerely
activistic, energetic, and in many ways captivating.[13] But it was from
an outsider position; Duthuit always went against the grain. Newman
never claimed that this editorial statement was the reason for choosing
Onement as his title for that painting of 1948, but the lexical similarities between "at-one-ment" and "onement" are self-evident, and the
journal was in his possession while he came to terms with the conse-
quences of his acts of 29 January.[14] More compelling, perhaps, are the
sympathetic parallels between Duthuit's "call to arms" and Newman's
highly principled social conscience. Duthuit's idea that a unifying
awareness brought forth by art would allow a new consciousness was
at the heart of Newman's own program. Duthuit argued for a new
"wholeness" that would arise out of the ashes of the war experience,
for "virtue" to be reclaimed for modern society, and, most strikingly
under the circumstances, for an "at-one-ment" – a neologism meant
to imply a permanent state of concord – to prevail.

These ideals, these markers of a utopian society, had real resonance for Newman, but they also struck a general chord among intellectuals reacting to an increasingly chilly climate of public conformity
and complacency. Such ideals stand in stark relief to the backlash

against the buying of modern art by the State Department for international exhibitions in 1947 and, of course, to growing support for
redbaiters like Joseph McCarthy.[15]

Newman's essay, "The Sublime is Now," published in December
1948 (though very likely written well in advance), matched his artistic
breakthrough with an articulated theoretical initiative. Now was the
time, he declared, for "making [cathedrals] out of ourselves, out of our
own feelings."[16] Here was a radically individualistic theoretical stance
that asserted self-awareness as the necessary goal of all persons. That
self-awareness was generated not only through making *Onement I*, but
also through seeing it honestly and conscientiously: "The image we
produce is the self-evident one of revelation, real and concrete, that
can be understood by anyone who will look at it without the nostalgic
glasses of history."[17] Newman's position was a fully realized program of
creation and being that would be a state of personal "at-one-ment." A
society composed of such individuals in states of "at-one-ment" was
the vision of Duthuit in his harmonious taverns, the togetherness of
festivities, that would lead to a new "wise wholeness."

If those visions can be seen to have concordance, and *if* Duthuit's
proclamation led Newman to articulate his painting's enterprises in
certain ways, Duthuit and Newman diverged over attitudes to the
past. Newman was a fierce proponent of the freedom of the New
World from the burdened past of Europe, while Duthuit was an
extremely cultivated European, equally at home defending Matisse as
he was evoking the charms of Coptic sculpture. Who else could,
without any overreaching at all, compare the impact of Fauvism on
European culture to the Franks taking Constantinople in 1204?[18] The
radical return to the anti-classical was comparable in his eyes to the
opening of Frankish eyes to the splendors of Byzantium. His investment in the past is likewise signaled at the end of his editorial statement of 1948 when he called for a "return to the sense of rapture."
The key word is return, not in a nostalgic sense, but for the reclama-
tion of the honest emotion possible at times in the past.

Such desire for restitution of harmony in modern society marks
much of Duthuit's writing, and it found its way into his discussions of
Byzantine art and society in such a way that Byzantium emerged as a
thoroughly unified and even classless society, a view at odds with the
vision of most practicing Byzantinists today. That version of the
Byzantine world emerged in his earlier work, to be sure, for example

in his monograph misleadingly entitled *Byzance et l'art du XIIe siècle.*[19] It was put forth most clearly and programmatically, however, in his own journal, *Transition* again, as "Matisse and Byzantine Space," published in 1949.[20] His description of Byzantine culture and society is idiosyncratic, but it was consistent with his leftist views. Moreover, his deep identification with non-mimetic art revealed connections to him between the great French painter Henri Matisse (1869–1954), who was his father-in-law and with whom he had not spoken since 1935,[21] and a style of art he admired highly, particularly the Early Byzantine mosaics of Ravenna. The Byzantium of Duthuit is admittedly compelling, based as it is on a view of that society as truly communal, but it is unrecognizable in terms of the relative absence of religious devotion and the strong role of theology most laymen associate with that culture. For instance, the essay included this claim, "Byzantium, abandoning aesthetics for ethesis, created primarily not art, but history – so that its citizens were no longer mummers, but played a game of which the stake was no vague heaven, but earth itself."[22]

The non-mimetic qualities Duthuit praised in Byzantine art were naturally echoes of what he admired in Matisse's painting. As he exclaimed, the art object is "A living organism, incommensurable with any model!"[23] And his account of pictorial space is modernist to the core, but brilliantly insightful about Byzantine art at the same time. How space implicates and acts on viewers has been a natural concern of Byzantine art historians, like the great Austrian art historian Otto Demus (1902–90), because the extant monuments with mosaics or paintings are so vivid and fulsome.

Duthuit identified one monument in particular for his analysis of the shift from Old Rome to New Rome, from one way of seeing and being to another: the so-called Mausoleum of Galla Placidia, formerly attached to the church of Santa Croce, but now a freestanding monument in Ravenna (dated 425–50).[24] The shift was nowhere more evident for him than in a comparison of the representation of space between the Good Shepherd lunette over the entrance at the north side of the building and the domed core of the building with the cross revealed in the apex and surrounded by evangelist symbols and apostles (Fig. 2). For Duthuit, as for others since, the Good Shepherd mosaic is an example of a self-sufficient image cordoned off from the viewer by its frame and perspective elements.[25] Unlike the

Fig. 2 Interior view, Mausoleum of Galla Placidia, Ravenna, 425–50.
Photo: Scala/Art Resource, NY.

conventional easel-painting effect that the lunette parallels (despite the lunette's placement above a door), the interior mosaics are inclusive and absorbing to the point that the distinction between represented and real space disappears. Here, Duthuit wrote, "The Orient receives us" (which naturally raises other questions that readers of Edward Said [1935–2003] will recognize), but he also argued, more interestingly, that the mosaics "invade us to the very root of our being" and "all conspire to produce self-communion." Such claims raise issues of subjectivity created by viewing experiences, and they rest in part on the breakdown of distinctions between representation and reality, when pictorial invasion and self-communion take place.

Granted, the Mausoleum of Galla Placidia is not a perfect example for what Duthuit was trying to posit: because it was never a church with liturgies, its context has been broken, and identification of subjects is still contested. But in terms of pictorial space, the distinction between the Good Shepherd lunette and the star-studded interior suffused with light from windows with alabaster panes exists insofar as the experience of absorption intensifies as one goes further into the building. And the small scale of the building makes the experience even more marked because the proportions of the interior are human-scaled. In these terms, a subjectivity is generated where the viewer's body is more aware of its bodiedness, taken into that "self-communion."

Now, the fifth volume of *Transition*, in which the "Matisse and Byzantine Space" article appears, was not in Newman's library. Nonetheless, the writings of Duthuit and Newman stress self-awareness of the viewer before works of art. Each theorist aimed at a radical subjectivity of the viewer before art, self-awareness and self-communion in important ways similar to the results of viewing. As Newman said about the experience of a whiteout he had once encountered, "You're not looking at anything. But you yourself become very visible."[26] A connection between the theories of Newman and Duthuit on viewer transformation is ultimately unprovable. The sense of a viewing body being made more immediate to itself through its viewing of art was common to both writers.

These ideas of trying to establish a modernist sense of pictorial space and subjectivity were not by any means restricted to those two men, and another reader of *Transition*, Willem de Kooning, was also at this same time proposing a subjectivity radically opposed to western understanding based on Renaissance models. He delivered a lecture in 1950, "The Renaissance and Order," in which he contended that a space deep enough for the artist, "to *be*, so to speak, on the inside of his picture," was the goal of a modernist aesthetic.[27] de Kooning, moreover, had read the "Matisse and Pictorial Space" article, and he seems to have absorbed some of its positions. This idea of Byzantine mosaic as an engulfing medium is given voice with a special fervor by Duthuit, but he was not the only Byzantinist making the case from a modernist point of view. Otto Demus wrote an essay in 1948 titled "The Methods of the Byzantine Artist," explored further in his (still) widely read book of the same year, *Byzantine Mosaic Decoration*.[28] The essay was much anthologized, and the fact that it was in the library of Robert Smithson (1938–73) speaks to its appeal for some American artists.[29] The appeal rested in part on Demus's analysis of Byzantine space as the antithesis of a Renaissance conception of illusion. For the Byzantines, Demus wrote, mural art was based on a "negative" perspective, where no barrier or distance existed between represented and real space.

de Kooning claimed in public to hold similar views to Demus

and Duthuit, yet such views were not only within their purview. Duthuit's essay made a sufficiently strong impression that Duthuit's arguments for a culturally integrated, classless society infiltrated de Kooning's own understanding of his adopted city, for he later said New York City was "really like a Byzantine city."[30] This reference is not perfectly transparent, and as Richard Shiff has written, "Like his painted figures, de Kooning's verbal analogy is all-inclusive and very compressed."[31] But de Kooning claimed even later to remember the Duthuit article of 1949, and the simile "New York is like Constantinople" appealed on some level to the cosmopolitan painter. It allowed, perhaps, a perception of an art world integrated into a society that had good pedigree and positive associations.[32]

Certainly at the time of the appearance of the essay, de Kooning was exploring pictorial equivalents to the dynamism of post-war New York, in pictures like *Excavation* (1950, 203.5 × 254.3 cm, oil on canvas, Art Institute of Chicago). Duthuit's evocation of a capital distant and familiar in which a "social structure where every genius, every talent, mingling with peoples of every race and land could find expression" hit home for de Kooning.[33] Not only did that evocation leave traces in de Kooning's memory, but the one Byzantine illustration to Duthuit's article made an impression, too.[34] The black-and-white plate is labeled simply "Byzantine Coin: 12th Century" (Fig. 3)[35] No reference is made to it in the text, and it stands alone, exaggeratedly large and anonymous, since by showing the obverse only and giving no further information the coin has no specific identity. Both those features made the coin available for formal integration of art-historical data at which de Kooning was so accomplished.

And indeed at this point in his career, de Kooning was about to make his own revolutionary breakthrough in his *Woman* series, most forcefully in his *Woman I* (1950–52, 192.7 × 147.3 cm, oil on canvas, Museum of Modern Art, New York) (Fig. 4). This series, like the *Onement* series, evolved from previous work, naturally, but it also represented a decisive and major advance in the painter's work. *Woman I* depended on many models for the final composition, but one must take into account that the Byzantine coin stayed in de Kooning's memory as a visual source into the 1970s. Formal characteristics like the strongly verticalized and frontal pose is derived in part from the coin. The strong contrast between the right angles of the supporting throne and figure on the coin are echoed in *Woman I*,

Fig. 3   Interior Plate, *Transition*, V: Byzantine coin, twelfth century.

Fig. 4   Willem de Kooning, *Woman I*, 1950–52. Oil on canvas, 192.7 × 147.3 cm. © The Museum of Modern Art/Licensed by Scala/Art Resource NY. © Willem de Kooning Foundation/Artists Rights Society (ARS), New York.

especially in the upper right-hand corner. The strongly accented striations on the coin, the clearly marked furrows that constitute Christ's garment, and the bands and markings in the halo are paralleled in the stripes and streaks of the woman's body and the passage around her head.

Such a comparison between an easel painting nearly two meters high and a coin may appear unlikely, but this is just the sort arthistorically self-conscious act artists like de Kooning would perform. And it was, moreover, described in detail by André Malraux (1901–76) in his *Musée imaginaire*, where he wrote about "fictitious arts," for instance, that "the unfinished quality of the execution resulting from the very small scale of these [photographic] objects, now becomes a style, free and modern in its accent."[36] The visual gain from such an act of embedding this reference in *Woman I* might also appear slight, but seen in the light of de Kooning's attraction to "Byzantine New York" or "American Constantinople," the associations are rich. The power of the figure in its iconic pose, exaggerated in its magnified form, combined with the forceful lines constituting the figure, however scumbled in the paint on canvas, marks a potent emblem for a modernist in search of a positively analogous visual culture.[37]

Such a search was not limited to de Kooning, it must be said. New York in 1944 had witnessed a major exhibition at the Metropolitan Museum of Art on Byzantine art, which caught the attention of the French master Fernand Léger (1881–1955). Léger's review of the show was a highly condensed version of some of the ideas Duthuit circulated for his American audience slightly later.[38] Léger admired non-Renaissance approaches to visual art on the basis of their avoidance of mimetic qualities, but he particularly admired Byzantium, he wrote, because that culture respected the mural integrity of mosaic. These views were apparently derived not only from the objects but also from replicas made for the Met.[39] In any case, such versions of Byzantine art allowed him to conceive a social contrast between contemporary western culture and that foreign past: "The art of mosaic is unhappily almost condemned by modern social evolution, our architecture no longer having the conception of the permanence of ancient times." After the war is completed, Léger wrote, mosaic will be the art of the future. In a very short review, he managed to arrive at key points of utopian visions of Byzantium that Duthuit would elaborate several years later.

These interested notions in what Byzantium could mean to moderns were by no means restricted to New York City at the end and in the aftermath of the war. With some help, Henri Matisse had been contending with some of these ideas nearly forty years previous. Memory of that connection between Matisse and Byzantium was never lost, and indeed Georges Duthuit wrote in 1928 that Thomas Whittemore (1871–1950) was using Matisse in his lectures on Byzantine art at New York University.[40] The social network generating these views of Byzantium's relevance to modernist life was strikingly close, for Duthuit, Whittemore, and Matisse were each trained in different ways by an English intellectual, Matthew Stewart Prichard (1865–1936).[41] Prichard was a highly idiosyncratic but charismatic presence in Paris before the First World War, and one of his specialties, which caught the attention of all in his circle, was Byzantine art. He published little, but his tutoring appears strong in Matisse, to whom he was devoted. He spent a great deal of time in Matisse's company in the years before the First World War, and he took the master to school to see the compelling features of Byzantine culture and art.[42]

Indeed, in these years, Matisse took to Byzantine coins more directly and viscerally than did de Kooning almost forty years later, but to equally important effect for their painting. In Matisse's case, the exposure was through actual inspection and understanding, through Prichard's tutelage, of coins as material objects. The mediation of the Byzantine coin for de Kooning through distorting photography lends a very different character to that project and the paintings that resulted from it. For Matisse, the contact implied some understanding of the specific formal and cultural values of the objects, however Prichard arbitrated that culture for him. The two visited museums and dealers' showrooms together, and Matisse became well versed, it would seem, in Byzantine art, for Prichard wrote:

> June, 23, 1914. To-day Matisse said that Byzantine expression and his have the same aim, and that he likes Byzantine coins without any reservation. He looks at them and seizes their meaning without any artistic interruption.[43]

The effect on Matisse's painting is also discernible, for Byzantine coins were on his mind when he was painting certain portraits in the period before the war, like *Le Rifain* (1913, oil on canvas) (Fig. 5).[44]

Fig. 5 Henri Matisse, *Le Rifain*, 1913. Oil on canvas. Photo: Erich Lessing/Art Resource, NY. © Succession Henri Matisse, ARS, New York.

Byzantine style freed Matisse, as he chose many forms from world art. Among other traditions, then, it ratified Matisse's freedom with historical precedent, from strictures of a realist figure style, and it afforded him the chance to create portraiture not invested in individual characteristics but in the expressive aspects of the human form. Such characteristics were strongly pronounced in the iconic and powerful figure style found even in Byzantine minor arts like coins. Unlike Roman portraiture, which often used personal references to locate imperial power, in Byzantium the person was subsumed into the office of emperor and was presented in state art as an impersonal representative of God on earth. Likewise, Christ was described in terms immediate and strikingly forceful through the frontality and expressive lines of clothing and features. In that way, the visual source of authority of the figure of *Le Rifain* is evident through comparison to the small model adapted by Matisse. The power of Christ's iconic presentation gave Matisse a way to represent force of personality

Fig. 6 Henri Matisse, *Portrait of Mme Matisse*, 1913. Oil on canvas, 146 × 97.7 cm. Photo: Art Resource, NY. The Hermitage, St. Petersburg, Russia. © Succession Henri Matisse, ARS, New York.

without gesture, attributes or specific facial expression, like his portrait of his wife from 1913 (Fig. 6). Prichard had shown him a paradigm, and – along with others like African tribal masks – Matisse had developed them with all the visual intelligence he had at his disposal.

Despite the fact that both Matisse and de Kooning were great colorists, those painters chose a linear and iconic figure style from the Byzantine visual tradition to imitate. In de Kooning's case, his capacious approach to source material perhaps dictated his use of the coin from *Transition*, though he did study some Byzantine art when he was a student.[45] Matisse knew the material more extensively than did de Kooning, primarily through Prichard's guidance. But both painters selected aspects that suited their immediate purposes, and those positive attitudes towards the past are, of course, self-interested and self-serving. Clearly both were attracted to Byzantine art, coins most directly and most strikingly; and both were brought to it through some form of mediation, for de Kooning, *Transition*, and for Matisse, Prichard.

Both were led to their awareness by Prichard in different ways, for Prichard was a strong determinant on the development of Duthuit's thinking when he was a young man. For Prichard, Byzantium was a route to a newly activated modernism:

> I look at an object of Byzantine art with affection. As a student of art I am pleased by its evocative character. The action which suggests Christianity under the guise of love and not of dogma appeals to me also. But there is no justification for me to possess it. Our action to-day must find other symbols and we must remember that our psychology has changed [...]. We cannot react to Byzantine art as did the Byzantine. We feel the slight psychological insufficiency of its constitution as well as our estrangement from its meaning. *Art must always be modern.*[46]

This statement is a remarkably vivid description of the appeal of Byzantium as utopia, for it presents that culture with both distance and proximity at the same time, which gives Byzantium a special aura. Prichard clearly kept his distance, and he wrote as a sober historian of the distant past, but he also responded emotionally, "with affection," to the evocativeness of the art. In that vein, he idealized aspects of the culture in his appeal to the love of its Christianity and in its orientation toward real action, a response brought out in other letters he wrote.[47] This last aspect, the activist element latent in Byzantine art, appealed greatly to Prichard, as it came to appeal to Duthuit also, who stressed that characteristic of Byzantium both in his 1926 book on Byzantine art and in his 1949 *Transition* essay. In that sense, Prichard instilled in Duthuit a life-long view of Byzantium as a dynamic and cohesive society and culture. That integrated energy was perhaps not so appealing to Matisse on a social level – he did not appear as a politicized artist at all – but the formal dynamism certainly was. In America in the years after 1945, as Léger had hoped, Byzantium was presented by Duthuit as a signpost for social evolution. Prichard had not presented Byzantium in Arcadian terms, but he had thought of Byzantium as a kind of utopia that could supply a similar dynamism to modern art and society. Duthuit was more romantic in his writing, as he presented that culture as a paradox, a cosmopolitan place of actorless theatre where the stage was real life, where art was seamlessly integrated into the lived world. By all appearances, these utopian ideals of an integrated and dynamic society resonated for Newman and de Kooning, and Duthuit's Byzantinized utopia left singular traces in some of the greatest American art yet produced.

Byzantine Heterotopias

The grounds of the Menil Collection in the Montrose district of Houston, Texas, reveal another site of Byzantine America (Figs. 7–9). The Collection, which was opened to the public in June 1987, is surely one of the most interesting museum experiences in North America, and many of its compelling features are due to the commitments to spirituality in art and to public outreach that were positions fervently held by the founders Dominique and John de Menil (respectively, 1908–97 and 1904–73).[48] The opening inaugurated the Collection's principal pavilion, which was designed by Renzo Piano (1937–), but other pavilions are found in the neighborhood, and these are dedicated to favorite artists of the Menils, such as Dan Flavin (1933–96) and Cy Twombly (1928–). Moreover, only several city blocks away, on the campus of the University of St. Thomas, is another remarkable building from the standpoint of Byzantine America, the Chapel of St. Basil, designed by Philip Johnson (1906–2005) and consecrated in 1997.

An extraordinary cityscape for modernists and Byzantinists alike, but the two pavilions even more relevant to this discussion are also found in orbit around Piano's main building in Montrose: the Rothko Chapel, dedicated in 1971, and the Byzantine Fresco Chapel Museum, opened to the public in February 1997. Each of these spaces is remarkable; no other space like them exists; and certainly, given perceptions of the state that are commonplace, each space is jarringly un-Texan. One could argue that all museum spaces are heterotopian, according to Foucault's description of that category of space as "counter-sites, a kind of effectively enacted utopia in which the real sites, all the other real sites that can be found within the culture, are simultaneously represented, contested and inverted."[49] Within the context of this discussion of Byzantine presence in American modernism, these two museum spaces are unique counter-sites. Each was created to make special conditions for remaking consciousness, one might say, or

Fig. 7 Exterior view, Byzantine Fresco Chapel Museum,
The Menil Collection, Houston, Texas. Photo: Paul Warchol Photography.

Fig. 8 Exterior view,
Byzantine Fresco Chapel
Museum, The Menil
Collection, Houston, Texas.
Photo: Paul Warchol
Photography.

Fig. 9 Exterior view, Byzantine Fresco Chapel Museum,
The Menil Collection, Houston, Texas. Photo: Paul Warchol Photography.

awakening a spiritual awareness, special concerns of the Menils who
commissioned both buildings. Each operates in distinct ways, naturally, as the Rothko Chapel belonged to the same intellectual milieu
as Newman, and Mark Rothko (1903–70) shared similar goals for his
art. Indeed, the Newman sculpture outside the Rothko Chapel,
Broken Obelisk (1963–67), makes a comparison of methods and aims
of the two artists inevitable for visitors.[50]

The Byzantine Fresco Chapel Museum, as the name states, relates
to a different context in which a tension is established and maintained
between a living Byzantine spirituality and museum preservation of
precious artifacts of the past. It is their singular qualities that set these
two buildings apart. The Rothko Chapel is a kind of *summa theologica*
of the artist's project, and in its programmatic presentation, it stands
apart from the other works of its time. Newman's contemporary
Stations of the Cross (1958–66, National Gallery of Art, Washington,
D.C., all approximately 198 × 152 cm) was conceived as a unity, and
even though Newman had clear ideas about the paintings' hanging
and disposition, the *Stations* have had a difficult exhibition history.

And the Byzantine Chapel is both a careful representation of the original setting of the frescoes, and a constant reminder to viewers of its essential dislocation. These two places work as heterotopias in that they represent other spaces, churches one might say in both cases, and they contest them in their carefully prepared presentations by offering unique solutions to understanding divinity, solutions arrived at nowhere else. Recognizable by their references to other spiritual spaces, the chapels explore singular routes by attempting to place questing bodies in intensely self-aware situations.

The Byzantine Fresco Chapel Museum is a re-presentation of two areas of fresco from an otherwise obscure rural chapel at Lysi in what is still the Turkish sector of Cyprus. Ripped from the walls by art smugglers in the 1980s, the frescoes were purchased by the Menil Foundation with the permission of Cypriot authorities and are on long-term loan to the Collection in Houston. The two passages of fresco, from the sanctuary apse and from the dome over the central crossing of the small cross-shaped chapel, are thirteenth-century renderings of the Virgin and Child flanked by two angels, and of the Pantocrator above a register containing the Deesis and worshipping angels (Figs. 10–11). The frescoes are of remarkably high quality given the character of the Cypriot chapel, a small funerary structure dedicated to an obscure saint, Themonianos, and the art-historical significance of the frescoes was beautifully presented by Annemarie Carr in a monograph of 1991. The restoration challenges are of no small interest, too, because the frescoes had been sliced into small sections for transport, and the perfect condition they appear in now attests to that fine work, too.[51]

The apparently flawless preservation of the medieval frescoes is striking to Byzantintists, who are accustomed to seeing most of the extant monuments in less than ideal conditions. In that sense, the chapel is a remarkable artifact, perfect for teaching Texan students about the beauty, as well as the function, of Byzantine art. In other words, the frescoes stand out for their state of preservation, for the clarity and access of presentation, and for the pleasure their high aesthetic order gives. And yet the experience of viewing and understanding the frescoes is entirely, inescapably conditioned by the urban American setting constructed to house the frescoes as long as they are in Houston. The design of the chapel itself was undertaken by François de Menil (1945–) between 1991 and 1997, and it performs a

Fig. 10 Interior view, Byzantine Fresco Chapel Museum,
The Menil Collection, Houston, Texas. Photo: Paul Warchol Photography

masterful balancing act of being both evocative of that Cypriot chapel and stating its mission as museum.[52] The building is a consecrated space as well, but entering the building means going past a museum guard.

Such tensions are irresolvable, perhaps, and that irresolution gives the chapel another special character not known in churches normally visited by Byzantinists. In that sense, the chapel belongs to Foucault's category of a heterotopia of compensation, which is "to create a space that is other, another real space, as perfect, as meticulous, as well arranged as ours is messy, ill constructed, and jumbled."[53] That compensation takes place for two main reasons, the first being the destruction of the original context, and the second being the stated mission of the Menil Collection, articulated by Dominique de Menil, as a museum "[…] dedicated to the transcendence of borders and the unification of all people in their common humanity."[54]

The means of compensation, moreover, are the specifics of the experience of the building as conceived and designed by François de

Fig. 11 Interior view,
Byzantine Fresco
Chapel Museum,
The Menil Collection,
Houston, Texas.
Photo: Paul Warchol
Photography

Menil. The Chapel Museum occupies a corner lot in the Montrose neighborhood, several hundred meters from the main building of the Collection, but it has no real architectural relation to that Piano-designed building. The outer shell is composed of squared grey masses; the entrance is indicated by a footpath and the location of the car park, rather than any markers used in the Middle Ages, like sculpture placed around an entryway. The relation of the outer shell to the frescoes is not revealed by the exterior of the building, therefore, but the process of entry was designed in such a way as to determine the experience of viewers. One crosses several thresholds in the approach to the frescoes, over water, which forms a partial moat, and then through a vestibule with museum guard and an entrance to a small garden on the other side, very like a minimalist cloister (Fig. 9). In order to enter the sacred space, one has to make a right-hand turn into the building and pass through another vestibule, which has a tower over it that allows light to descend. Visitors are advised to pause in these "decompression chambers" to adjust eyes and mind to the inner sanctum about to be penetrated.[55]

Once inside, the contrast between outer and inner shell is dramatically clear, for the outer shell is in fact a "liner box," a reliquary-like container, that creates a rectangular sanctuary within which the small-scale chapel is housed.[56] The outer shell is dark for the most part, except for the two-foot light shafts around the exterior walls. Called an "infinity box" by François de Menil, it creates the sense of aura within and completes the progression of visitors into the inner space where the frescoes are found. The frescoes themselves are only partially visible until one steps into the center space. Here the dislocation is most pronounced. The frescoes are set into an etched-glass enclosure that reproduces the dimensions of the original Cypriot chapel, but the etched glass is held together by sutures, which are readily apparent.

The chapel is present but strangely disembodied at the same time; one is constrained by the chapel walls, but vision and sense of space are more expansive than the chapel walls would normally permit. As François de Menil described it, the plan of the inner chapel was based on the original, "only exploded and pulled apart."[57] That aspect of semi-opaque walls for the chapel is clearly a solution to a search for authenticity and self-conscious recognition of the impossibility of that search. But it does have some resonance for medieval church architecture on Cyprus, because many mountain churches do still have wooden roof coverings for protection against heavy snow. This resonance was consciously evoked by Menil in his design, but without reference to the fact that the chapel belongs on the island's northern littoral, and not in the mountains like the church of the Panagia Phorbiotissa at Asinou, for example, where snow, in fact, is an issue. The functional aspect of the covering, then, was evoked, but not followed literally in the outer shell, which is really concerned with the aura of a reliquary.

All of these aspects can be interpreted as compensatory, making up for loss of context, tragically undermined by the ongoing conflict between Greek and Turkish Cypriots, and of thoroughgoing spirituality in modern society like that integrally and dynamically evident in the medieval eastern Mediterranean. The contrast between chapel and museum was intended by the architect to create "a mystical union and historical arc between the past and present, between Cyprus and America."[58] The frescoes are part of an enacted heterotopia within which circulate conflicting notions of museum and living art, secular and sacral art, nationalism and ecumenicalism. Traversing the "mystical union and historical arc" here means occupying a liminal space between the worlds of Houston and Lysi. The chapel-museum

space is well ordered, without reference to the tragic history of the original context, and indeed familiarizes that foreign Christianity by
installing an altar seen through an obtrusive, yet transparent, version of
an iconostasis. These conflicting elements within the chapel-museum
space are not found in concert anywhere else, and they make the
Byzantine Fresco Chapel Museum a unicum, a place without a place.

The building kitty-corner to the Byzantine Fresco Chapel
Museum, the Rothko Chapel, belongs to the pre-history of the Menil
Collection, but is emblematic of the aims of the Menils in making their
collection public. The Chapel was conceived in the first place as a
collaboration between the painter and Philip Johnson, who was to
design the building to house the cycle of paintings. Disagreements
arose early in the design process, and the chapel was completed by
Howard Barnstone (1923–87) and Eugene Aubry (1935–). Dedicated
in 1971, the chapel and paintings have been the subject of subsequent
restorations, as the building developed structural problems and the
paintings needed consolidation on account of some unstable materials
used by Rothko. The lighting inside the chapel has changed since it
was opened, but the arrangement and hanging of the fourteen canvases
by Rothko remains the same as he dictated before his death. The paintings themselves have no titles, and they constitute a unity formed by
their gathering in the octagonal space of the chapel (Fig. 12).

In distinction to Rothko's program, the other great cycle of
profoundly spiritual abstraction of the 1960s is Barnett Newman's *The
Stations of the Cross: Lema Aabachthani*, which was hung together at
the Guggenheim in 1966 for the first time.[59] This cycle comprises
fifteen pictures, so they were presented on a scale comparable to
Rothko's cycle, but they were not commissioned, nor were they originally intended, for any particular space. The fourteen canvases were
not meant to be read consecutively as conventional stations, but as a
cumulative, communal cry referring to that great intertextual moment
when, in his dying moments, Christ recites the line from the Psalm,
"why have you forsaken me?" (Psalm 22:1, Matthew 27:46). The
collective element does not make clear any progression within the
paintings or program. Typical of Newman, the work is about the individual person before it, "The Painting should give man a sense of
place: that he knows he's there, so he's aware of himself [...]. To me,
the sense of place has not only a mystery but has that sense of meta-
physical fact."[60]

Fig. 12 Mark Rothko, Rothko Chapel, Interior view. © ARS, NY.
Photo: Nicolas Sapieha/Art Resource, NY. © Kate Rothko Prizel and Christopher
Rothko Foundation/Artists Rights Society (ARS), New York.

That sense of self-awareness was key to Newman's understanding
of how his painting should work, but that emphasis on the individual
consciousness before the painting contrasts strongly with the intentions of Rothko and his great suite of works.[61] Rothko's pictures
surround viewers in that chapel, and the scale of the paintings, which
dwarfs viewers, gives a sense of overwhelming presence. The fact that
no single viewpoint exists in the chapel adds another element of
disorientation, so that the totalizing sense of presence of those paintings is underlined by their apparent similarity. Each seems to be a
copy of the others, and they do share qualities, but upon closer examination, their individual characteristics also emerge. A subtle play
between frames, shades, and grounds within the pictures gives a strong
sense of viewers' relationships to the paintings. As the light shifts in
the chapel, different readings of the paintings become possible, which
in turn brings to the fore the relational element of viewer before
object. Lacking a perfect viewpoint and an immediately comprehensible reading, the program makes demands of the body of the viewer
to move, evaluate, and enter fully the field of representation. If the

program is working on a viewer as it was intended, it brings out a
sense of immensity and limitation, of infinite and finite space. The
knowledge of being before a painting is never lost, for the materiality
of the surfaces is strong, but that serves only to intensify the sense of
self, of the specificity of that experience, which no one else can share
in precisely the same way. While the sense of self is strong, like in
Newman's work and writing, Rothko also invested his cycle with a
strong universalizing element, which gives the impression of melting
into a larger, irresistible reality within the pictures. Specifics of
content were never of much interest to Rothko, and silence seems a
natural response, indeed, to his work. Apophatic or negative theology
comes closest to Rothko's aims: to reach the point where only silent
contemplation and communion is possible and where individuality is
subsumed into that eternity of unknowingness revealed by that
immense surround of somber color fields.[62]

Representation of unknowingness, one might say, was not
restricted to modernism, and Byzantine art had as one of its goals a
mystery of vision that overwhelmed figural grounds with gold-suffused
halations. In that aura, Byzantine viewers saw an unspeakable, divine
reality.[63] These notions may have been part of the effect Rothko was
seeking when he designed the paintings for his chapel, for, as Carol
Mancusi-Ungaro has eloquently argued, he appears to have been
exploring color, transparency, viscosity, and reflectance of paint, and
the effects are often a wavering play between glowing sheen and color
values.[64] Moreover, Rothko had traveled and seen Byzantine monuments, perhaps in some ways inspired by Duthuit's bête noir, André
Malraux, to do so.[65] One monument that Rothko was particularly
impressed by was the medieval cathedral on the island of Torcello in
the Venetian lagoon. The juxtaposition between the church's two elev-
enth-century mosaics, of the Virgin and Child in the apse (Fig. 13) and
the very active Last Judgment on the west wall opposite, created a
particularly strong impression on the painter.[66] He wanted, as he said,
to translate the same tension he felt in that building to his chapel in
Houston. Dominique de Menil wrote vividly of the impact that experience had on Rothko's chapel paintings and the disposition of those
paintings within the chapel space: "In the final chapel arrangement, he
accomplished this dichotomy by creating a large black rectangle for the
panel at the entrance, and by making the middle panel of the apse trip-
tych, facing the entrance, slightly lighter, with a hint of pink."[67]

Fig. 13 Virgin and Child with Apostles, Mosaic, Cattedrale di S. Maria Assunta,
Torcello, Italy, eleventh/twelfth century. Photo: Alinari/Art Resource, NY.

The epiphanic quality of those mosaics needs to be kept in mind,
also, because the durational element of encountering the mosaic in the
apse by processing the length of the nave is essential to the experience
of medieval mosaic. Such processing also takes place in the Rothko
Chapel, where time is needed for the subtle workings of the paintings
to play out. The unfolding of the vision, as it clarifies itself while one
walks eastward, is a process of enlightenment. Initially, the mosaic will
appear as a glowing indistinct presence and then gradually coalesce
into a legible vision, but even in certain conditions, when the light
comes from certain directions, the process does not end with clarity.
The mystery of medieval seeing is that it sometimes denies understanding and articulation. The power of the active Last Judgment
scene derives in part from the contrast with its iconic counterpart in
the east, and it too, as mosaic, was subject to similar processes of
obscurity and revelation. The massive panels in the Rothko Chapel
possess the balance and counterbalance found at Torcello, as well as

the mysterious oscillation between clarity and murkiness. In that passage between the two, between light and darkness, is formed that enveloping and dynamic entry into unknowingness.

The Cypriot chapel across the street also partook of that element of apophatic seeing, which provoked strong senses of bodiedness at the same time. In figural art, that sense of bodiedness is perhaps too obvious, but the incarnational element of Byzantine art rests on an ultimately inarticulable paradox, that the Lord of Creation humbled himself to the degree that he became a human being. At the same time that the child in time is shown with its mother in the apse, dynamically emerging from between the angels, the adult and pre-eternal Christ is in the process of making himself known at the building's apex.[68] But Byzantines recognized the partial quality of their understanding, and they communicated that impasse non-verbally through the irresolvable contradictions of their figural art. Even in a limited program like the frescoes at the Menil, the contradictions of Christ's representations raised the issue of the deeply elusive basis of figuration. And the mysterious qualities of light and reflective grounds, especially but not only gold, gave an essential characteristic of obscured vision in medieval churches generally. In other words, the artistic means in the Rothko and Byzantine chapels diverge fundamentally, but some concurrence in goals does exist. The experience of limitlessness and of unspeakable dimensions to the world we know, and of a necessary reliance on one's bodiedness to realize that experience, are essential qualities to both programs.

Boat-building in Byzantium

Those heterotopias in Houston can be approached as sharing essential characteristics, based in part on the material evocativeness of their programs. Rothko himself praised the way in which Byzantine artists conveyed their meanings directly through their materials.[69] Those chapels can also be seen to share the characteristic of compensation for spiritual emptiness in modern life. By creating such heterotopic space, Rothko and Menil have constructed perfectly ordered spaces for viewing bodies to experience themselves in transcendence. In one sense, then, those viewers climb aboard a boat, Foucault's perfect heterotopia, at once "closed in on itself and at the same time given over to the infinity of the sea."[70] That metaphor of the boat is a perfect way of realizing that sense of being in a place without a place, of being in transit from one kind of existence or consciousness to another. The destination is remarkably unclear: salvation for the Byzantine viewer, and presumably a kind of transcendence and placeless contemplation for the modern viewer of the Rothko Chapel and of the Byzantine Fresco Chapel Museum.

In what sense was that utopian ideal of Byzantium also a means of passage for post-war American art, too, one might ask? To answer that question, returning to the Byzantinized freedom of Matisse casts some light on the strange pull of that tide. In 1911, Prichard wrote a letter from Paris to Isabella Stewart Gardner (1840–1924) in Boston in which he attempted to describe the process of viewing a Matisse:

> A Matisse painting is a *hint* of creative action, its seed, germ, and the determination, at the same time, of your state of mind. In *Hamlet* (à la Craig), the action is guided and carried through: in the Matisse painting it is started only. You are put into a boat and pushed off: the boat may stick in the mud or reeds or may reach the stream. The artist pulls the trigger, you go off or you miss fire. The result is your affair and not his. If you respond the distance you carry depends on the nature of your gun, its aim and its charge. Think of the evocative power of a Byzantine Christ on a double loaded conscience![71]

This letter pre-dated the engagement of Matisse with Byzantine art at the hands of Prichard, but it showed the connection already formed in Prichard's mind between the prospective qualities of the art of Matisse and Byzantium. Each is a starting point, a catalyst, and although Prichard left the goal of that start not fully stated, clearly creative action is an ideal of that artistic engagement with Matisse. The comparison with a Byzantine Christ is telling: if only the person viewing were fully set, loaded, and ready to detonate, then the "evocative power" would be unleashed.

Such ideas of passage from one state of consciousness to another are implied again in the boat metaphor, the potent image of a journey that may or may not reach its destination according to the will of the sailor. And the destination came to have power for Prichard's disciple Duthuit, for the voyage to Byzantium was about finding again that creative energy and infusing a modern world desperately in need of such binding force that Byzantium possessed in his mind. For these intellectuals – Prichard, Duthuit, and others – Byzantium was a utopian world of perfect community formed through art, where no divisions existed between representation and life: Byzantine bodies were corporate and permeable with art. This ideal came to find expression through Duthuit in post-war New York, and it resonated with idealists there, too, though for American reasons. Newman and de Kooning both appear to have found sympathetic elements in Duthuit's journal, for Newman a social ideal of concord, and for de Kooning an urban ideal of diversity and a visual paradigm of power and energy in that Byzantine Christ. Strange journeys indeed, from the eastern Mediterranean to western Europe to the New World, from Constantinople to Paris to New York to Houston, that saw the boat reach the stream, as Prichard wrote. To borrow from Kurt Weitzmann (1904–93)[72] and William Butler Yeats (1865–1939), sailing from utopian Byzantium to America was a charged crossing for modern art.

NOTES

1. For their guidance and interest, I must express warm thanks to Massimo Bernabò, Yve-Alain Bois, Charlotte Cousins, Helen Evans, Caitlin Haskill, Herbert Kessler, Asen Kirin, Kostis Kourelis, Rémi Labrusse, Robert Nelson, Brigitte Pitarakis, Elisabetta Povoledo, Jean-Michel Spieser, Chelsea Weathers, Annabel Wharton, Gerhard Wolf, and Michael Zimmerman. I am grateful to Laura Schwartz, Martha González Palacios and Shiela Winchester for their patient help in the library work that was needed for this essay. More than anyone, however, my colleague Richard Shiff helped and encouraged at every stage; for his mentoring, I have nothing but gratitude and for his work, enormous admiration.

2. In a posthumously published lecture, originally given in 1967, Foucault examined what he called "the space of emplacement." See M. Foucault, "Of Other Spaces," trans. J. Miskowiec, *Diacritics* 16 (1986): 22–27. On this essay, see T. R. Flynn, "Partially Desacralized Spaces: The Religious Availability of Foucault's Thought," in *Michel Foucault and Theology: The Politics of Religious Experience*, ed. J. Bernauer and J. Carrette (Aldershot: Variorum, 2004), 149.

3. Highly recommended on related contexts are K. Kourelis, "Byzantium and the Avant-Garde: Excavations at Corinth, 1920s–1930s," *Hesperia* 75 (2007): 391–442.

4. For Duthuit's career and thought, see R. Labrusse, "Le muséoclaste," in *Autour de Georges Duthuit. Galerie d'Art du Conseil Général des Bouches-du-Rhône, Aix-en-Provence, 11 avril–22 juin 2003* (Arles: Actes sud, 2003), 57–86, as well as his "Byzance et l'art moderne: la référence byzantine dans les cercles artistiques d'avant-garde au début du XXe siècle," in *Présence de Byzance*, ed. J.-M. Spieser (Paris: Infolio, 2007), 77–81, and "Samuel Beckett and Georges Duthuit," in *Samuel Beckett: A Passion for Painting*, ed. F. Croke (Dublin: National Gallery of Ireland, 2006), 88–91.

5. See *Le Collège de Sociologie 1937–1939*, ed. D. Hollier (Paris: Gallimard, 1995), 746, where the editor, as he introduces the text of a talk Duthuit delivered on "Grandeur du ceremonial" in 1939 (753–61), gives this characterization of Duthuit: "Georges Duthuit incarne une variété rare du dandy modern, un des Esseintes d'extrême gauche ou presque. Byzantin subversif, esthète anti-culturel, c'est le type même de l'amateur extrémiste." For a sympathetic reminiscence, see Y. Bonnefoy, *Le nuage rouge: Essais sur la poétique* (Paris: Mercure de France, 1977), 159–67, and the reminiscence by Sam Francis (1923–94) in an interview with Yves Michaud, in *Art press* 127 (July–August, 1988): 18: "C'était un dandy, un vrai dandy, un dandy baudelairien, très émotif, toujours sur la scène. Il était très passioné par Matisse, par l'art byzantin. Nous passions de formidables après-midis au café. It était toujours heureux ou déprimé de quelque chose. Enthousiaste ou déprimé."

6. M. Stevens and A. Swan, *de Kooning: An American Master* (New York: Knopf, 2004), 94–96.

7. *Barnett Newman: A Catalogue Raisonné*, ed. E. C. White (New York, New Haven, CT: Yale University Press, 2004), 645.

8. See the analysis in Y.-A. Bois, "Perceiving Newman," in *Barnett Newman: Paintings* (New York: Pace Gallery, 1988), I–XIII.

9. See G. Didi-Huberman, "The Supposition of the Aura: The Now, the Then, and Modernity," in *Negotiating Rapture: The Power of Art to Transform Lives*, ed. R. Francis, trans. J. M. Todd (Chicago: Museum of Contemporary Art, 1996), 48–63.

10. In R. Shiff, "To Create Oneself," in *Barnett Newman: A Catalogue Raisonné*, 46. See also R. Shiff, *Doubt* (New York, London: Routledge, 2008), 68–76.

11. Incidentally, Greenberg wrote a short article that is relevant to the argument at hand: "Byzantine Parallels," in *Art and Culture. Critical Essays* (Boston: Beacon, 1961), 167–70. However, the article is not included in *The Collected Essays and Criticism*, 4 vols., ed. J. O'Brian (Chicago, IL, and London: University of Chicago Press, 1986–93). R. S. Nelson, "Byzantine Art vs. Western Medieval Art," in *Byzance et le monde extérieur: Contacts, relations, échanges*, ed. M. Balard, É. Malamut, and J.-M. Spieser (Paris:

Publications de la Sorbonne, 2005), 257, also remarks on Byzantine art and its appreciation by modernist pioneers.

12. Duthuit's editorial statement in *Transition* 1 (1948): 5–6.

13. Bibliography in *Autour de Georges Duthuit*, 87–91. One apparent misstep for the outsider Duthuit was the publication of his *Le musée inimaginable: Essai*, 3 vols. (Paris: Corti, 1956), which sank with little notice – pace *Autour de Georges Duthuit*, 90. The book was intended as a response to the widely read work of André Malraux. See O. Todd, *Malraux: A Life*, trans. J. West (New York: Knopf, 2005), 449–51, 514 n. 10. See, however, the balanced appreciation by André Chastel (1912–90), "The Revolt against Malraux," *New York Times* (26 May 1957): 8, although the book was never translated. And an unsigned appreciation in *Apollo* 78 (July 1963): 68–69, reveals strong sympathy for his work, as well.

14. The possibility has to be admitted that the journal came into Newman's collection as a used book.

15. For the general context, as well as the history of that episode of state manipulation of art, see T. D. Littleton and M. Sykes, *Advancing American Art: Painting, Politics and Cultural Confrontation at Mid-Century*, 2nd ed. (Tuscaloosa and London: University of Alabama Press, 2005); M. L. Krenn, *Fall-Out Shelters for the Human Spirit: American Art and the Cold War* (Chapel Hill and London: University of North Carolina Press, 2005); as well as P. M. Von Eschen, *Satchmo Blows Up the World: Jazz Ambassadors Play the Cold War* (Cambridge, MA: Harvard University Press, 2004).

16. See *Barnett Newman: Selected Writings and Interviews*, ed. J. O'Neill (New York: Knopf, 1990), 170–73. The whole passage under discussion reads, "We are reasserting man's natural desire for the exalted, for a concern with our relationship to the absolute emotions […].We are creating images whose reality is self-evident and which are devoid of the props and crutches that evoke associations with outmoded images, both sublime and beautiful. We are freeing ourselves of the impediments of memory, association, nostalgia, legend, myth, or what have you, that have been the devices of Western European painting. Instead of making *cathedrals* out of Christ, man, or 'life,' we are making [them] out of ourselves, out of our own feelings. The image we produce is the self-evident one of revelation, real and concrete, that can be understood by anyone who will look at it without the nostalgic glasses of history."

The editorial from *The Tiger's Eye* 6 (December 1948): 57, the volume in which Newman's essay appeared (51–53), reads in part: this issue on the sublime was "shaped by the idea that sublimity is the visitor of many and not exclusive guest of the rhetorical thinker or of religiosity. There is importance, too, of finding new symbols, for medieval definitions have long been outmoded"; and "Of the two general rooms of thought, whether sublimity is a *beyondness* signifying man as eternal, or whether it is a *hereness* denoting a reverence or rare understanding of life, this magazine readily enters into the latter." On Newman and the journal, see A. E. Gibson, *Issues in Abstract Expressionism: The Artist-Run Periodicals* (Ann Arbor and London: UMI Research Press, 1990), 30–31.

17. *Barnett Newman: Selected Writings and Interviews*, 173. See also R. Shiff, "Newman's Time," in *Reconsidering Barnett Newman*, ed. M. Ho (Philadelphia, PA: Philadelphia Museum of Art, 2005), 174.

18. G. Duthuit, *Les Fauves* (Geneva: Éditions des Trois Collines, 1949), 13, with other references to Byzantine and Early Christian art at 39–45 and 210–11. A new edition of this work has been prepared by Rémi Labrusee, who also provides historical context for Duthuit's thought in an essay and notes (Paris: Michalon, 2006). The American version of the book was published in 1950 by Robert Motherwell (1915–91) with uncredited translation done by Samuel Beckett (1906–89): Labrusse, "Samuel Beckett and Georges Duthuit," 89.

19. Published Paris: Stock, 1926, and never translated, but reprinted without illustrations in his *Représentation et présence: Premiers écrits et travaux (1923–1952)* (Paris: Flammarion, 1974), 105–59.

20. "Matisse and Byzantine Space," *Transition* 5 (1949): 20–37. See also *Matisse: "La revelation m'est venue de l'Orient"* (Florence: Arteficio, 1997), 322–35.

21. See H. Spurling, *Matisse the Master. A Life of Henri Matisse: The Conquest of Colour, 1909–1954* (New York: Knopf, 2005), 364.

22. Duthuit, "Matisse and Byzantine Space," 23.

23. Duthuit, "Matisse and Byzantine Space," 22.

24. Duthuit, "Matisse and Byzantine Space," 23–24. For a broader sense, see also Labrusse, "Samuel Beckett and Georges Duthuit," 90. On the mausoleum, see G. Mackie, *Early Christian Chapels in the West: Decoration, Function, and Patronage* (Toronto: University of Toronto Press, 2003), 22–35; and also C. Rizzardi, "Il cielo stellato del Mausoleo di Galla Placidia," in *Studi in Memoria di Patrizia Angiolini Martinelli*, ed. S. Pasi (Bologna: Ante Quem, 2005), 277–88.

25. See G. Peers, *Sacred Shock: Framing Visual Experience in Byzantium* (University Park: Pennsylvania University Press, 2004), 2–6.

26. From Shiff, "Newman's Time," 166.

27. Published in *Transformation: Arts, Communication, Environment. A World Review* 1.2 (1951): 86. The passage continues, "He took it for granted that he could only measure things subjectively, and it was logical therefore that the best way was from the inside. It was the only way he could eventually project all the happenings on the frontmost plane."

28. O. Demus, "The Methods of the Byzantine Artist," in *Art History:*

An Anthology of Modern Criticism, ed. S. Wylie (New York: Vintage, 1963),
100–15. [= *The Mint: A Miscellany of Literature, Art and Criticism*, ed. G.
Grigson, 2 vols. (London: Routledge, 1946–48), 2:64–77], and *Byzantine
Mosaic Decoration: Aspects of Monumental Art in Byzantium* (London: Paul,
Trench, Trubner, 1948; repr. New Rochelle, NJ: Caratzas Bros., 1976).

29. See C. Weathers, 'From Parmigianino to Andy Warhol, or Conceptions of Mannerism in the 1960s as Reflected in the Writings of Robert
Smithson' (MA diss., University of Texas at Austin, 2005).

30. D. Sylvester, "De Kooning's Women," *Sunday Times Magazine* (8
December 1968): 51.

31. R. Shiff, "Water and Lipstick: de Kooning in Transition," in
Willem de Kooning, Paintings (Washington, D.C.: National Gallery of Art,
1994), 52.

32. See J. Zilczer, "De Kooning and Urban Expressionism," in *Willem
de Kooning from the Hirshhorn Museum Collection* (Washington, D.C.:
Hirshhorn Museum and Sculpture Garden, Smithsonian Institution, 1993),
41–42; and S. Yard, *Willem de Kooning: The First Twenty-Six Years in New
York, 1927–1952* (New York: Garland, 1986), 182.

33. Duthuit, "Matisse and Byzantine Space," 21.

34. Shiff, "Water and Lipstick," 70 n. 110.

35. Duthuit, "Matisse and Byzantine Space," opposite 33.

36. See A. Malraux, *Museum Without Walls*, trans. S. Gilbert and F.
Price (Garden City, NY: Doubleday, 1967), 86.

37. Meyer Schapiro (1904–96) played a role in June 1952 in de
Kooning's acceptance of *Woman I*'s progressive value. See Stevens and Swan,
de Kooning: An American Master, 330; E. A. Carmen, Jr., "Willem de
Kooning: The Women," in *American Art at Mid-Century: The Subjects of the
Artist*, ed. E. A. Carmen, Jr., E. A. Rathbone, and T. B. Hess (Washington,
D.C.: National Gallery of Art, 1978), 158; and T. B. Hess, "de Kooning
Paints a Picture," *ARTNews* 52 (March 1952): 30.

Schapiro also made claims for connections to be made between
Byzantine mosaics and Newman paintings like *Onement I*. He alluded to
these connections in *Worldview in Painting: Art and Society. Selected Papers*
(New York: George Braziller, 1999), 189–90; see 191, where it states that the
lecture was delivered in 1963 and published first in 1969, and that that
lecture was attended by the Menils and Philip Johnson. Schapiro's views
were dismissed by other modernists, however; see B. Glaser, "Questions to
Stella and Judd," ed. L. R. Lippard, *ARTNews* 65 (September 1966): 61.

38. F. Léger, "Byzantine Mosaics and Modern Art," *Magazine of Art*
(April 1944): 144–45.

39. For now, see H. Evans, "Byzantium at The Metropolitan Museum
of Art," in *Abstracts of Papers. Thirty-First Annual Byzantine Studies*

Conference, 28–30 October 2005, The University of Georgia, Athens, Georgia (Athens: University of Georgia, 2005), 80.

40. R. Labrusse and N. Podzemskaia, "Naissance d'une vocation: aux sources de la carrière Byzantine de Thomas Whittemore," *Dumbarton Oaks Papers* 54 (2000): 50.

41. Spurling, *Matisse the Master*, 50; R. S. Nelson, "Private Passions Made Public: The Beginnings of the Bliss Collection," in *Sacred Art, Secular Context: Objects of Art from the Byzantine Collection of Dumbarton Oaks, Washington, D.C.*, ed. A. Kirin (Athens: University of Georgia Press, 2005), 43, 44; idem., *Hagia Sophia, 1850–1950: Holy Wisdom, Modern Monument* (Chicago, IL, and London: University of Chicago Press, 2004), 159–64; Labrusse and Podzemskaia, "Naissance d'une vocation," 52–56; J. B. Bullen, "Byzantinism and Modernism 1900–14," *Burlington Magazine* 141 (1999): 665–75; as well as G. Dagron, *Décrire et peindre: Esai sur le portrait iconique* (Paris: Gallimard, 2007), 80–83. On Byzantine art and modernism in the early twentieth century, see also *Sacred Art, Secular Context*; and M. Bernabò, *Ossessioni bizantine e cultura artistica in Italia. Tra D'Annunzio, fascismo e dopoguerra* (Naples: Liguori, 2003).

42. R. Labrusse, *Matisse: La condition de l'image* (Paris: Gallimard, 1999), 94–115. Important, too, is M. Antliff, "The Rhythms of Duration: Bergson and the Art of Matisse," in *The New Bergson*, ed. J. Mullarkey (Manchester and New York: Manchester University Press, 1999), 184–208. Naturally, Islamic art also provided models for Matisse; see, for example, R. Labrusse, "The Desire of the Line," in *Henri Matisse, Ellsworth Kelly: Plant Drawings*, trans. T. Selous (Paris: Gallimard, 2002), 17–49.

43. Labrusse, *Matisse: La condition de l'image*, 108–9, 280 n. 192.

44. See *Matisse: "La revelation m'est venue de l'Orient"*, 148–51.

45. Stevens and Swan, *de Kooning: An American Master*, 40.

46. Labrusse, *Matisse: La condition de l'image*, 279 n. 184 (his italics).

47. Labrusse, *Matisse: La condition de l'image*, 102.

48. On medieval objects and museum experience, see now M. P. Brown, "The Modern Medieval Museum," in *A Companion to Medieval Art: Romanesque and Gothic in Northern Europe*, ed. C. Rudolph (Malden, MA: Blackwell, 2006), 639–55.

49. Foucault, "Of Other Spaces," 24.

50. *Barnett Newman*, ed. A. Temkin (Philadelphia, PA: Philadelphia Museum of Art, 2002), 280–81.

51. See A. W. Carr and L. J. Morrocco, *A Byzantine Masterpiece Recovered: The Thirteenth-Century Murals of Lysi, Cyprus* (Austin: University of Texas Press, 1991).

52. François de Menil very kindly discussed some of his ideas about the chapel in a telephone interview, which took place 3 March 2005, but he has

also written an essay on the chapel, "The Belief in Art as Faith," in *Sanctuary: The Spirit In/Of Architecture*, ed. K. Shkapich and S. de Menil (Houston: Byzantine Fresco Foundation, 2004), 39–59.

53. Foucault, "Of Other Spaces," 27.

54. From Menil, "The Belief in Art as Faith," 39.

55. Menil, "The Belief in Art as Faith," 57–59.

56. See the essay, also, of N. Laos, "Sanctuary," in *Sanctuary: The Spirit In/Of Architecture*, 21–37.

57. Menil, "The Belief in Art as Faith," 51–53.

58. Menil, "The Belief in Art as Faith," 55.

59. See A. Temkin, "Barnett Newman on Exhibition," in *Barnett Newman*, 60–65.

60. See R. Shiff, "Whiteout: The Not-Influence Newman Effect," in *Barnett Newman*, ed. Temkin, 110 n. 194, and 101. And see now on these paintings, M. Godfrey, *Abstraction and the Holocaust* (New Haven, CT, and London: Yale University Press, 2007), 51–77. Newman distinguished between the messianic Jesus, the son of God, and the historical Jesus, and he appears only to have used the latter in his writings. See T. B. Hess, "Barnett Newman: The Stations of the Cross-Lea Sabachthani," in *American Art at Mid-Century*, 187–213, at 208–9.

61. In *The Rothko Chapel Paintings: Origins, Structure, Meaning* (Austin: University of Texas Press, 1997), S. Nodelman has written an extraordinarily sensitive and evocative analysis of this cycle.

62. See also Y.-A. Bois, "The Limit of Almost," in *Ad Reinhardt* (New York; Rizzoli, 1991), 28–29, as well as Ad Reinhardt (1913–67) himself, who wrote, "Painting that is almost possible, almost does not exist, that is not quite known, not quite seen," and "No ordinary seeing but absolute seeing in which there is neither seer nor seen." These passages are from an undated poem-essay; see "Imageless Icons," in *Art-as-Art: The Selected Writings of Ad Reinhardt*, ed. B. Rose (New York: Viking, 1975), 108–9.

63. See R. Franses, "When All That is Gold Does Not Glitter: On the Strange History of Looking at Byzantine Art," in *Icon and Word: The Power of Images in Byzantium. Studies Presented to Robin Cormack*, ed. A. Eastmond and L. James (Aldershot: Variorum, 2003), 13–24, as well as essays in *Visuality Before and Beyond the Renaissance: Seeing as Others Saw*, ed. R. S. Nelson (Cambridge: Cambridge University Press, 2000). I have also tried to explore this aspect of Byzantine viewing conditions in my *Sacred Shock: Framing Visual Experience in Byzantium*.

64. C. Mancusi-Ungaro, "Material and Immaterial Surface: The Paintings of Rothko," in *Mark Rothko*, ed. J. Weiss (New Haven, CT, and London: Yale University Press, 1998), 282–300. See also Bois, "The Limit of Almost," 25–26.

65. See Nodelman, *The Rothko Chapel Paintings*, 349–50. See also the evocative pairing of a painting by Rothko with a calendar icon in S. Brenske, *Ikonen und die Moderne/Icons and Modern Art* (Regensburg: Schnell und Steiner, 2005), 77–82.

66. See Nodelman, *The Rothko Chapel Paintings*, 92–93; and S. Fox, "Visionary Builders: John and Dominique de Menil as Architectural Patrons," in *Image of the Not Seen: Search for Understanding. The Rothko Chapel Series,* ed. K. C. Eynatten, K. Hutchins, and D. Quaintance (Houston: The Rothko Chapel, 2007), 32; as well more generally, D. E. Brauer, "Space as Spirit," in *Image of the Not Seen*, 43–53.

67. In Nodelman, *The Rothko Chapel Paintings*, 9.

68. Even in situations like the nursing Madonna, one should not read overly human qualities into the child at breast, for this is a sign of divinity, according to medieval viewing: a Virgin giving birth and nursing can only be possible if God willed it. See E. Bolman, "The Enigmatic Coptic Galaktotrophousa and the Cult of the Virgin Mary in Egypt," in *Images of the Mother of God: Perceptions of the Theotokos in Byzantium*, ed. M. Vasilaki (Aldershot: Variorum, 2005), 13–22.

69. See M. Rothko, *The Artist's Reality: Philosophies of Art*, ed. C. Rothko (New Haven, CT, and London: Yale University Press, 2004), 51.

70. Foucault, "Of Other Spaces," 27.

71. From Labrusse, *Matisse: La condition de l'image*, 278 n. 178.

72. K. Weitzmann, *Sailing with Byzantium from Europe to America: The Memoirs of an Art Historian* (Munich: Editio Maris, 1994).

Queer Crusading, Military Masculinity, and Allegories of Vietnam in Richard Lester's *Robin and Marian*

Tison Pugh

In their 1976 film *Robin and Marian*, screenwriter James Goldman and director Richard Lester retell the legend of Robin Hood, but not to celebrate the romantic possibilities of military or vigilante heroism; rather, this post-Vietnam film posits the Crusades as a queering experience, one that unravels fictions of heteronormative romance and military masculinity.[1] The debilitating effects of crusading in the Holy Land, notably in the ways in which it confuses relationships between lovers (as well as between enemies), undermines the mythic cast of the Robin Hood legend which, writ large, depends on patriarchal gender roles of brave men rescuing maidens fair. Moreover, the gendered confusion resulting from crusading abroad is revealed to be a peripatetic affliction, as it also corrupts the idyllic depiction of England, despite its ostensible position as a land culturally and geographically removed from the barbarities of war. Revising heroic conceptions of war and military conquest in light of the immeasurable suffering of Vietnam, *Robin and Marian* exposes the queer potential of battle to estrange warriors from themselves, their communities, and their genders. The protagonists of the film, including Sean Connery as Robin and Audrey Hepburn as Marian, are older than their typical cinematic incarnations, but the wisdom of age does not readily assist them as they struggle to understand the ways in which wars have shifted their sense of gender and, thus, of one another.

At its most powerful, and, I would argue, in its most productive applications, queer theory encourages investigations into the maintenance of gendered and sexual normativity, as well as the ways in which such cultural practices service particular ideological regimes. Queerness interrogates systems of normativity through myriad perspectives – including sexuality but expanding to additional constituent factors of personal identity that can be deemed non-normative.[2] In this protean adaptability, its utility in addressing questions of political import defines its subversive relevance, as Judith Butler suggests:

> If the term "queer" is to be a site of collective contestation, a point of departure for a set of historical reflections and future imaginings, it will have to remain that which is, in the present, never fully owned, but always and only redeployed, twisted, queered from prior usage and in the direction of urgent and expanding political purposes.[3]

With its political edge, queerness offers a praxis and a metaphor for reading texts – literary, cinematic, or other – by confronting ideological institutions of normativity through the position of the gendered and sexual Other. Although it is unlikely that the creators of *Robin and Marian* saw their film as particularly queer, since the film comes only a few years after the Stonewall Riots of 1969 (which inaugurated the modern Gay Rights Movement) and predates the rise of queer theory in the academy during the 1980s and 1990s, it nonetheless reveals queer affinities in its disavowal of modern warfare through a relentless questioning of heroic sexuality and masculinity, as well as their political ramifications. Alex Doty argues for queer readings as a resistant interpretive strategy and uses the term *queer* "to mark a flexible space for the expression of all aspects of non- (anti-, contra-) straight cultural production and reception."[4] In finding himself with a new and unexpectedly beleaguered masculinity after the Crusades, Robin Hood must confront the ways in which life on the erotic margins can be forced upon one, despite his steadfast attempt to view himself through a lens of mythic and heroic masculinity. Thus, the goal of this essay is to explore how crusading paradoxically undermines the constructions of aggressive masculinity that war should ostensibly uphold. At the same time, cultural constructions of masculinity frequently depend on heteronormativity in male sexuality, and, so subverting masculinity often raises issues of homoeroticism. This dynamic emerges in *Robin and Marian*, in that the subversion of Robin's masculinity, as evidenced from his crusading experiences, climaxes in a homoerotically inflected duel with the Sheriff of Nottingham (Robert Shaw).

Recent theoretical work on queerness in the Middle Ages questions the applicability of modern theories of homosexuality and heterosexuality to medieval life and art, and these investigations have productively problematized the transferal of modern sexual hermeneutics to the past.[5] Normativities of all stripes have shifted throughout the centuries, and it is essential to gauge these accretional differences and their effect on our understanding of gender and sexuality in the past. *Robin and Marian*, situated as it is between the medieval (in terms of the film's setting) and the modern (in terms of the film's production), exposes the cultural construction of normativity in the cinematic world as it also plays with the cloudiness of such apparently demarcated standards: which version of normativity – the medieval or the modern – do the filmmakers establish for their characters? "Medieval" films frequently teeter between medieval and modern genders, creating a space in the past to consider issues deeply relevant to the present, but to do so, they nonetheless establish paradigms of normativity – although perhaps fluid ones – through which to analyze their fictions. Numerous films featuring the Middle Ages showcase this dynamic of oscillating gender roles between the medieval and the modern: *A Kid in King Arthur's Court* (1995), in which young "girl-power" characters more representative of 1990s teenagers than medieval princesses must nonetheless be negotiated into their eventual subservience to historical masculinity;[6] *A Knight's Tale* (2001), in which a mostly homosocial grouping forges the historically implausible heroic masculinity of the film's protagonist;[7] or *Monty Python and the Holy Grail* (1975), in which young Prince Herbert longs to resignify the typical gendered positionings of medieval romance into a modern-day musical theater number more suitable to his queer sensibility.[8] These brief examples, to which numerous others could be added, testify to the frequent amorphousness of gender in "medieval" films, in which historical visions of gender are reformulated to reflect both the film's zeitgeist and an anachronistic longing for yesteryear's values. Queer potential emerges in this gendered play, as the foundations of gendered identities are rendered unstable, sometimes unrecognizable, in the transversals between medieval and modern.

From a historical perspective and in terms of typical cultural practice, queerness is ostensibly cordoned off from war. War defends an ideological superstructure through the enactment of violent forms of masculinity: in the propagation of a culture's beliefs it serves as an aggressive and forceful (albeit, in certain situations, necessary) intervention to protect, or perhaps to disseminate, a society's values. In this manner, wars are fought to uphold the normative structures of a society, to allow a culture to continue to define itself rather than to be defined by others, whether such identity be related to its sovereignty, its mores, or any other attribute deemed worth dying for by the hierarchical structures in command. In regard to the Middle Ages and today, a peasant or a poor man cannot declare a war, but a king or a president can, and thus the enactment of ranges of masculinity – none of them considered queer – makes warfare possible.[9] Furthermore, wars often construct a corresponding vision of masculinity aligned to the goals of the conflict, as Leo Braudy observes of the Crusades: "a significant achievement of the Crusades was to bring a spiritual manhood – albeit in military guise – onto the stage of European culture."[10] War is declared and waged by men who enact roles of martial masculinity with the normativity of their culture, and thus the normativity of their masculinity, at stake.

As wars reflect and create particular versions of heroic masculinity with little room for queerness, so too do many films about such conflicts that lionize martial masculinity as inherently triumphal. In regard to Hollywood's Vietnam films, however, a crisis of masculinity emerges in the historically accurate depiction of American defeat, and films of this ilk, including *The Deer Hunter* (1978), *Coming Home* (1978), *Apocalypse Now* (1979), and *Full Metal Jacket* (1987), portray men suffering from shattered versions of masculinity, in which myths of martial manhood are revealed as bravado rather than truth. In contrast, other examples of Hollywood's Vietnam films, such as *Uncommon Valor* (1983), *Missing in Action* (1984), and *Rambo: First Blood, Part II* (1985), imaginatively reconstruct the war as an American victory, as Stephen Ducat observes:

> The American defeat in Vietnam seemed to induce a culture-wide malaise of wounded masculinity that was to be only partially remedied by the spate of revisionist Vietnam War films, such as *Rambo*. In these movies, hypermasculine *Ubermenschen* won fierce battles against enormous odds, which enabled the mostly male audiences to momentarily forget about the real war's final outcome.[11]

Films addressing the Vietnam War cannot be divorced from a corresponding depiction of masculinity, but the urge to depict American military heroism and machismo is counterbalanced by the history of the war itself. Consequently, tensions arise between the type of victorious masculinity celebrated in war and the historically enervated masculinity witnessed in the actual conflict.

Of course, *Robin and Marian* is not a Vietnam film in the typical sense of the term, as it is set in a medieval past roughly 800 years prior to the actual conflict; it nonetheless addresses the cultural repercussions of the Vietnam War and military masculinity in terms of its loose allegorical superstructure. Eben Muse describes the contours of "Vietnam allegory" films, which are "set in other wars and other lands" yet nonetheless "comment [...] on the war in Vietnam," in that the "audience could hardly fail to view them as either referring to the current military situation or having their description influenced by it."[12] In terms of allegory and history, the Vietnam War need bear no deep historical parallels to the Crusades in order to situate the cultural context of *Robin and Marian* as a criticism of both conflicts simultaneously. Richard Lester's commentary on his protagonist is relevant here, as his description of the masculine heroism depicted in his film parallels the experience of numerous American veterans. He describes "the concept of Robin Hood as a small-time robber," one "who had been inspired by a great emotional ideal that sent him off to the Crusades. Now he's back, disillusioned, trying to relive the past – trying to live up to an old image which was probably just a myth in any case."[13] Through the Crusades, Lester questions the effects of war against a medieval background, but for the viewers of the film, especially during its initial release in 1976, Vietnam operates as a more topical lens through which to consider the nature of war and its effects on martial masculinities.[14]

In terms of their generic history, the films of the Robin Hood legend are typically identified as swashbucklers, a genre that celebrates masculine derring-do and heroism,[15] and some notable works in this cinematic oeuvre include Allan Dwan's 1922 *Robin Hood*, starring Douglas Fairbanks and Wallace Beery; Michael Curtiz and William Keighley's 1938 *The Adventures of Robin Hood*, starring Errol Flynn, Olivia de Havilland, and Basil Rathbone; and Kevin Reynolds's 1991 *Robin Hood: Prince of Thieves*, starring Kevin Costner, Morgan Freeman, and Mary Elizabeth Mastrantonio. These films are celebrated for their acrobatic action scenes and sparkling humor, in which a tongue-in-cheek temperament leavens the more dramatic elements emphasized in the film's conflicts between Robin Hood and his adversaries. Although swashbucklers are typically lighter in tone than war films, they nonetheless embrace a standard construction of masculine heroism, with the distinction that the protagonists in this genre are celebrated as much for their pluck, wit, and daring as for their strength in combat. Despite their levity, swashbucklers often address a political plot, as Brian Taves observes: "A political consciousness underlies [...] these films [that] follow a pattern of despotism, subversion, and the establishment of a government system to protect the rights of its citizens."[16] Thus, the allure of the genre results from its hybridity of levity and seriousness, of light action coupled with deeper political significance.

Resisting the jovial swashbuckling of most films of the Robin Hood legend, *Robin and Marian* is, if anything, an anti-swashbuckler, and Stephen Knight defines the film's genre as "anti-romantic realism," in that its "autumnal credibility" brings about "the fullest version of realism in the whole myth."[17] Through its consistent deflation of genres that glorify violence sensibility, *Robin and Marian* punctures moments that appear to build up to climactic scenes of valiance enacted through daring displays of heroic masculinity. For example, when Richard the Lion-Hearted (Richard Harris) imprisons Robin and Little John (Nicol Williamson), Robin quickly determines to escape. He succeeds in opening a hole out of the prison's wall, but at the moment he appears ready to liberate himself (and will consequently need to undertake daring battles with inept guards to complete his quest for freedom), the jailer enters and peacefully brings him to Richard, thus deflating the escalating tension of the scene. Likewise, after Robin and Little John return to Sherwood Forest, they mistake Friar Tuck (Ronnie Barker) and Will Scarlett (Denholm Elliott) for enemies and engage in battle, but this conflict of mistaken identities offers no opportunities for adventurous antics and martial heroism; it is a rather pathetic scuffle among middle-aged men. As Richard Stapleford notes in his comparison of *Robin and Marian* to Curtiz and Keighley's *The Adventures of Robin Hood*, the former's climactic battle between Robin and the Sheriff eschews the capering celebrated in Curtiz and Keighley's film:

> When Flynn fought Basil Rathbone, the evil Guy of Gisbourne, they thrust and parried according to the highly artificial and chivalrous rules of fencing. [...] But when Connery fights his antagonist Robert Shaw as the Sheriff, they flail at each other clumsily with monstrously heavy broadswords. Forcing themselves off balance they stagger and heave and pant, in clear contrast to the clean, articulate duel of Flynn and Rathbone.[18]

A swashbuckler should be spry and lively, as the action sequences of *Robin Hood* and *Robin Hood: Prince of Thieves* establish, but in the dour climax of *Robin and Marian*, the grim nature of a fight to the death is stripped of its illusory lightheartedness. Any hopes a viewer might hold for *Robin and Marian* to play with its comic roots in the swashbuckler tradition are dashed in this scene, and the movie soon moves to its tragic (yet in some ways uplifting) conclusion.

If war ostensibly provides a measure of a man's masculinity as counted in medals and citations of bravery, in *Robin and Marian*, the Crusades are shown to be a queering force that renders men emasculated. This theme is established in the film's opening sequence, in which two soldiers dig a rock from the arid ground and place it in a trebuchet to attack their enemy. The shot is fired, but, rather than the dramatic display of military puissance viewers are likely to expect, it impotently falls short of its target. Weapons in war films frequently build metaphorical meaning – such as is hilariously evident in Slim Pickens's performance as Major J. T. "King" Kong, with his phallic torpedo drop in *Dr. Strangelove* (1964) – but this trebuchet suggests, if anything, premature ejaculation rather than phallic strength. Beyond merely a botched salvo in an ongoing battle, this opening confrontation also calls to mind the persistent question that dogged the Vietnam War, in that the soldiers did not really know against whom or for what they were fighting, as evident in this dialogue between Robin Hood and Little John:

> Robin Hood: See anything?
> John: You think it's deserted? [...] If they've gone off with the treasure, Richard isn't going to be pleased.
> Robin Hood: If there ever was a treasure.

Robin learns that the small castle holds no jewels or riches, merely a rock in a turnip field, and he mock heroically determines to retrieve this prize for Richard: "We're fighting for a rock. [...] I want to give that rock to Richard. Let's find the turnip field."

Richard, however, will not leave without a slaughter, no matter that victory, if achieved, would be meaningless:

> Richard: I ordered you to take this castle.
> Robin Hood: Yes, my lord.
> Richard: Well, take it. Bring it down and get my statue.
> Robin Hood: They surrender, and your statue is a rock.
> Richard: I want it done.
> Robin Hood: There is no treasure.
> Richard: Do it.
> Robin Hood: There are no soldiers in there – just some children and a mad old man.
> Richard: Oh. And what is that to me?
> Robin Hood: It should mean something.
> Richard: Oh. Is that disapproval, Robin? Am I in the wrong?
> Robin Hood: I followed you for twenty years. I fought for you in the Crusades, I fought for you here in France. Show me a soldier, and I'll fight him now. But I won't slaughter children for a piece of gold that never was.
> Richard: I ordered it. I command you.

The screams of women and children then dramatically underscore the fall of the castle, but no heroism leavens the conflict; it is merely a slaughter undertaken to satisfy the ruler's whims. Indeed, the word *castle* inappropriately describes the site of this battle, as it is a barren, desolate, and singularly unluxurious construction, and, consequently, indicates Richard's tenuous sanity as a ruler in desiring so violently a prize so worthless. Richard Harris's performance as Richard the Lion-Hearted accentuates the historical figure's antiheroic and tyrannical qualities, which upends the legendary cast of the character as established in much film and literature, particularly Sir Walter Scott's novels.[19] Frequently in films of the Robin Hood legend, Richard's reemergence signifies the renewal of good governance in England; here, this myth is doubly denied, both in the depiction of Richard's tyranny and in his death prior to his return to England.

Also somewhat disjointing in Robin's dialogue with Richard regarding the castle is that Robin reveals the conflict takes place in France, although the topography of the scene iconographically suggests more the sandy and arid landscape of the Middle East than the verdure of France. Obviously, France is not entirely a land of forests, farms, and vineyards, but in terms of semiotic shorthands, the landscape of these opening scenes of *Robin and Marian* more readily conveys the Middle East, and the effect of this geographical confusion is to muddy the vision of war in the film. (Andrew Yule notes that the film was shot not in the Middle East, nor in France, nor in England, but in the "parched, arid fields of Spain."[20]) As little as Robin knows about his enemies, so too do viewers share their protagonist's discombobulation, as they are required to ponder against whom, for what, and even where their hero fights. Throughout the film, little mention is made of Richard's French campaigns, even though they are depicted in these opening scenes; in contrast, the shadow of the Crusades looms in the consciousnesses of the characters, who often refer to it as catalyzing their actions and their sense of the world. The Crusades have rendered war the *de facto* condition of life not merely in the Middle East but in Europe as well, despite the meaninglessness of the ensuing battles' objectives.

War depends on the acceptance of masculine hierarchies, and *Robin and Marian* punctures the gravitas accorded to this myth of male aggression. Robin's metamorphosis, from defender of the downtrodden to powerless onlooker, leaves all conceptions of military heroism suspect. When he and Marian discuss their separation from each other, he shares with her in gruesome detail the horrors he witnessed during the Crusades:

> On the 12th of July, 1191, the mighty fortress that was Acre fell to Richard, his one great victory in the Holy Land. He was sick in bed and never struck a blow. And on the 20th of August, John and I were standing on a plain outside of the city watching while every Muslim left alive was marched out in chains. Then Richard spared the richest for ransom, took the strong for slaves, and he took the children – all the children – and had them chopped apart. When that was done, he had the mothers killed. When they were all dead, 3000 bodies on the plain, he had them all opened up so their guts could be explored for gold and precious stones. Our churchmen on the scene – and there were many – took it for a triumph. One bishop put on his miter and led us all in prayer. And you ask me if I'm sick of it?

Robin's description of the Crusades reveals the violent and ugly truths underneath a purportedly just and holy war: the military leader too ill to fight, rather than enacting a stirring and inspiring display of masculine prowess; the slaughter of children and women, rather than the merciful treatment of soldiers fallen in battle; the clergy reveling in bloodshed, rather than tending to the dying. Marian senses the traumatic effects the war has taken on Robin and tenderly asks, "Why didn't you come home then?" Somewhat surprised by the question, Robin replies, "Be[cause] [...] he was my king." Following his diatribe against the horrors of crusading, Robin's protest of his innocence in a philosophically weak justification of his actions – "he was my king" – seems little better than the oft-repeated defense of concentration-camp guards in Nazi Germany, who just followed orders. Robin here claims his allegiance to patriarchal and authoritarian governance: as his king proclaims, so must he and his fellow vassals act.

But, of course, Robin's identity and appeal as a legendary hero are predicated upon his resistance to such transparent ploys of the patriarchy. As Kevin Harty notes, "Traditionally, Robin Hood has been an anti-authoritarian figure. His deeds fly in the face of the political and ecclesiastical establishment,"[21] but this vision of Robin Hood, which viewers are conditioned to expect, is merely a spectral presence in *Robin and Marian*, one alluded to at several moments but lost due to Robin's crusading. Indeed, the Robin Hood of *Robin and Marian* appears relatively surprised by his celebrity status, by remembering the man who he used to be, and he remarks with surprise to Little John, "They've turned us into heroes, Johnny." He reminisces about his life prior to the Crusades, recalling with nostalgia his relationship with his enemy, the Sheriff: "Those were good days, fighting him." *Robin and Marian* thus re-creates Robin Hood into a character who acts in allegiance to the dominant hierarchies and must learn, in effect, to become the Robin Hood of legend once more. In terms of his metamorphosis, he embraced the secondary masculinity accorded him in his role as a crusader, a masculinity determined by following orders in deference to a corrupt and patriarchal hierarchy rather than fighting that hierarchy. Prior to the Crusades, he was such an anti-authoritarian figure, but the war transformed him into a man who supported the status quo, as demanded by Richard, but who now finds his life devoid of meaning or purpose.[22]

Beyond his confused sense of heroic masculinity, Robin also

rejects religion as an antidote against suffering, despite his past vocation as a *miles Christus* in the Crusades. When Marian declares, "God's with me," Robin pointedly responds, "He was with us in the Crusades. It didn't help," which highlights his loss of faith due to this purportedly holy war. Robin also paradoxically clings to the idea that crusading has not changed him, despite the overwhelming evidence that it has. The Sheriff asks him, "How was the Crusade?" to which he responds, "A disappointment. After all these years, look at us. I'm nothing but a former captain. You're still the sheriff." Robin, however, is incorrect in his assessment of the Sheriff, who has learned to read and write during their long separation. If anything, the Sheriff has metamorphosed into an intellectual over the years, but Robin fails to recognize his enemy's transformation, as he (Robin) attempts to reclaim the heroic masculinity of his past rather than to establish a new future. He is mired in his historical manhood and thus unable to see how conditions have shifted him into a queered avatar of his former puissance; he does not want war and the suffering it effects, yet he can envision no alternatives for he must, above all else, retain his sense of masculinity, attenuated as it is.

As an anti-swashbuckler, *Robin and Marian* refuses to glorify warfare, and Robin repeatedly denies his interest in battle. When Will asks him why he returned to England, he succinctly responds, "Not to fight," and when Little John encourages him to relive his glorious past, wistfully wheedling, "Still, it would be something, wouldn't it, Robin?" Robin proclaims that he can no longer successfully perform the requirements of derring-do heroism: "Not at my age." Given these rejections of military answers to social problems, the moral complexity of *Robin and Marian* arises in the ways in which it unsettles models of martial masculinity while nonetheless pointing to their continued appeal. Robin sporadically realizes he is no longer the legendary hero of his youth, but he also repeatedly claims this position, especially in regard to his renewed courtship of Marian:

> Robin Hood: You think I'm old! Gray and old. Well, I'm not.
> Marian: Robin, I'd be twenty for you if I could.
> Robin Hood: I'm all I ever was.

What Robin misunderstands is that Marian would welcome a more mature lover whose identity is no longer entangled with notions of military masculinity that the Crusades have rendered archaic and unattractive. During one of his unwanted attempts to rescue her, she grows exasperated with him and snaps, "Robin, are you ever going to grow up?" The scuffle that follows, in which Robin must fight Marian as well as her captors and unheroically kicks one of these men in the groin, points to the devolution of Robin as a masculine ideal, one who attacks a woman and uses puerile tactics against men in a battle deemed unnecessary by the woman for whom it is fought.

Robin's heroic masculinity is also undercut throughout the film by scenes that accentuate his boyishness (despite the fact that he is middle-aged). Upon his return from France, the green fields of England revitalize him, and his reinvigorated childishness is readily apparent when he exclaims to Little John, "I'll race you," as they ride their horses across the meadow. After the two men steal a peddler's cart to gain entry into Nottingham, John tells Robin, "You look ridiculous," and this loony scheme appears more the invention of a boy's overactive imagination than the detailed military strategy of a seasoned campaigner. In terms of Robin's boyishness, it is apparent that he is also, somewhat inexplicably, sexually immature, in that he is intimidated at the prospect of seeing Marian again: "John, you go in. I never really said good-bye. She might be angry. Better yet – leave it for another day," Robin decides prior to reuniting with his lost love. In these scenes, Robin's heroic past is undermined by his boyishness in the film's present. Instead of becoming more manly from crusading, he has regressed into a pre-heroic and puerile figure.

The film's backstory establishes that Robin and Marian were lovers prior to his departure, but the homosocially inclined Merry Men nonetheless appear to be rather naive about heterosexual relationships. Will tells Robin that the people are rejecting King John's authority, and he uses John's relationship with his wife as evidence of his unfitness to rule: "Even his own kind have turned against him. The kingdom is falling apart. His queen is only twelve years old, and they say that all he does all day is stay in bed with her." Robin and Will chortle at this depiction of their king's sex life, and this excessive carnality defines John's unattractiveness as a ruler; however, given the typical depiction of John in the legendary materials as a ruthless tyrant, this portrayal of him as enjoying too frequently the sensual pleasures of heterosexual intercourse in effect queers Robin and his newly reconstituted band of merry men more than the king. What exactly are they laughing at, if not heterosexuality? Within the medieval contours of the film, the queen's youth should not attract such sniggers: as is well known, girls as young as twelve frequently married in the Middle Ages. D. L. D'Avray succinctly notes of medieval marital practices, "It was common for women to marry young, not long after puberty."[23] The men's laughter is an ahistorical response to a social phenomenon common to the Middle Ages, designed to mark John for modern audiences as sexually perverse due to behaviors unremarkable in their day. If one views John's relationship with his wife within medieval paradigms, it is sufficiently normative not to garner such snickering by a group of men living in a homosocial and sylvan commune. Also, within the trajectory of this film, it is never clearly explained why allegiance to John would trouble Robin after he so blindly followed a morally bankrupt Richard for twenty years of crusading.[24]

War typically upholds rather traditional gender roles, a dynamic that remains evident in contemporary debates about the roles of women and homosexuals in the military,[25] but in *Robin and Marian* the Crusades have undermined longstanding concepts of gender. Most significant in this regard is Marian's increased independence from Robin.[26] During his long absence crusading, Marian, beyond her vocational shift into Church life, has rejected the traditional feminine role of the damsel in distress and thus no longer depends on Robin to fight her battles:

> Robin: If you're in trouble, I can save you.
> Marian: I've nothing to be saved from. I don't want you, Robin.
> Robin: But you've got me. I like the way you look.

Robin's words here border on the pathetic as he clings to their traditional roles and cites his sexual attraction to her as a motivating factor in his actions. After Robin "rescues" Marian from the Sheriff, he tells her that he "couldn't let them take you," to which Marian responds with surprise, "Take me? I was going." Marian acts in response to her own sense of justice, and she refuses to play the helpless feminine role that Robin expects of her. Instead, she threatens him with violence: "I wish to God I were a man. I'd knock you down." She succeeds in "knocking him down" at the movie's end when she poisons him, proving that she understands the trap of masculinity that incites him to violence and that she is strong enough to halt its apparently endless cycle. Within this film, it takes a woman to stop a warrior, which highlights the oscillating potential of genders in regard to the bodies through which they are performed.

In its thematic treatment of bodily scars, *Robin and Marian* debunks the notion that soldiers are the only ones who physically suffer in battle and further destabilizes gendered notions of military sacrifice. When Marian sees Robin's scars, she laments the ways in which they register his transformation from innocence to experience: "So many [scars] […] you had the sweetest body when you left. Hard, and not a mark. And you were mine." The connection between physical and emotional scars is made explicit when she describes her suicide attempts after his departure: "When you left, I thought I'd die. I even tried"; she connects the past to the present when she laments, "It's too much to lose you twice." Viewers see Marian's scars on her wrist from her suicide attempt, and this demonstrates the physical effects of war on women supposedly safe from such violence as they await their lovers at home, but she separates herself from this prior identity: "To want to die from wanting you – some other girl, it must have been." In both cases, the scars represent the effects of battle, but they register emotional loss more than martial conquest; Robin's and Marian's mutual metamorphoses into new gender roles that alienate them from each other makes their reunion, although mutually desired, impossible to effect.

Further disrupting the gendered dynamics of love, crusading has queered the romantic relationships among the main characters of the film, leaving them in a state of erotic disarray. Eve Sedgwick's foundational work on the erotic triangle is relevant here, in its presumption of the messy dynamics and slippery desires sparked by competitions for affection.[27] What is intriguing about *Robin and Marian*, however, is the sheer multiplicity of such triangulated desire: Robin loves Marian, but leaves her to serve Richard the Lion-Hearted; Marian loves Robin, but devotes herself to Jesus and the Christian Church to replace her crusading lover; after Robin reunites with Marian, his homosocial yet aggressive bond with the Sheriff of Nottingham (as well as this man's conflicting desire to arrest Marian) leads him to forsake her yet again; and Little John ultimately confesses his long-standing yet unfulfilled affections for Marian, which he has squelched in favor of his friend. Instead of attempting to sate their romantic desires with their beloveds, the characters find surrogates to fulfill their needs, often those caused by the voids of separation necessitated by crusading.

For instance, Marian describes her motivations for becoming a nun in terms of an erotic competition between Robin and Jesus: "I suppose I took the Church up out of anger. And it's a blur now, but I think that I thought that of all men you'd mind most if I married Jesus." She then mentions that she fantasized of Robin while going to bed and suggestively adds, "My confessions were the envy of the convent." As Marian expects, Robin is surprised by her religious vocation – "A nun? She can't be. Not my Marian" – but even more troubling to his self-image and sense of masculinity is her rejection of him: "I don't think about you anymore, Robin." Likewise, Little John later confesses his love for Marian and, in doing so, discloses that he would have treated her better than Robin did: "You're Rob's lady. If you'd been mine, I never would have left you." Marian, in turn, reveals her jealousy over Little John's attachment to Robin: "You've had him for years, and I'm going to lose him." The encounter between Little John and Marian concludes as John throws away the apple he is eating, a sign that the seductive fruits of sexual passion should now be cast aside in favor of new possibilities.[28] So many competing desires are circulating among the primary characters of the film – Robin, Marian, Richard, the Sheriff, Little John, and even (latently) Jesus. In the final analysis, love cannot be entirely divorced from concepts of gender, but these characters are, in essence, queered from the fictions of their genders into a miasma of sexual identity in which they no longer recognize themselves or their lovers due to the topsy-turvy effects of crusading.

In the film's climax, the latent erotic triangle among Robin, Marian, and the Sheriff brings about their deaths. The submerged homoeroticism between Robin and the Sheriff, sublimated as it is through their conflict with each other, becomes explicit through the imagery of their final confrontation. When the viewer sees the Sheriff performing his daily hygienic rituals, he is naked while surrounded by many men; moreover, when he shaves himself with his knife, the positioning of the knife vis-à-vis his mouth, along with his puckered cheeks, suggests the iconography of fellatio. Certainly, the Sheriff's nudity and detailed attention to his hygiene marks him as fastidious and somewhat precious in comparison to Robin's more rough-

and-tumble version of masculinity. The two men then meet to discuss
the conditions of their impending battle, and it is apparent that the
bond between enemies is as strong as the bond between lovers:

> Sheriff: I knew you'd come.
> Robin Hood: Of all men, just for you.
> Sheriff: I know.

If stripped from their martial context, these lines would resonate with
romantic and affective emotions, and one can readily imagine them
transferred to the climax of a classic Hollywood melodrama in a scene
reminiscent of the one shared between Cary Grant and Deborah Kerr
at the close of *An Affair to Remember* (1957). The scene unfolds
slowly, as the two men adhere to the rules of engagement, and their
mutual patience for their final conflict establishes the predestined
nature of their violent union. Robin and the Sheriff then fight their
climactic battle, with the Sheriff slicing Robin in the side. This injury
gives him a Christ-like wound, but the metaphoric construction of
Robin as Christ is then undone when he stabs and penetrates the
Sheriff, an iconic consummation of their aggressive bond.

In the end, it appears that Marian's real competition for Robin's
love was not a living person, neither Richard the Lion-Hearted nor the
Sheriff of Nottingham – but death itself. Robin is too mired in
crusading, too alienated from the foundations of his legendary identity, to imagine any other form of attachment, erotic or otherwise.
After his battle with the Sheriff, he tells Marian of his plans for their
future: "You'll tend me 'til I'm well again. And then – great battles!" As
much as the Crusades have upended his sense of self and masculine
identity, he cannot imagine any other paradigm around which to
structure his life, and he now reveals that he has consistently refused to
learn any lessons about dying. Early in the film, while imprisoned
with Little John and expecting Richard to order their executions, the
two men discuss the ramifications of death:

> John: Well, if we go, we go.
> Robin Hood: Is that your idea of dying?
> John: I don't know. You'd think I'd learn, I've seen enough of it.
> Robin Hood: Well, I tell you something. I won't go quietly.

For Robin, death appears to be the ultimate enemy, the one to be resisted above all others. But the Sheriff knows Robin better than Robin knows himself when he claims of his foe, "He's a little bit in love with death. He flirts, he teases." Repeatedly, too, Robin's sexual interest in Marian is trumped by his military passion that bears fatal possibilities. He provocatively propositions Marian – "I've never kissed a member of the clergy. Would it be a sin?" – and Marian removes her wimple to kiss him, but a horn blows, and the moment is lost. In a similar scene, Marian pleads with him, "Don't go," to which he responds, "I just want to look. See who's hunting me." Again Robin turns his interest away from sex and life to conflict and death, and Death, latently and allegorically, wins his hand, despite Marian's best erotic efforts to the contrary.

Robin's erotic attachment to death defeats Marian's love for him, and at the film's conclusion, she frees him from defending her by ceding him to her necrotic rival for his affections. As Robin realizes that Marian has poisoned him, he croaks, "Why?" to which she responds, "I love you … I love you … more than God." Robin defeats God in their amatory competition for Marian, and, in complementary contrast, Marian surrenders to Robin's necrotic drive for battle and gives him what he has been seeking. The two are left as each other's lovers, and in their death throes, their fingers reach for each other's, recalling the famed imagery of Michelangelo's Sistine Chapel in which God's and Adam's fingers almost touch. The two are together forever, but given Robin's conflicted and queered masculinity, they can only be together in death.[29]

Robin's premature death consequently links him to his initial adversary in the film, Richard the Lion-Hearted, as both men die before they succeed in procreating or resolving the conflicts that ensnare them. Richard wonders as his death appears imminent, "Christ, why did I have no children?" Robin, too, dies without offspring, thus reenacting his ruler's infertility. In Richard's death scene, he frees Robin from the weight of their relationship:

Robin Hood: Richard, it's me.
Richard the Lion-Hearted: I know it's you. You couldn't leave me, could you? (Robin shakes his head.) You're free of me. I let you go. What are you going to do without me now, jolly Robin? Now I'm dead …

Richard's death ostensibly enabled Robin to escape from their patriarchally inflected relationship of hierarchical masculinity, but ultimately, the pattern established through queer crusading, of war disgusting yet no less inspiring men and thus rendering gendered identities suspect, leads Robin to seek death in battle more than life with Marian. Through its subtext of martial conflict rendering men infertile and alienated from heterosexual and procreative passion, *Robin and Marian* undermines myths of masculinity – those of both the Crusades and Vietnam – thereby constructing these alien lands as contaminatively queer places, where western myths are confronted with their gendered bravado, and punctured.

NOTES

1. *Robin and Marian*, dir. Richard Lester, screenwriter James Goldman, perf. Sean Connery, Audrey Hepburn, and Robert Shaw, DVD (1976; Culver City, CA: Columbia 2002). Goldman also wrote the screenplay for Anthony Harvey's *The Lion in Winter* (1968) – featuring Peter O'Toole as Henry II and Katharine Hepburn as Eleanor of Aquitaine – another film that tackles the meanings of medieval masculinity. Likewise, Lester's interest in historically inflected masculinities is evident in his films inspired by Alexander Dumas's *The Three Musketeers*: *The Three Musketeers* (1974), *The Four Musketeers* (1975), and *The Return of the Musketeers* (1989).

2. For example, one of the more recent deployments of queer theory involves its intersection with disability studies, such as in Robert McRuer's *Crip Theory: Cultural Signs of Queerness and Disability* (New York: New York University Press, 2006).

3. Judith Butler, *Bodies That Matter: On the Discursive Limits of "Sex"* (New York: Routledge, 1993), 228.

4. Alexander Doty, *Making Things Perfectly Queer: Interpreting Mass Culture* (Minneapolis: University of Minnesota Press, 1993), 3.

5. For example, see James A. Schultz, *Courtly Love, the Love of Courtliness, and the History of Sexuality* (Chicago, IL: University of Chicago Press, 2006), esp. 51–62; and Karma Lochrie, *Heterosyncrasies: Female Sexuality When Normal Wasn't* (Minneapolis: University of Minnesota Press, 2005), esp. xi–xxviii.

6. Tison Pugh, "Marginal Males, Disciplined Daughters, and Guinevere's Adultery in *A Kid in King Arthur's Court*," *Arthuriana* 13.2 (2003): 69–84.

7. Holly Crocker, "Chaucer's Man Show: Anachronistic Authority in Brian Helgeland's *A Knight's Tale*," in *Race, Class, and Gender in "Medieval" Cinema*, ed. Lynn T. Ramey and Tison Pugh (New York: Palgrave Macmillan, 2007), 183–97.

8. Donald Hoffman, "Not Dead Yet: *Monty Python and the Holy Grail* in the Twenty-First Century," in *Cinema Arthuriana*, rev. ed., ed. Kevin Harty (Jefferson, NC: McFarland, 2002), 127–35; and Kevin Harty, "The Damsel 'in Dis Dress': Gender Bending in the Arthuriad," *Arthuriana* 14.1 (2004): 79–82.

9. As with all generalizations, exceptions disrupt this blanket statement about the dominant masculinity of war, ranging from Joan of Arc's campaigns for Charles VII to Margaret Thatcher's role as Prime Minister during the 1982 Falklands War. Still, war remains primarily a normatively masculine domain, although women are increasingly entering the fray.

10. Leo Braudy, *From Chivalry to Terrorism: War and the Changing Nature of Masculinity* (New York: Knopf, 2003), 77.

11. Stephen J. Ducat, *The Wimp Factor: Gender Gaps, Holy Wars, and the Politics of Anxious Masculinity* (Boston: Beacon, 2004), 14.

12. Eben J. Muse, *The Land of Nam: The Vietnam War in American Film* (Lanham, MD: Scarecrow, 1995), 46–47. See also Linda Dittmar and Gene Michaud, *From Hanoi to Hollywood: The Vietnam War in American Film* (New Brunswick, NJ: Rutgers University Press, 1990); and James C. Wilson, *Vietnam in Prose and Film* (Jefferson, NC: McFarland, 1982).

13. Richard Lester, quoted in Andrew Yule, *The Man Who "Framed" The Beatles: A Biography of Richard Lester* (New York: Fine, 1994), 260. It should be noted that, in the parallel I am drawing between Lester's Robin Hood and America's Vietnam veterans, the relevant axis of comparison focuses on initial idealism and subsequent disillusionment, not on Robin's past as a "small-time robber."

14. Traces of Vietnam can be found in other "medieval" films as well. See Tom Shippey, "Fuqua's *King Arthur*: More Myth-making in America," *Exemplaria* 19.2 (2007): 310–26, esp. 316–17, in which he reads Antoine Fuqua's *King Arthur* (2004) as "yet one more reflex of the generation-old trauma over Vietnam."

15. As a genre, the swashbuckler has not proved particularly amenable to female protagonists. Renny Harlin's *Cutthroat Island* (1995), starring Geena Davis, is a notable exception to this rule, and the British television series *Maid Marian and Her Merry Men* likewise re-imagined the gendered dynamics of the Robin Hood legend.

16. Brian Taves, *The Romance of Adventure: The Genre of Historical Adventure Movies* (Jackson: University Press of Mississippi, 1993), xi.

17. Stephen Knight, *Robin Hood: A Complete Study of the English*

Outlaw (Oxford: Blackwell, 1994), 237. For a glossy overview of Robin Hood movies, see David Turner, *Robin of the Movies: A Cinematic History of the Outlaw of Sherwood Forest* (Kingswinford, England: Yeoman, 1989).

18. Richard Stapleford, "Robin Hood and the Contemporary Idea of the Hero," *Literature/Film Quarterly* 8.3 (1980): 182–87 (183).

19. For a biography of Richard I that focuses on his dual heroism and tyranny, see John Gillingham, *Richard I* (New Haven, CT: Yale University Press, 1999). In terms of Richard's depiction in other films, Sean Connery plays the role in a much more triumphantly masculine incarnation, albeit in a cameo role, at the close of Reynold's *Robin Hood: Prince of Thieves.*

20. Andrew Yule, *The Man Who "Framed" the Beatles*, 264. For Richard's campaigns in the Middle East and France, see Gillingham, *Richard I*, esp. 155–92 and 283–320.

21. Kevin J. Harty, "Robin Hood on Film: Moving beyond a Swashbuckling Stereotype," in *Robin Hood in Popular Culture: Violence, Transgression, and Justice*, ed. Thomas Hahn (Cambridge: D. S. Brewer, 2000), 87–100 (97).

22. This timeline of events muddies the standard trajectory of the Robin Hood legend, in that Robin typically takes up his defense of the poor and downtrodden in response to John's usurpation of the throne during Richard's absence while fighting (or returning from) the Crusades. That Robin undertook such battles against injustice prior to the Crusades, and hence prior to Richard's departure for them, suggests that Richard did not fully protect his people during his time in England (which, in the historical record, was quite brief).

23. D. L. D'Avray, *Medieval Marriage: Symbolism and Society* (Oxford: Oxford University Press, 2005), 182. See also Frances and Joseph Gies, *Marriage and the Family in the Middle Ages* (New York: Harper & Row, 1987).

24. For an overview of John's reign, see Ralph V. Turner, *King John* (London: Longman, 1994). Many of the typical depictions of John in the Robin Hood legend, including his attempt to usurp the throne and his conflict with the Church, are loosely based on the historical record.

25. Debates addressing the propriety of women in combat and of gays and lesbians in the armed forces fractiously continue in the American political sphere. For overviews of these arguments, see *Gender Camouflage: Women and the U.S. Military*, ed. Francine D'Amico and Laurie Weinstein (New York: New York University Press, 1990); *Wives and Warriors: Women and the Military in the United States and Canada*, ed. Laurie Weinstein and Christie C. White (Westport, CT: Bergin & Garvey, 1997); *Gays and Lesbians in the Military: Issues, Concerns, and Contrasts*, ed. Wilber J. Scott and Sandra Carson Stanley (New York: Aldine de Gruyter, 1994); and the

essays of Martin Binkin, "Minorities and Gays in the Military: Who Will Fight the Next War?" and the Servicemembers Legal Defense Network, "An Overview of Don't Ask, Don't Tell, Don't Pursue, Don't Harass," in *America's Military Today: The Challenge of Militarism*, ed. Tod Ensign (New York: New Press, 2004).

26. In modern retellings of the Robin Hood legend, the character of Marian often offers insight into the shifting role of women in contemporary society. See the studies of Lorinda B. Cohoon, "Transgressive Transformations: Representations of Maid Marian in Robin Hood Retellings," *The Lion and the Unicorn* 31 (2007): 209–31; and Lorraine K. Stock and Candace Gregory-Abbott, "The 'Other' Women of Sherwood: The Construction of Difference and Gender in Cinematic Treatments of the Robin Hood Legend," in *Race, Class, and Gender in "medieval" cinema*, 199–214.

27. For the erotic triangle and its relationship to queer desire, see Eve Sedgwick, *Between Men: English Literature and Male Homosocial Desire* (New York: Columbia University Press, 1985).

28. The iconographic trope of fruit as a sign of sexuality runs throughout *Robin and Marian*. The film's first shot focuses on three apples, but the second shot shows that two of the apples have rotted, with only one remaining fresh. The general iconography of the apples forms a woman's body, a crude pictogram of apples for breast and vagina suggestive of a fruity Venus of Willendorf. The film returns to this imagery in its closing shot of one ripe and two withered apples (which reveals a continuity problem, since an earlier shot shows one apple and the chalice of poison).

29. *Robin and Marian* is only very loosely based on the Robin Hood of medieval literature, but in this death scene, Goldman includes two key points of Robin's lore: that he was killed by a prioress and that he shot an arrow to mark the place of his burial. For the Robin Hood legends, see *Robin Hood and Other Outlaw Tales*, ed. Stephen Knight and Thomas Ohlgren (Kalamazoo, MI: Medieval Institute, 1997), in particular "A Gest of Robyn Hode," lines 1801–20, for the Prioress's role in Robin's death, and "The Death of Robin Hood," lines 127–32, for the arrow marking his grave.

Getting Reel with Grendel's Mother: The Abject Maternal and Social Critique

David W. Marshall

Recent film adaptations of *Beowulf* offer interpretations of Grendel's mother that seem to defy any grounding in the text. In one retelling, a net-clad Playmate slinks into Hrothgar's room while he sleeps and mounts him in a soft-core display of sexual delight. In another, Beowulf stands cautiously in a dark cave as Grendel's mother rises naked from the water, voluptuous, gold, and buxom. There may be logic in adding a measure of sex to screen adaptations of the poem, since, as Roger Avary confesses, "in Hollywood [...] *Beowulf* was considered something of a joke. A sword-and-sandal hoity-toity lesson in ancient literature."[1] A story associated with the pains of senior English left the book a punchline for producers seeking success in a competitive market.[2] To some extent, casting Angelina Jolie adds a draw for the young male demographic. More substantively, however, the rather unorthodox re-imaginings of Grendel's mother join scholarly attempts to interpret her role in the story.

While the above images of Grendel's mother are, perhaps, the most eye-catching, each of the *Beowulf* adaptations rewrites the character in different ways, ranging from a grudge-holding beast or alien in the most recent adaptation, *Outlander* (2008), or the Sci Fi channel production *Grendel* (2007) to an "uncivilized" tribal leader of *The Thirteenth Warrior* (1999) or a magical, ancient being in the two films titled *Beowulf* (1999 and 2007). Despite that variety, they consistently foreground the character well beyond her role in the original poem. This article examines the way that representations of Grendel's mother have changed in some recent film adaptations of *Beowulf*. It argues that each of the films constructs the character as a threat to masculine social structures, but that the films' responses to that threat differ. John McTiernan's *The Thirteenth Warrior* offers a monstrous image of destruction contained by male heroes, while two others, Robert Zemeckis' *Beowulf* and Sturla Gunarsson's *Beowulf and Grendel*, offer a figure that questions patriarchy and leaves it unsettled. Ultimately, however, only Gunnarsson's film succeeds in using the maternal figure as a tool for critiquing hyper-masculine iterations of power. I will suggest that the films evince Julia Kristeva's idea of *abjection*, with the latter films employing it as a position of active resistance.

Abjection is not a new concept in relation to analyses of Grendel's mother, but scholarship on her character does not begin there. Academic discussions of Grendel's mother have largely revolved around establishing her function as both woman and monster, with two distinct positions emerging. First, scholars such as Janet T. Buck, Elaine Tuttle Hansen, and Setsuko Haruta argue that women in *Beowulf* tend to be weak and victimized figures who are tragic, pathetic, lonely victims of forces outside their control.[3] In this reading, Grendel's mother functions as a shocking violation of gender norms, insofar as she unnaturally perpetuates a masculine imperative to feud. The second critical strand asserts that (some) women in the poem are strong, active figures. Jane Chance and L. John Sklute, for example, argue that women in the world of the poem are different from men, wielding a feminine authority secondary to that of men but significant nonetheless.[4] For Chance that authority expresses itself in the mead hall, while Sklute sees in the idea of peace-weaving a sort of diplomatic power. Grendel's mother in this framework is an "anti-type" (to use Chance's term) for the "proper" action of diplomatic peace-weaving. Helen Damico claims that the women of *Beowulf* find their origins in the Valkyrie reflex, while Gillian Overing argues that Modthryth enacts authority associated with masculine norms.[5] Grendel's mother, therefore, is another representative of the fierce woman or warrior-maiden that discomfits masculine structures. Similarly, Christine Alfano's reassessment of translations and glosses for the epithets describing Grendel's mother concludes with a desire to see her not as monstrous, but as a powerful woman.[6]

Use of Julia Kristeva's notion of abjection is more recent. Critics have employed it to demonstrate the ways in which Grendel's mother destabilizes the otherwise masculinist agenda of the poem. In *Powers of Horror*, Kristeva explains that abjection is the process by which subjectivity is established. Heavily indebted to Lacan, Kristeva claims that a subject must push the mother and the maternal body away in the process of aligning itself with the symbolic system, which is associated with the Law of the Father. That process, however, creates a simultaneous desire for the primal connection to the maternal and utter revulsion produced by becoming a subject in the symbolic order. Overing invokes Kristeva's ideas, though she chooses not to address Grendel's mother, because the character creates category confusion that blurs the lines between female and monster.[7] Inspired by that absence, James Hala seeks to "put her in the poem as an active, dynamic force in the creation of the poem's shifting meanings."[8] He positions Grendel as the Kristevan *deject* through whom "the abject, the ambiguity which threatens the demarcation of the subject from the object, flows back and forth."[9] As a Kristevan *chora*, Grendel's mother is a site of indeterminability that the poem attempts to resolve through Beowulf's battle with her.[10] More recently, Paul Acker argues for the similarity between what he calls "Anglo-Saxon psychodramas" and our own, basing that claim on the observation that attacks of the abjected mother figure threaten "the whole system of male dominance."[11] In response, Renee Trilling suggests that Acker's use of abjection leaves intact a simple binary structure that ignores the slippery signification of Grendel's mother. She claims that "Grendel's mother stands in for that which exceeds representation – and hence exceeds the totalizing grasp of criticism as well."[12] She claims that, as a signifier of ideas clustered around the feminine, Grendel's mother is a figure repressed by masculine authority, even as her presence ruptures that authority.

Scholarship on Grendel's mother thus highlights women in Anglo-Saxon culture and in its only surviving epic poem as distanced from power structures associated with masculinity; Grendel's mother (or Modthryth, for Overing) unsettles that masculine economy of power, but in monstrous terms that ultimately confirm the correctness of that power being held by men. Hala, Acker, and Trilling each read Grendel's mother as troubling Anglo-Saxon power structures that constrain female agency and that relegate women to the margins. The film adaptations I will discuss below locate the character in a similar dynamic. While not all of them adhere to the reifying of authority as masculine, they consistently locate the maternal figure on the margins, abjecting her. As such, the haunting presence of the maternal becomes the unsettling force it is in the readings of Hala, Acker, and Trilling.

The Thirteenth Warrior

The Thirteenth Warrior, an adaptation once-removed, offers a dramatic rewriting of Grendel's mother. As Nickolas Haydock describes, it combines "evolutionary biology and even genetics [...] to offer what are in essence euhemeristic interpretations of the supernatural [...]."[13] Director John McTiernan follows Michael Crichton's novel *Eaters of the Dead*, in which a cannibalistic group of Neanderthals (the Wendol) who follow a figure called "The Mother" begin raiding Hrothgar's domain. *The Thirteenth Warrior's* cinematic portrayal of the Neanderthals, observes Hugh Magennis, gives the impression that the Wendol are "a primitive and benighted tribe," being "like the relentless Indians in early Westerns."[14] Whatever the precise effect, Magennis hints at the cultural distinction drawn between the production's Scandinavian heroes and the Wendol. Lynn Shutters argues that the Wendol culture is a polar opposite of the masculine ethos of the Scandinavian culture; according to Shutters, "gender distinctions reinforce the cultural lines that the film seeks to draw."[15] Shutters is certainly correct, though she understates the gendered relationship between the two cultures in the text.[16] In *The Thirteenth Warrior*, masculine identity is not simply in contrast to the feminine Wendol, but constituted by a figural abjection of the Wendol association with the maternal that constructs boundaries by which a communal subjectivity is formed.

A schema of female roles emerges throughout *The Thirteenth Warrior* that locates safe and threatening female functions. Within that schema, the film emphasizes the maternal as a disturbing force that destroys when functioning outside the sanction of masculine authority structures. We see women as consorts, as demonstrated by both the liaison between Ahmed and Olga and by the maiden who is sacrificed for her dead lord early in the film. In this capacity, their function is unproblematic and does not threaten male authority, but confirms it. In their role as nurse-maids, women are more ambivalent. Because of the maternal nature of that position and the association of monstrosity with the Wendol Mother (of which I will say more below), *The Thirteenth Warrior* consistently authorizes women as care-takers. For example, after first meeting with Rothgar, Buliwyf and his men race to meet a small, naked child fleeing a farmstead after a

Wendol attack. Rethel (Mischa Hausserman) and Weath (Tony Curran) attempt to question the child before Buliwyf tells them to "find somebody who knows him." Weilew steps forward and states, "I know him." The recurrence of "know him," first from Buliwyf, then from Weilew, highlights the way in which the maternal figure (though significantly not the mother) operates in relation to male initiative rather than as an independent agent. We see a similar authorizing of maternal action prior to the first anticipated Wendol mass-attack, when Buliwyf directs Weilew to take the children to safety with the other women. As these examples indicate, motherly activity in the Danish setting is made acceptable by male mediation (the small child) and by male instruction (Buliwyf's directions). Even when a nurturing figure challenges masculinity, as when Olga mocks Ahmed's whining about pain, she operates within the story's Danish expectations, which Shutters has identified as admirably masculine, and the comment addresses Ahmed's failings more than Olga's deviation from a prescribed role.

Outside this sanctioning of nurturing activities the maternal appears unnatural and destructive. The only character, in fact, who is clearly identified as a mother is the Wendol leader, whom Buliwyf and his men first encounter via proxy after investigating the attack on the farmstead. In addition to gnawed-upon bodies and claw marks, they find a small fetish object reminiscent of the Willendorf Venus, though intentionally headless. Later in the film, an aged oracle identifies the maternal nature of the object, saying, "This is the mother of the Wen." The northmen refuse to touch the object; they spit on it and hurl it away with the blade of a sword. Two responses seem entwined here. First, the veneration of a mother figure is perceived as not just suspicious, but unnatural and threatening. The reaction of the northmen suggests anxiety over a power inherent in the feminine-maternal figure of the fetish object, with its distended womb and engorged breasts. Second, the association of the fetish object with the cannibalistic attack renders the maternal a perversion of not just social order but natural order. This violation of order is emphasized further in the Wendol caves, wherein Buliwyf and his men see a massive version of the fetish object in a chamber littered with human skeletal remains. As Shutters remarks, "instead of associating the female body with fecundity, [the Wendol] associate it with death, and this statue insistently connects the violence and irrationality of the Wendol to the feminine."[17] The scene suggests, then, an angst produced by the sudden confrontation with a rival power from which the northern heroes are barred, a power that inverts the proper relations of male/female and life/death.

The dual association of the Wendol Mother with life and death, in particular, draws attention to the way in which McTiernan's film seems to play with a Kristevan sense of abjection to construct the Wendol and the Mother. As noted above, for Kristeva, abjection is the process by which subjectivity is established. She suggests that a subject must push the mother and the maternal body away in the process of acquiring language and thereby align itself with the symbolic system, which is associated with the Law of the Father.[18] We find this idea enacted figuratively in the behaviors of the Wendol. While Grendel's Mother actually invades Heorot in the poem, *The Thirteenth Warrior*'s corollary figure never enters the hall or the lands of the Danes. Instead, her presence is a haunting effect that troubles them through the awareness of both the fetish object and the reverence given it by the cannibals that prey on them. The Wendol Mother remains pushed to the margins with her people, who, as Ahmed observes, "think they're bears." The Wendol are a totemic people, working in simple representations. Their animalistic nature points to the constitution of subjectivity delineated by Kristeva. They exist in a primitive state, living like bears in caves, communally. They utter shrieks and howls rather than intelligible words; it appears they have not fully entered the symbolic order. As the second oracle in the film observes, "She is their will," and their reverence for the maternal, their ceding of power to her, leaves the Wendol in a barbaric state.

The film reasserts a civilized, male authority by figuratively enacting abjection of the maternal in a three-step sequence. First, McTiernan creates this effect in the cave setting of the Wendol home, through which Buliwyf and his men must descend. The cave complex is a hidden space in which maternal power is concealed and protected, a site of power that displaces masculine authority. The mysteriousness of the space is conveyed by Herger asking, "How deep in the earth are we?," conveying notions of intruding into an unknown realm. Moreover, by locating the Mother's cave in nearly the deepest point, the imagery suggests a penetration down from the mouth into the womb. The invasion of that space by six men bespeaks a masculine desire to root out the threat inherent in that maternal space, which advances the associations between the maternal womb and death. The caves are jagged rock, bare of life other than the primitive Wendol, and shots of the Mother's cave encapsulate these associations. She crouches over a small fire, among staked heads, a snake slithering across her shoulders. Second, the action begins to resolve the horror of the destructive maternal in the exchange of blows between the Mother and Buliwyf: she scratches him with a poison-dipped bear claw; he decapitates her with a single stroke of the sword. Buliwyf's killing of the Mother destroys the living presence of the fetish object among the Wendol, and with that sacrifice, the Danes assert the primacy of the masculine/paternal over the maternal. All that remains is to fully distance Scandinavian manliness from the physical realm of the maternal. The symbolic psycho-drama finds its conclusion with imagery that suggests the separation of mother and child in birth. Kristeva explains that "evocation of the maternal body and childbirth induces the image of birth as a violent act of expulsion through which the nascent body tears itself away from the matter of maternal insides,"[19] and that imagery is invoked by the heroes' escape from the lair. They retreat deeper through the caves, which become increasingly tight, until they arrive at a narrow, flooded tunnel. The camera shifts to a sequence of underwater shots as each of the men swims through the tunnel until, finally surfacing outside the cave, they rise to the surface and gasp for air. The suffocating claustrophobia invokes associations with the birth canal, so that their final emergence into the ocean implies a final separation from the maternal figure. The film's jump cut from the shot of the men treading water in the ocean stamps this figurative abjection by lingering over the edifice of Heorot perched on its hill.

With its associations with power and law, Heorot in this context completes the process by returning the warriors – and, importantly, our attention – to what is deemed their rightful place: a civilized space defined not by organic, meandering caverns, but by rigidly organized composition. Masculine authority, having cut down the source of matriarchal power, successfully reasserts itself by escaping and rejecting the maternal geography of the Wendol cave structure, and thereby recontains the threat of the perverse power associated with the maternal in the film. The editing moves from rejecting the procreative power and its associations with smothering, consumption, and death into reifying the authority represented by Heorot's assertion of order on a wild land. The progression of the imagery conveys a drawing of boundaries by which the male-dominated, masculine community forms its collective identity, even if such boundaries remain permeable in regards to Ahmed's place with them. Similar confrontations with the abject serve a similar function in Ahmed's witnessing the northmen's morning ablutions, which involve men sharing a bowl into which they blow their noses and from which they wash their faces and rinse their mouths. Ahmed, for the northmen, seems closer to the abject in both his touching the fetish object and in their calling him "little brother," with its implication of retarded maturation.

The retelling, then, examines the uncertainty of such boundary-drawing as a means of establishing both individual and collective subjectivity. McTiernan's film creates a gendered dynamic in which specifically masculine identity is jeopardized and defined in confrontations with the abject maternal, which returns to threaten the definition of civilized, masculine forms by consuming them. Boundary violation manifests most dramatically in the death of Buliwyf, and here McTiernan's Crichton-based film intensifies gendered anxieties over the poem's own concerns. Whereas in the original poem Beowulf successfully confronts Grendel's mother in the aquatic cave and is slain decades later by the dragon, in *The Thirteenth Warrior* the mother slays Buliwyf. While the poison does not kill him until after the final battle with the Wendol, the mother is responsible for the destruction of the hero. *The Thirteenth Warrior* thus defines the abject maternal as a destroyer of the noblest images of the masculine. Even so, the film does not allow the maternal to displace the heroic in an attempt to challenge Western masculine structures. McTiernan's film invokes the poem as read by Overing and Clare A. Lees, each of whom has read *Beowulf* as proffering a decidedly masculinist agenda that limits female agency. While the psychoanalytic notion of abjection suggests a perpetual ambivalence, a continual unsettling of the subject, McTiernan's film attempts closure to the conflict by allowing for the final elimination of the mother figure in much the same way that the source text does. That closure is illusory, however, because in her final moment the mother wreaks a final trauma on the northmen by securing the hero's death. Buliwyf's death and the poem (which we are led to believe grows from this "true" story) hint at the perpetuation of the mother's disruption of secure male authority: she, too, will live on alongside Buliwyf in tradition.

Beowulf (2007)

The confrontation between hero and abject maternal announces itself early in Robert Zemeckis' adaptation, when the titular character, standing on the prow of a storm-wracked ship, bellows, "The sea is my mother! She will never take me back into her murky womb!" Subsequently, the film is driven by a return to a horrifying womb, but the gendered ambivalence towards the Other in *The Thirteenth Warrior* marks the depiction of the monstrous in Zemeckis' adaptation too. The ambivalence takes the surprising form of a simultaneous sexual desire for and violent rejection of that Other, and Grendel's mother is the character around which this dual response resolves. Rather than offering two different characters, as in McTiernan's *Olga and the Mother*, this *Beowulf* gives Grendel's mother two distinct images: a monstrous mother and a sensual seductress. The dichotomy, however, does not serve to reify Western notions of civilization. On the contrary, Zemeckis' production deploys a similar notion of the abject (m)other, coupled with the sex object, to destabilize those notions by critiquing expressions of power. Authority in the movie is coded as masculine, and masculine desires and impulses ultimately corrupt it.

Neil Gaiman and Roger Avary's script, an imaginative "truth" behind the poem, maintains fidelity to its source in a limited thematic engagement, even if the narrative development deviates wildly at times.[20] From the very beginning, their rewriting emphasizes the masculine space of the mead hall and locates its source in the figure of King Hrothgar (Anthony Hopkins). In the opening scene, Hrothgar proclaims that he has made good on a year-old promise to "celebrate our victories in a new hall, mighty and beautiful" where they might "divide the spoils of their conquest." Scholarship has for decades commented upon the decidedly masculine nature of the mead-hall community. James W. Earl, for example, uses Freud to construct a contrast between the world of the hall, masculine in its associations with "civilization" or "consciousness and rationality," and the feminine world of the hut, "a natural representation of the unconscious and the irrational."[21] From a more anthropological perspective, Mary Jane Luecke argues that the hints of matrilocal power in the depiction of the Geats is entirely absent in the poet's treatment of the Danes.[22] As the site of community, or civilization in Earl's thinking, this Heorot derives its personality from its center: Hrothgar. As the poem puts it: "Then Hrothgar was given luck in war/ [...]/ It brought to his mind/ that he should command a hall-building [...]." (64, 67b–68 translation mine).[23] In both texts, Hrothgar's authority as king yields victory, expressed in the construction of the hall. The setting of the film's first scene, thereby, threads together conquest, power, and wealth.

Contrary to the poem, however, the gendering of this cinematic hall is so narrow in its sense of masculinity as to shift it away from the cerebral associations identified by Earl and towards the bodily. The vulgar image of masculine power is evinced by the opening shots, in which a toga-clad, drunk Hrothgar encourages a fraternity party atmosphere. Proclaiming Heorot to be a place of "merriment, joy, and fornication," he tosses treasure about and praises Unferth as the "violator of virgins and bravest of brave brawlers." His warriors pound mead tankards on tables and grope the women who serve them in a display of masculine subjectivity expressed in bodily terms. The image appears much closer to the physical and irrational operations associated with the world of the hut that Earl bases on Freud's discussion of the cellar. The power exhibited in the warriors' display, led by Hrothgar, amounts to an unconstrained freedom to act on terms of not reason and civilization, but base physical desire. Beowulf (Ray Winstone) intensifies this gendering of power in vulgar masculinity during his fight with Grendel (Crispin Glover), bellowing, "Mine is strength and lust and power – I am Beowulf."[24] The line suggests that Beowulf is not simply strong, amorous, and powerful, but that he is the embodiment of those traits. Beowulf, thus, names himself as the physical manifestation of a masculine notion of power that is brutal and driven by desire.

The effectiveness of Zemeckis' critique derives from a further inversion of the rational/irrational, masculine/feminine correlation. Strong feminine subjectivity expresses itself in refusal of base desires. Wealhtheow (Robin Wright Penn), for example, perhaps the strongest and most admirable character in the film, strives to distance herself from the bacchanalia of Heorot. More central, art director Doug Chiang's designs for the cave cast a sense of feminine subjectivity as marked by a balance between the instinctual and the rational. The design of the cave complex consists of four separate sections. The entrance resembles a vaginal opening, littered with human bones, that leads to a flooded chamber spanned by ribs and a spine, a womb-like space in which Grendel's mother (Angelina Jolie) scolds in anger and cradles in grief.[25] It is a physically abject image of the maternal body, a site of gothic horror. But this is not the chamber in which Grendel's mother appears most clearly. That happens in the chamber of the cave filled with gold. The scenery very subtly reveals itself to be the skull of some ancient being, with eye and nose cavities. Chiang refers to this location as "the brain area," and a production map describing the cave structure labels this site "Grendel's mom."[26] While the womb may convey primal power, Zemeckis' production team locates a joint feminine/maternal threat in the seat of the mind. The dialogue Jolie's character speaks to Beowulf in the seduction scene underscores this point. She appeals to Beowulf's self-professed identification with strength, lust, and power, tempting him with promises of worldly power. The manipulation of the hero emphasizes the shrewd plotting of Grendel's mother. As a result, the film suggests that Grendel's mother functions rationally and that she is not solely driven by the instinct of the womb. Instinctive behaviors are linked to Beowulf and the men of Heorot.

Actualizing the latent critique embedded in the inversion of gendered functions hinges upon the way in which Gaiman and Avary's rewriting of the story splits Grendel's mother between two distinct images that correlate to their related roles. The division between roles in Grendel's mother is not an idea original to this film.[27] Scholarship has noted a similar feature in the poem. Jane Chance argues that she manifests the fallen half of a pervasive dichotomy of Mary and Eve (which she labels Ave/Eva) to parody both the Anglo-Saxon mother/kinswoman in her attack on Heorot and the Anglo-Saxon queen/hostess in her struggle with Beowulf.[28] Helen Damico observes that the valkyrie tradition, from which Grendel's mother, she argues, has her origins, contains a similar division between woman as sacral guardian and woman as threatening warrior.[29] For this film, the split in Grendel's mother takes the form of monstrous mother and sensual seductress – and in each case, she is threatening.

As in McTiernan's *The Thirteenth Warrior*, the monstrous maternal threatens separate subjectivity and neuters attempts to express power. The monstrous mother in Zemeckis' film is a gold lizard woman. She is never fully visible, always hidden. She lurks in reflections and hides among piles of golden treasure. When we see her most directly, it is only her hands that appear or, later, her form is camouflaged against treasure. For example, when Grendel is wounded, lying on a stone pedestal in the cave, sobbing over the loss of his arm, her golden lizard hands extend and gently stroke his head. She speaks soft words of comfort to him. What interests me is that this form is how we first experience the character: as a sometimes scolding, sometimes soothing voice, then as caressing hands. The gold lizard woman is the monstrous reality of the character; she is the maternal. This half of the fractured image positions the maternal as abject horror, relegated to haunt the shadows that impinge on the borders of subjectivity. Maternal gestures become an unsettling mingling of both tenderness and the terror of suffocation, exemplified in her sultry scolding of Grendel, which takes the form of a disembodied voice, resonating in (mostly) Old English throughout the cave.

That sound envelopes Grendel in Kaja Silverman's use of the term. Silverman explains that in cinema the "fantasy of the maternal-voice-as-sonorous-envelope" can be "an emblem of infantile plentitude and bliss," but can also be "an emblem of impotence and entrapment."[30] The film conveys this simultaneous lure and revulsion through Grendel, who whimpers a defense when she scolds him. For Grendel the voice relegates him to the position of deject (as Hala argues of him in the poem), unable to fully define the boundary between mother and self, fighting the law of his own father, Hrothgar. Grendel's return to the cave, his being enveloped, suggests "the desire to return to the original oneness of things, to return to the mother/womb, [which] is primarily a desire for non-differentiation," to use the words of Barbara Creed.[31] As such, Grendel, in the relationship with his mother, becomes an example of the constricting powers of the maternal on the effecting of one's will. As such, he is the counterpoint to the expression of power exemplified in the mead hall and in Beowulf's self-identification.

Unlike McTiernan's production, however, this film attempts a critique of power by balancing the monstrous image with the sexualized one, particularly in scene eight, in which Beowulf is enveloped by the sultry, sensual voice of the seductress that resonates throughout the cave. She says, "I see you've brought me treasure." Distinguished from the maternal by the use of Modern English, the line shifts the context of the voice by characterizing the golden mead horn as something like a courtship gift. Jolie then rises from the water, naked, with a shimmering gold sheen dripping from her digitally enhanced body. She asks if he is Beowulf, decoding the kenning of "bee-wolf" for "bear" proposed by Henry Sweet.[32] Beowulf meets her challengingly by asking, "What do you know of me?" The verbal exchange that ensues concerns the role of "grandeur" in establishing one's reputation as a path to power. Grendel's mother tempts him both with her body and with smooth words of earthly power in exchange for his giving her another son. She promises "riches beyond imagination," that she will make him "the greatest king that ever lived," and that he "will forever be king, forever strong, mighty, and all-powerful." As she makes these promises, she strokes Beowulf's sword with her fingertips and melts its blade, invoking the melting of the giants' blade in the poem. Here, though, the camera focuses on the dripping hilt, held near Beowulf's groin and pointing to hers, tapping the image of the castratrice described by Barbara Creed as a common horror motif.[33] The next shot reveals the reflection of Beowulf taking Grendel's mother in his arms in the puddle of melted sword.

The imagery in the scene is complex if not subtle. The final shot, Beowulf taking Grendel's sexualized mother, invokes sexual penetration as a violence that asserts masculine dominance. At the end of the scene, Beowulf responds to seduction aggressively, suggestive of taking destiny by force. The embrace and sexual union implicitly establish a masculine identity that appears to use the feminine as a means to an end. However, the dominant imagery of the scene, the fingertips and sword, highlights the centrality of power as the focus of Beowulf's desires. The promises of worldly power coupled with the melting blade visually suggest Beowulf's sexual climax, not over her physical form, but over the idea of having wealth and total authority. Power, coded in terms of masculine subjectivity, is therefore critiqued as being driven by *cupiditas*. Jolie as Grendel's mother conflates sexual desire and yearnings for material wealth and power. The gold sheen that covers her breasts and groin associates her with gold itself, the metal most popularly valued for centuries. A similar confusion between woman and treasure is actually made earlier in the film, as Hrothgar promises Beowulf a beautiful gold drinking horn. In the scene, Hrothgar stares at Wealhtheow, remarking about beauty while Beowulf covetously eyes the vessel. The scenes together convey a generalized notion of male desire as liability, effectively pillorying ego-driven masculinity as a social form that builds power through acquisitiveness. Masculine desires for dominance – evoked explicitly in Beowulf's naming himself "lust", "strength", and "power" in the fight with Grendel – mark masculinity with a pathological will to power at the same time that it identifies the flaw in that demeanor. Zemeckis' and Baker's films position desire as a weakness that corrupts power and its uses. Moreover, the links between desire and power, *cupiditas* as a misdirected or selfish will, make those who seek or hold authority vulnerable, insofar as desire can be exploited. The craving for command destabilizes itself, revealing power to be plagued by its own monstrous structure.

If in the cave we see Grendel's mother and her interactions with her son as expressing the failure of the Kristevan deject to fully establish subjectivity by abjecting the mother, then in Beowulf's entry into the cave we find an Oedipal play; his return to the maternal body, his own envelopment in her voice, and then confrontation with the gold fetish of the sexual woman express a desire to possess the mother sexually. A separate, masculine subjectivity asserts itself by reorienting the female role from enveloping-maternal to sexual, from containing in the womb to being contained in the male embrace. The Zemeckis film does not draw its interest simply from this Freudian/Kristevan psychodrama. Rather, desire and its relation to power motivate the action of the narrative. Uncontrollable desire or power renders the hero abject in the Kristevan sense of the interiorization of abjection that occurs within what she calls "evangelical attitudes."[34] The sexualized exchange between Beowulf and Grendel's mother (whom I have noted is situated in the seat of reason) displays masculine subjectivity as unable to control its own desires and, as a result, not in control of its own destiny, despite the intentions of Beowulf. The film tries to suggest power, coded in masculine terms, is corrupted by a misdirected will, one that loves the self unduly.

Ultimately, however, the film fails to actualize such a critique. The prurient spectacle of Angelina Jolie's digitally-enhanced, gold-sheened, naked body caters to the same hyper-sexualized function of masculine desires that drives Beowulf in Zemeckis' film. Splitting the sexual off from the maternal effects a monstrosizing of female sexuality, similar to the ways in which the maternal is rendered terrifying through associations with animalistic imagery in the lizard woman. Rather than creating space for strong feminine roles, the film polices female sexuality and renders sexual agency in women horrific. This is confirmed by the portrayal of Wealhtheow, who preserves her chastity throughout the film. As a result, Zemeckis' *Beowulf* more fully restricts the authority ascribed to the women of the film. With both the sexual and maternal facets of the feminine demonized, the film ends up undercutting the potential efficacy of their subversion of hyper-masculine power structures. This film attempts a clever inversion of gendered images of authority, but fails, in part because of the problems inherent in notions of feminine power derived from sexuality. Female agency is thus contained by localizing two sites of feminine authority and demonizing both to create a compounded horror.

Beowulf and Grendel

So far I have argued that film adaptations of *Beowulf* emphasize the role of the maternal – specifically the abject maternal – beyond its role in the original poem. For McTiernan, the increased attention to the role of Grendel's mother enables *The Thirteenth Warrior* to reify Western cultural values that emphasize strong masculinity by drawing the boundaries between human and non-human and policing acceptable and unacceptable difference. Zemeckis' *Beowulf* violates those boundaries to unsettle the moral economy of masculine power structures, even if in the end the film ultimately resubscribes to them. Sturla Gunnarsson's *Beowulf and Grendel* evinces similarities with each of these films, but, finally, attempts to offer a more enlightened political view. Like *The Thirteenth Warrior*, Gunnarsson's film sets the tale within the euhemeristic world of racial or genetic difference. Like *Beowulf* (2007), his film seeks a critique of authority coded as masculine in its aggressive will to power. *Beowulf and Grendel* distinguishes itself in the way it deploys abjection to construct boundaries that allow the sort of community-subject formation of McTiernan's film; yet Gunnarsson utilizes the permeability of the boundary inherent in abjection to challenge that means of community definition. Rather than leaving the maternal as horrific, Gunnarsson posits it as offering a hopeful alternative to destructive conceptions of community and power.

Gunnarsson achieves this idea by locating three characters outside the realm of the fully human: Grendel (and his father), Grendel's mother, and the outcast woman Selma. In the euhemeristic rewriting of the story, the Grendel-kin are a small collection of genetically malformed individuals whose physical traits and actions ostensibly locate them beyond the boundary of human. Grendel and his father are animalistic in appearance, Neanderthal in depiction, wearing skins and furs. In the opening scene, the young boy Grendel sports a respectable beard and both characters produce guttural grunts rather than comprehensible language. Grendel's mother is first seen only as a claw reaching up towards Beowulf from the water as he approaches Denmark. When we see her fully, her body is grotesque, large and pallid. Only Selma, whom I shall discuss further below, is recognizably human, although her hair gives the appearance of someone untamed and wild. Despite these malformed appearances, the actions of the Grendel-kin are recognizable, uncanny images that challenge our perception of them as monsters. That seeming discontinuity actually initiates the film, in the scenes of the young boy Grendel and his father. Grendel's father flips him around, smiling at the delight taken by the playful young boy. When Hrothgar and his men ride the two down, the grotesque father defends his child, who cowers in fear and witnesses the slaughter. The opening scene muddles the boundaries between human/non-human as based on actions rather than image. The question of what makes a monster orients the entire film, as Beowulf (Gerard Butler) comes to grips with the humanity of Grendel and Hrothgar's originary monstrosity. By humanizing the adult Grendel (Ingvar Sigurdsson) as engaged in a justified feud, Gunnarsson follows Seamus Heaney, who translates the poem's "se ellengǽst earfoðlīce/ þrāge geþolode [...]" (86–87b) as "a powerful demon [...]/ nursed a hard grievance" to suggest an earlier incitement to his feud.[35] Regardless, Gunnarsson suggests Danish authority to have grown from violent rather than civilizing impulses.

While Zemeckis' film centers its critique on the mother by gradually revealing fault, Gunnarsson's assigns blame at the outset. That decision opens space to use the maternal differently, as a contrast to hyper-masculine, violent authority. *Beowulf and Grendel* employs two different iterations of the mother, the first being Grendel's mother. Grendel's mother appears twice prior to her entering Heorot: once when the Geats sail to Denmark as an eerie claw that rises from the water and grabs at Beowulf's hand; then again when, after Grendel flees the mead hall, a shot shows his body floating, and the same hand reaches out to retrieve Grendel's body from the water where the mother swims. Two associations emerge. First, the scary claw denotes a threat that produces both fear and revulsion of the unknown. Second, a maternal hand reaches from its environment to grasp the lifeless body of a child. The first image certainly establishes viewer expectations that a price will be exacted for the death of the troll when, in the second image, the hand reaches for Grendel's body. Yet, in the maternal gesture, the hand reaches up from the water into the empty space where the self-amputated arm should be. That subtle detail directs the motivation of Grendel's mother when she enters Heorot. Upon entering the hall, she looks about the room of sleeping men and shrieks at the sight of her son's arm. She strides over, tears it from its nail, and defends herself from Aeschere's attack before fleeing. Compassion to restore her dead son's missing arm appears to direct her actions as much as revenge. This is, of course, not to suggest that the Grendel's mother of *Beowulf and Grendel* is not monstrous. She does kill in a single blow the Irish Christian, Brendan (Eddie Marsan), outside the hall, and in her battle with Beowulf she threatens to destroy the hero. Those violent acts notwithstanding, Gunnarsson ascribes quite human traits to the character. Her face may be frightening as she screams in the mead hall, but it is decidedly human, clearly feminine. The motivation implied by her actions indicates not inherent violence, but protective acts of aggression born out of circumstance and not bloodlust. An emotional interiority similar to that suggested by the poem's describing her as dwelling on her "yrmþe" ("misery", 1259), "sorhfulne" ("sorrowfull", 1278) complicates the image of the horrific maternal figure and makes her an object of sympathy.

Selma (Sarah Polley) is the second mother in the film, and the film's assertion of an alternative to violence and aggression resolves around her. She initially appears to be a simple product of formulaic screenwriting guidelines: the hero's love-interest. The red-haired consort to a deceased Dane has been cast away from the Danish mead-hall community, because her ability to foresee the circumstances of men's deaths renders her a witch. Fear of the mysterious woman does not prevent men from stealing out to her hut and raping her, she tells Beowulf.[36] From her outcast position, Selma speaks as the film's moral voice. She challenges the logic that directs Beowulf's pursuit of the wily "troll" and suggests that Beowulf simply does not understand his foe. In the process she highlights the lack of recognition in

Hrothgar, who fails to see the feud for what it is and refuses to accept responsibility for initiating it. Selma's role as moral compass allows Gunnarsson to level criticism against a civilizing system, represented by the Danes, that defines itself by responding to difference violently.[37]

The feminine-maternal image offered by Selma provides a counterpoint that begins a transformation of Beowulf, reorienting his own sense of humanity. That sensitivity becomes heightened after Grendel's death, when Beowulf and Selma discuss mourning:

> Selma: One Geat's life worth what? Hm? Two Danes … three
>   Swedes … ten trolls? Hondscio's life had worth to you, because
>   you knew him. Others know others.
> Beowulf: You mourn the troll.
> Selma: I knew him.

The film then cuts to a flashback of a night Grendel visited Selma's hut, ultimately producing their son. He enters the hut cautiously and inspects Selma like an animal before copulating with her in the same fashion. Effort seems to have been made to depict the act as non-violent.[38] Aside from its obvious problems, if we read the act as a "non-violent" rape, then Grendel is simultaneously made similar to and different from the Danes. Selma suggests the Danes were less gentle in their assaults, and that Grendel became her protector. The sexual union of Grendel and Selma, therefore, establishes the Danes' foe as driven by the same desires as themselves, but less violent in his satisfying them. The preceding discussion of mourning establishes the non-violent, moral context; Selma's teary-eyed remonstrance to Beowulf states that the variable valuing of life functions within a relative scheme rooted in familiarity. The psycho-emotional distance produced by foreignness does not erase the significance or value of that alien life. Gunnarsson thus uses Selma to level the field between monster and hero by equating them within a shared appraisal of their lives. The absence of knowledge, therefore, becomes the engine of monstrosity.

Gunnarsson employs Selma to advance the textually subversive agenda of the film by paralleling her to Grendel's mother as abject. As noted above, aside from her motivation to seek out Heorot, Grendel's mother seems to follow the original poem rather faithfully. Her large form, horrific shriek, and inhuman appearance locate her decidedly outside human society – not to mention her apparent ability to spend most of her time under water. Selma, too, is outcast, at least in part for her supernatural abilities. Her hut separate from the Danish settlement, Selma lives alone on a heath. Sustaining herself with only Grendel as a defense, she rejects Wealhtheow's offer to bring her back into the village community. Even her physical appearance is made Other. Gunnarsson's film casts Polley as the female sex-symbol, decidedly feminine with soft features and makeup, but her hair has been turned into a wild red mane, somewhere between tangles and dreadlocks. She becomes simultaneously the male fantasy figure and the abject maternal. Her role as abject, however, is the source of the moral voice. If the abject returns to haunt the subject, then, in Gunnarsson's film, that haunting is not in terms of the horrific; rather, what returns is a notion of love, compassion, and mercy inherent to the mother.[39]

This privileging of "maternal values" finds its fullest expression in Beowulf's transformation in the final scenes of the film. While the character spends the film shifting his sense of the monsters, his adoption of a more enlightened sense of human relations takes form after he slays Grendel's mother only to confront the son of Grendel and Selma (Benedikt Clausen), who emerges to defend the body of Grendel. Beowulf recognizes the potential for the feud cycle to continue, but attempts to circumvent it by returning to the shore near Grendel's cave and building a stone monument to him. The gesture indicates his growing into a more nuanced understanding of difference, a sort of maturation resembling that identified by Gwendolyn A. Morgan in the original poem. She interprets it as "an allegory of male maturation, a struggle against the stifling power of the Great Mother" that finds its resolution in Beowulf's killing of Grendel's mother.[40] While Beowulf builds, the son witnesses an action that implicitly professes the value of Grendel's life. As the Geats then sail away, Beowulf looks to the rocky shore, where Selma and the son stand together. The image of Selma and the son together re-invokes, however indirectly, the image of Grendel's mother reaching up to the (literally) disarmed son. A potential feud relationship parallel to Hrothgar and Grendel's exists between Beowulf and the son. Though, in a move that turns away from Morgan, who sees maturation coming by way of eliminating the Great Mother figure, Gunnarsson's sentimental monument-building shot may suggest that newfound respect will quell ongoing violence, because it derives its meaning from the lessons Beowulf has learned from the mother Selma.[41]

Locating both mother figures (the only explicitly identified mothers in the film) outside human society allows Gunnarsson to create a complex maternal image and, as a result, an alternative to what the film paints as a masculine, aggressive, reactionary social system. We find in Polley's Selma an object of desire, a conflation of the sexual and the maternal, underscored by her confession that Danish men periodically used her to satisfy sexual impulses; yet aligning her with Grendel and paralleling her with his mother complicates the picture, though not in ways associated with ideas of abjection. Kristeva, as Acker points out, identifies abjection with the recognition of the mortality, and hence death, granted by the maternal.[42] The maternal gives life, but also sets stifling limits, as in the skull-filled womb-cave of McTiernan's *The Thirteenth Warrior* and the bone-littered opening of the vulva cave of *Beowulf* (2007). Gunnarsson's film does not evince such a simple correspondence to the theory, because death, although delivered by Grendel's mother, is not the limit against which the masculine cultural structures resist. To adopt Kristeva's terms, "fear of the [archaic mother's] generative power" appears uplifting and victimized by "patrilineal filation" and its "burden of subduing" that power.[43] Recall the image of Selma and her son standing contentedly as Beowulf sails away. The scene offers an alternative to the rivalry that produces dead Danes, Geats, and trolls. While Grendel's mother presents a fluid, reactionary image of protective bonds, Selma evinces a moderate, sexual-maternal power that chooses (as Selma rejects Wealhtheow's offer) to exist according to standards of mutual understanding rather than fear and violence. The Paternal Law of the Father, which draws distinctions and assigns symbolic meaning, is the assertive death-giver here, not the maternal.

Conclusion

If the scholarship that has investigated questions of gender in *Beowulf* has sought to clarify the cultural dynamics of its Anglo-Saxon audience, it has also attempted to locate a place for feminine modes of authority within those cultural dynamics. The work by Chance and Sklute in particular seems exemplary in this interest. Their examination of feminine expressions of power as subsidiary to dominant, masculine modes assumes an active place for women. Even when that role is a passive one, scholars such as Joyce Hill and Elaine Tuttle Hansen have located purpose within it. The films I have discussed, then, follow a critical tradition that expands the function of female characters, Grendel's mother in particular, though perhaps not in consistent directions. While *The Thirteenth Warrior* denigrates feminine authority in the interests of elevating masculine structures, Zemeckis' *Beowulf* establishes something like an equality in the destructive potential of both types of power. Only *Beowulf and Grendel* activates the feminine authority located in the maternal as a rival type of authority that has the potential to transform dominant expressions. More generally, however, recent adaptations of *Beowulf* seem to follow the tendency found in Zemeckis' and Gunnarsson's films to use the original story as a means of critiquing modern corollaries to the poem's topics, particularly the definition of communities (in relation to their "others") and the use of violence. For example, *Star Trek: Voyager*'s episode 12, "Heroes and Demons" (1995), Graham Baker's *Beowulf* (1999), and Howard McCain's *Outlander* (2008) all challenge the glorification of expansionism that the poem can be seen as promoting in Scyld's and Hrothgar's extension of influence. Similarly, graphic novels take up that issue in works such as *Kid Beowulf*, by Alexis Fajardo, or the three-issue, manga-styled series *Beowulf* by David Hutchison, which raises questions about violence as a tool for community-building.

While both the poem and its progeny often take up ambivalent positions on these topics, the locus of that ambivalence shifts. Hrothgar and Beowulf are both elevated characters through whom positive uses of violence or productive exclusions of the other (for example) are manifested. In the adaptations, the racist implications of "othering," the oppressive nature of expansionism, or, as this paper has argued, the destructive potential of masculine authority all coalesce around the heroes. The means of these critiques derive from abjection of the poem; current tastes and values require the shunting of potentially offensive medieval predilections to the margins. Retellings such as *Beowulf and Grendel* – or John Gardener's *Grendel*, with its cynical view of human society – perform a drawing of boundaries that allow the modern to separate itself from one site of its origins, which is deemed unenlightened, if not horrible. But just as the maternal in these *Beowulf* films haunts those boundaries, so too does the source text lurk within the adaptations. That haunting serves to underscore the ways in which the harshness associated with the Anglo-Saxons persists as an unsettling part of the present. The efficacy of the critique, in other words, derives from recognition in ourselves of what we perceive as distasteful in the past.

NOTES

Thanks to my colleague Chad Luck, who read drafts of this article, and to the readers at *SiM* for their very helpful observations.

1. Neil Gaiman and Roger Avary, *Beowulf: The Script Book* (New York: Harper Entertainment, 2007), 11.

2. Regardless of Hollywood's sense of the Anglo-Saxon poem as a joke, eight films have been made since 1998. The eight adaptations include: *Animated Classics: Beowulf* (dir. Yuri Kulakov, 1998), *Beowulf* (dir. Roger Baker, 1999), *The Thirteenth Warrior* (dir. John McTiernan, 1999), *Beowulf and Grendel* (dir. Sturla Gunnarsson, 2005), *Beowulf: Prince of the Geats* (dir. Scott Wegener, 2007), *Grendel* (dir. Nick Lyon for Sci Fi Channel, 2007), *Beowulf* (dir. Robert Zemeckis, 2007), and *Outlander* (dir. Howard McCain, 2009).

3. Janet T. Buck, "Pre-Feudal Women," *Journal of the Rutgers University* 34 (1971): 46–51; Elaine Tuttle Hansen, "From *freolicu folccwen* to *geomuru ides*: Women in Old English Poetry Reconsidered," *Michigan Academician* 9 (1979): 109–17 (116–17); Setsuko Haruta, "The Women in *Beowulf*," *Poetica* 23 (1986): 1–15.

4. John L. Sklute, " 'Freothuwebbe' in Old English Poetry," *Neuphilologische Mitteilungen* 71 (1970): 534–41, rpt. in *New Readings on Women in Old English Literature*, ed. Helen Damico and Alexandra Hennessey Olsen (Bloomington: Indiana University Press, 1990), 214–20; Jane Chance, *Woman as Hero in Old English Literature* (Syracuse, NY: Syracuse University Press, 1986), see 1–12 for discussion of queen's power and 95–108 for Grendel's mother as anti-type.

5. Helen Damico, *Beowulf's Wealhtheow and the Valkyrie Tradition* (Madison: University of Wisconsin Press, 1984); Gillian R. Overing, *Language, Sign, and Gender in Beowulf* (Carbondale: Southern Illinois University Press, 1990), 101–7.

6. Christine Alfano, "The Issue of Feminine Monstrosity: A Reevaluation of Grendel's Mother," *Comitatus* 23 (1992): 1–16.

7. Overing, *Language*, 81.

8. James Hala, "The Parturition of Poetry and the Birthing of Culture: The Ides Aglaecwif and Beowulf," *Exemplaria* 10.1 (1998): 29–50 (30).

9. Hala, "Parturition of Poetry," 37. Kristeva's deject is one who fails to absent the body of the mother, leaving more permeable boundaries.

10. Hala, "Parturition of Poetry," 42. See Kristeva, *Powers of Horror*, trans. Leon S. Roudiez (New York: Columbia University Press, 1982), 13–15.

11. Paul Acker, "Horror and the Maternal in *Beowulf*," *PMLA* 121.3 (2006): 702–16 (709, 708).

12. Renee Trilling, "Beyond Abjection: The Problem with Grendel's Mother Again," *Parergon* 24.1 (2007): 1–20 (20).

13. Nickolas Haydock, *Movie Medievalism* (Jefferson, NC: McFarland & Co. 2008), 27.

14. Lynne Shutters, "Vikings through the Eyes of an Arab Ethnographer: Constructions of the Other in *The 13th Warrior*," in *Race, Class and Gender in "Medieval" Cinema*, ed. Lynn Ramey and Tison Pugh (New York: Palgrave, 2007), 36.

15. Shutters, "Vikings through the Eyes," 85.

16. To be fair, Shutters' essay revolves around the gendering of Ahmed. She argues that, despite a favorable depiction of the Arabic figure, Crichton's film creates gendered poles between which Ahmed is situated. Ahmed learns to be a strong, Western male, effectively reifying that ethos while reasserting the Orientalist stereotype of the effeminate Arab.

17. Shutters, "Vikings through the Eyes," 85.

18. Kristeva, *Powers of Horror*, 44–55.

19. Kristeva, *Powers of Horror*, 101.

20. ääēathleen Forni has documented some of the ways in which the film adheres to the original poem; "Popularizing High Culture: Zemeckis' *Beowulf*," *Studies in Popular Culture* 31.2 (2009): 45–59.

21. James W. Earl, *Thinking About Beowulf* (Palo Alto, CA: Stanford University Press, 1996), 119–20.

22. Jane Marie Luecke, "*Wulf and Eadwacer*: Hints for Reading from *Beowulf* and Anthropology," in *The Old English Elegies: New Essays in Criticism and Research*, ed. Martin Green (Rutherford, NJ: Fairleigh Dickinson University Press, 1983): 190–203.

23. "Þā wæs Hrōðgār here-spēd gyfen/ […]/ Him on mōd bearn/ Þæt healreced hatan wolde […]." Quotations from *Beowulf* are taken from *Klaeber's Beowulf*, ed. R. D. Fulk, Robert E. Bjork, and John D. Niles (Toronto: University of Toronto Press, 2008).

24. Gaiman, *Beowulf*, Blue Revision, 40. Beowulf's declaration follows a string of identifiers rooted in violence, including "ripper, tearer, slasher."

Masculinity is thus entwined with destruction – an association that seems to tie this film to Gunnarsson's, in which Hrothgar exhibits destructively masculine behaviors.

25. Production designers established "the motif as the petrified remains of a gigantic ancient creature" that "began with [a] vagina-like opening into the 'womb' of the beast." Mark Cotta Vaz and Steve Starkey, *The Art of Beowulf* (San Francisco, CA: Chronicle Books, 2007), 95.

26. Vaz and Starkey, *Art of Beowulf*, 94.

27. Graham Baker's *Beowulf*, starring Christopher Lambert, also makes this division of Grendel's mother, played by *Playboy* Playmate Layla Roberts. On this film, see Kathleen Forni, "Graham Baker's *Beowulf*: Intersections between High and Low Culture," *Literature/Film Quarterly* 35.3 (2007): 244–49.

28. Chance, *Woman as Hero*, see in particular 97–101.

29. Damico, *Valkyrie Tradition*, 41–46.

30. Kaja Silverman, *The Acoustic Mirror: The Female Voice in Psychoanalysis and Cinema* (Bloomington: Indiana University Press, 1988), 73.

31. Barbara Creed, *The Monstrous-Feminine: Film, Feminism, Psychoanlysis* (London: Routledge, 1993), 28.

32. Henry Sweet, *Anglo-Saxon Reader in Prose and Verse* (Oxford: The Clarendon Press, 1884), 202.

33. Creed, *The Monstrous-Feminine*, 87. The most relevant portion of Creed's study to the above discussion is her treatment of the films *I Spit on Your Grave* and *Sisters*, 122–38.

34. Kristeva, *Powers of Horror*, 113.

35. *Beowulf*, trans. Seamus Heaney (New York: Farrar, Straus, & Giroux, 2000), 9.

36. The opposition between Hrothgar's Heorot and Selma's hut offers a cinematic rendition of Earl's arguments about the Anglo-Saxon cultural dichotomy between the mead hall and the hut. *Thinking About Beowulf*, 114–24.

37. Haydock describes both *Beowulf and Grendel* and *The Thirteenth Warrior* as "politically correct" (*Movie Medievalism*, 28). That phrase seems somewhat dismissive and minimizes the extent to which the films engage with specific contexts. McTiernan's film violates any sense of such "correctness" with its leaving the Wendol as grotesque other while attempting to preach tolerance through the character of Ahmed. See Shutters ("Vikings through the Eyes," 83–87) for more on the "Other" in this context. Gunnarsson's film, I would suggest, takes up specific concerns relating to the global "War on Terror" that proclaimed the evil of fundamentalist Islam.

38. In the DVD audio commentary, Gunnarsson and members of his production team discuss the scene ambivalently. First Assistant Director

Wendy Ord explains that she imagines Selma as not seeing the act as rape, while Gunnarsson and scriptwriter Andrew Rai Berzins rationalize it as either more gentle than the Danes' assaults or as symptomatic of a pre-courtly love culture.

39. The shifting of terms away from masculine aggression and violence towards love, compassion, and mercy also expresses itself in the character of Brendan, the Irish missionary who gradually converts the Danes. Gunnarsson discusses Brendan's role in these terms on the DVD audio commentary.

40. Gwendolyn A. Morgan, "Mothers, Monsters, Maturation: Female Evil in *Beowulf*," *Journal of the Fantastic in the Arts* 4.1 (1984): 54–66 (55).

41. In an interview among the DVD's special features, Gunnarsson indicates that his film raises questions about "who the real enemy is." His portrayal of Beowulf as mediating between Grendel and Hrothgar challenges the increasingly polarized relationship, for example, between the West and Islam. The film might be read as criticizing Western responses to a fundamentalist Islam that the U.S. helped create by funding fundamentalist schools to counter Soviet engagements in Afghanistan, among other things. In this context, the film participates in a larger trend within *Beowulf* adaptations of lodging such critiques by recasting Hrothgar as a flawed and guilty figure.

42. Acker, "Horror," 703–4.

43. Kristeva, *Powers of Horror*, 77.

The Colony Writes Back:
F. N. Robinson's *Complete Works of Geoffrey Chaucer* and the *Translatio* of Chaucer Studies to the United States

Richard Utz

> Heterogeneity [...] was a function of hegemony. The open-ended inclusiveness of the United States was directly proportionate to America's capacity to incorporate *and exclude*, and more precisely to incorporate by exclusion. The culture seemed indefinite, infinitely processual, because as America it closed everything else out, as being either Old World and/or not-yet-America. And vice versa: the process by which it closed out everything un-American was also the spur toward an ideal of *liberal* inclusiveness, a vision of *representative* openness that eroded traditional barriers of nationality, territory, language, and ethnicity, and eventually, perhaps, would erode even the barriers of race and gender [...].
>
> Sacvan Bercovitch, "Discovering America" (1996)[1]

In 1933 Alois Brandl, Professor of English at the University of Berlin, reviewed *The Complete Works of Geoffrey Chaucer*, published in the United States by Houghton Mifflin (Boston) and earlier in the same year in Britain by Oxford University Press. In his review, Brandl expresses his astonishment at the publication of an edition of Chaucer by "the biggest publisher in English studies" compiled by someone he does not know:

> Who is F. N. Robinson? *Minerva* calls him a professor of English at Harvard; one seeks his name unsuccessfully in the English studies bibliographies. But he must be a diligent reader and

compiler of that which others have written about Chaucer [...] and must have access to a wonderful library [...].[2]

Brandl's astonished condescension was not based on inexperience. Even at the age of seventy-eight, he was the chair of his department and the Nestor of English studies in the German-speaking world. In the 1870s and 1880s, he studied in Berlin and Vienna with the founders of English and German philology, Wilhelm Scherer, Karl Müllenhoff, Julius Zupitza, Jakob Schipper, and Erich Schmidt, and he later held positions at the universities of Vienna, Prague, Göttingen, Strassburg, and Berlin. His list of achievements includes studies on some of the major authors from the Middle English through the Romantic periods (e.g., Chaucer, Shakespeare, Coleridge), the essay on "English Philology" for the compendious tome *Die deutschen Universitäten*, through which the German universities proudly exhibited German academic accomplishments for the 1893 Chicago World Exposition, a hefty history of English literature, and the editorship of the prestigious *Shakespeare Jahrbuch* and *Archiv für das Studium der Neueren Sprachen und Literaturen*.[3] Small wonder Brandl cannot comprehend how a U.S. colleague without a similarly extensive scholarly record might have produced what he recognizes as a momentous event in the modern history of scholarship on Chaucer. In fact, Brandl's review expresses what had remained a typically German colonialist or hegemonist attitude toward non-German academics ever since the institutionalization and professionalization of *Anglistik* at the German universities in the 1860s and 1870s. And various features of Robinson's *Complete Works* of 1933 can be understood as part of a postcolonial response to such German attitudes in the gradual process of transition of the center of Chaucer studies from the "Old" to the "New World."[4]

English Textual Territories and the German(ic) Invasions

To claim that a hegemonist or colonialist attitude existed among the first generations of German professors of English may need some historicizing: The discipline of English studies in Germany was institutionalized in 1872, one year after Prussia and its allies had defeated France and proclaimed the Prussian King, Wilhelm I, Emperor of a unified German nation, and the first chair of English philology, Bernhard Ten Brink, was appointed at the Imperial University of

Strassburg (Kaiser Wilhelm Universität), an institution specifically meant to Germanize the newly annexed region of Alsace-Lorraine. Ten Brink's Strassburg appointment as chair was the beginning of the swift establishment of thirty-two other chairs of English philology between 1872 and 1914 all across the country. This movement suggests that national leaders believed, on the one hand, that strengthening the subject of English, a Germanic language, was one way of expanding the academic study of national subject matter and, on the other hand, that increased funding for Germany's universities would boost the country's progress in gaining a place among the world's most powerful nations.[5] German scholars, a vast majority of them reserve officers, were encouraged to emulate in their own profession their country's successful rush for imperial colonization around the world. While the German government's *Kanonenboot* diplomacy or outright invasions secured territories in Europe (Elsass-Lothringen), Africa (*Kamerun, Togoland*), and Asia (*Tsingtao*), scholars in language and literature study engaged in an academic form of colonization, the annexation of textual territories through the application of a scientistic theory of editing generally referred to as "philology." More than two decades before British and U.S. institutions developed their first chairs exclusively dedicated to the study of English, Germany boasted two dozen state-employed scholars who, together with their *comitatus* of graduate students, traveled to British libraries to copy, edit, and publish what most British scholars, predominantly private amateurs without state support or academic appointment, regarded to be their national heritage. British medievalists such as Henry Sweet and Walter W. Skeat recognized their German counterparts' work as part of a colonialist effort. Sweet, in 1885, speaks resignedly about abandoning all hopes to build an "independent school of English philology" because the "historical study of English was being rapidly annexed," leaving only a few areas "uninvaded" by German "dissertations and programs." The only role left to him and his colleagues was to serve as "purveyors to the swarms of young German program mongers turned out every year by the German universities, so thoroughly trained in all the mechanical details of what may be called 'parasite philology' that no English dilettante can hope to compete with them," the result of Britain's own "neglect" and "the unhealthy over-production of the German universities."[6] Skeat, also in reference to the German invasions of English textual territories, sarcastically stated that he might be "to some extent disqualified, as being merely a native of London, in which city Chaucer himself was born," to work on a critical edition of the father of English poetry.[7]

In addition to their actual incursions into English manuscript collections, German Anglicists also created an imposing academic infrastructure, including the first two journals devoted exclusively to English studies, *Englische Studien* (1877–1944) and *Anglia* (1878–), and a host of book series, grammars, dictionaries, textbooks, and bibliographies. As late as 1892, Arthur S. Napier, a Leipzig Dr. phil. who would go on to become Rawlinsonian Professor of Anglo-Saxon at Oxford, admitted that, compared with the German achievements, "we in England have very little to show," and that "a scientific study of English philology and literature is absolutely impossible without a knowledge of German."[8]

The impressive success story of Germany's scientistic study of English did not go unnoticed by U.S. institutions of higher learning. Not only did many of them, beginning with Harvard, Johns Hopkins, Michigan, Chicago, Yale, Indiana, and Northwestern universities, import the idea of graduate study from Berlin and other German institutions, they also actively recruited dozens of German scholars with degrees in English philology to build up their programs, among them Stanford's first Professor of English philology, the Chaucerian Ewald Flügel, who unabashedly professed, at a "German Day" speech in San Francisco and a Stanford commencement speech (both in 1903), that it was his mission to "inoculate" Stanford, California, and the entire United States with the German spirit and its academic representative, philological study, and to make German the official language of the United States.[9] And while missionaries like Flügel zealously proselytized "in country," hundreds of U.S. graduate students were infected with the philological virus when studying with the transatlantic paragons of philology in Germany. In the late nineteenth and early twentieth century such credentials proved to be a great asset for finding a position in the United States.[10] Thus, unlike British scholars, most of whom felt preempted in their scholarship by foreign specialists, American scholars, with somewhat less national pride at stake, did not perceive the dominance of German philologists over English studies as invasive, at least not until World War I. Beginning with that war, German scholars' academic hegemony in this specific discipline was increasingly recognized and rejected as synchronic and synergistic with Germany's political imperialism, and even the term "philology" was abandoned by many academics in Britain and the United States because of its alleged links with the German national character.[11] Thus, the same political conditions that had originally helped establish and fund the foundational moves of *Anglistik* would now contribute to its demise, as a country weakened by a lost war and the conditions of the Versailles Treaty had no money left to spend on the investigation of early English texts.

German Hegemonist Discourse and the Study of Chaucer

The German professors of English inherited from their teachers in Classical and German studies the arrogant notion that the particular scientistic mélange of diachronic linguistics (including dialect geography, phonology, grammar, etc.) and criticism (i.e., textual criticism based on a comparative analysis of all extant manuscripts, and the objectification of meter) they termed "philology" gave them an advantage over all other students of historical texts. Secured by tenure and the welcome assistance of graduate students, they competed with one another for the strictest application of philology and severely criticized and ridiculed colleagues who dared neglect their allegedly scientific methodologies.[12] Thus, not only a relative dilettante like Frederick Furnivall, who fervently facilitated German access to English manuscripts, but even Skeat, perhaps because he posed a recognizable threat to German hegemony in the field, was chided in caustic and condescending tones by the likes of Ten Brink, Ewald Flügel, and John Koch. The major points of criticism included producing editions that did not investigate all extant manuscripts, overlooking a recent critical article or monograph (especially when written by a German scholar), or writing essayistic, unscientific scholarship that concentrated too much on the content or the aesthetics of a text rather than on a text's linguistic or textual/editorial history. German Anglicists looked down on their British contemporaries in the final third of the nineteenth century as kindly, often enthusiastic, amateurs whose role was to assist them, "full of joy that the 'learned doctors' copied and edited their manuscripts."[13] Since the textual territories for German Chaucerians were situated in Britain and since it was British scholars who could claim Chaucer as part of their national heritage, the relatively few U.S. scholars who translated and interpreted Chaucer in the late nineteenth century practically never became the target of German attacks. However, after 1900, when more and more serious scholarship on the English poet was published, and even more so after 1917, when the United States entered World War I on the side of Germany's enemies and emerged as a world power militarily, economically, and intellectually, German Chaucerians attempted to reassert their priority and superiority over this new group of competitors in the field.[14] While U.S. critics were often lauded for their diligence and good methodology, the origins of these virtues was seen in the training they received at German universities. Those without an authorizing German educational background were branded as impertinent upstarts and unphilological dilettantes. John Koch, for example, a Chaucerian and Berlin school teacher with one of the most extensive publication records in the history of modern Chauceriana, keenly realized in the late 1920s that while British Chaucer studies had been on the decline, "our fatherland is by far outdone by North America, whose scholars have available several journals (Publ. Mod. Lang. Ass., Mod. Lang. Notes, Mod. Philology, Journ. Of Engl. and Germ. Philol., Rom. Review) which are exclusively dedicated to the study of modern languages." He immediately downplays his admission when he adds in typically paternalistic tone that "although the gentlemen – and ladies – over there can point to a variety of fine achievements, the old proverb that 'all that glitters is not gold' remains valid. In general, they intend to debunk all the results of Anglistics in the Old Europe as untenable and replace them with new and surprising discoveries."[15] Realizing that U.S. Chaucerians were using the same or at least similar foundational moves to build up a scholarly infrastructure that had established the hegemony of German Chaucerians only four decades earlier, he critiques Dudley David Griffith's 1925 *Bibliography of Chaucer 1908–1924* by opining that it only bulged into book length because it cited the same works several times in different categories and left enormous amounts of space between entries, both undeniable signs – in view of the German economic status quo – of the American "capacity for wasteful production."[16] He understands that the relocation (and hence future inaccessibility to European scholars) of the Ellesmere manuscript to California parallels the nineteenth-century German invasions into English textual territory.[17] And conveniently neglectful about his own decade-long preference for citing and praising German Chauceriana, Koch accuses John Manly, one of the

best-known American medievalists, of preferring scholarship by
British and U.S. colleagues:

> I see in this stratagem a disregard or disdain for foreign achieve-
> ments [...] which strikes me as, let us say, unpleasant. Should this
> attitude be a late consequence of the temper brought about by the
> war? I am almost tempted to think so, because the collegial
> offprints of Chaucer studies, sent to me earlier by the likes of
> Kittredge, Lowes, Tatlock, Young, Tupper, and others, have no
> longer been arriving since this division of nations. Or should my
> occasionally harsh criticisms be the cause for this change?[18]

*The Colony Resists: Medieval Philology/Germanity in New World
Academe*

Koch's patriotic *planctus* recognizes the descent into mediocrity of his
country and Chaucer studies in his country, the parallel ascent of the
United States and U.S. Chaucer studies during and after World War I,
and the insultingly hegemonist tone of his reviews.[19] In the anti-
German atmosphere of the war, during which various traces of scholarly "Germanity" were attacked and silenced, this hegemonist tone
was now often recognized and decried as Teutonic hubris. As Gerald
Graff has indicated, the growing animosity between Germany and the
U.S. during and in the decade after World War I awakened U.S. literature and language studies to their responsibilities in the area of
national leadership.[20] English professors like Stuart Sherman, at the
University of Illinois, warned the country against the "Prussianism
streaming into Anglo-Saxon communities through the forty volumes
of Carlyle," and college anthologies described their selections as "landmarks in the march of the Anglo-Saxon mind from the beginning to
the modern period," illustrating "the National Ideals of Freedom,
Faith, and Conduct."[21] This general anti-German climate found
support among those who, beginning as early as the 1890s, had
resisted Germany's most successful export item in the humanities,
scientistic "philology," from completely colonizing the study of
languages and literature at U.S. institutions.[22] These teachers, many of
them professors at liberal-arts colleges with an interest in creative
writing and the aesthetic, social, and political aspects of literary texts,
had thought it "bad enough to confine ourselves to the grammatical
features of Chaucer" and "little far from criminal to do so with our

mighty dramatist [Shakespeare]," and they had vigorously objected to making the "study of the most charming of the English classics [...] a mere starting-point for laborious investigations into antiquities, history, geography, etymology, phonetics, the history of the English language, and general linguistics."[23] More often than not, these strong ideological and methodological objections to Germanity and German philology joined forces with a growing desire to shake off the burden of European academic traditions in general: "Our research," M. D. Learned said in his presidential address to the twenty-seventh annual meeting of the Modern Language Association of America in 1909, "will not be content to follow foreign leads but will go down into the deeper study of the genesis of American culture; scientific inquiry will become creative and the truth newly discovered, creative energy."[24] Despite these tendencies, the major tenets of German philology remained foundational for graduate work at all major U.S. research institutions. Philology or, "the philological instinct," as J. R. R. Tolkien once defended the science-like study of historical language and literature against its discontents in the 1920s, was of course neither "a purely German invention" nor something "the late war was fought to end," but "as universal as is the use of language."[25] As such, all its elements, sometimes subsumed under different nomenclature and as moderately revised practices, are still important for medieval studies in the twenty-first century, and they certainly still dominated, often only available in the original German and in editions published in Leipzig, Tübingen, and Berlin, most U.S. curricula in English (medieval) studies as late as the 1930s, when F. N. Robinson published *The Complete Works of Geoffrey Chaucer*.[26]

The Emergence of U.S. Chaucer Studies and the Place of F. N. Robinson

U.S. Chaucerians, many of whom shared various features of the academic identities sketched above, quickly seized the chance to fill the vacuum left in the field by the disappearance of the British Chaucer Society and the marked decrease in the quality and quantity of German scholarship during and after World War I.[27] While they rarely ever expressed openly anti-German sentiments in their publications and while they based many of their own teaching practices and publications on Old World models, the New World Chaucerians excluded German scholars in the effort to make the United States the new home of scholarship on Chaucer by withholding review copies from their impoverished German colleagues, banning them from collaborative scholarly enterprises, and silencing their foundational achievements by "translating" them into English.[28] Perhaps assisted by the modest popular interest in Chaucer recently demonstrated by Candace Barrington, they built on the solid if secondary nineteenth-century tradition of U.S. Chaucerians to achieve the twentieth-century *translatio* from Europe to North America.[29] The Harvard scholar George Lyman Kittredge, for example, a preceptor-like proponent of strictly applied philological method to "extricate" literary study from "the druidical mist" and "fogbound labyrinth" of essayistic scholarship, had managed to beat German scholars at their own game and, in the absence of U.S. journals exclusively dedicated to the study of English literature, on their own territory.[30] In 1889, in the pages of *Englische Studien*, one of the two flagship journals of German *Anglistik*, he completely dismantled Alois Brandl's hardly convincing assumptions on some possible historical allusions in Chaucer's "Squire's Tale." He turned the tables on the typical German claims that American Chaucerians produced only newfangled theories, dismissed Brandl's "new and startling" claims as "impossible," "inconsistent with the language of Chaucer," "inconsistent with itself," and based "upon certain errors of fact," and concluded gleefully that "the world has been right for the last five hundred years in regarding the Squire's Tale as nothing more or less than a romance."[31] Others, like James Russell Lowell, while avidly receiving and reviewing the voluminous German and British publications on Chaucer, were eager to mitigate the science-like nature of purely philological Chauceriana and to redirect the results of such investigations to their own political, social, and aesthetic interests.[32] Similarly, Francis James Child, Kittredge's Harvard colleague, whom Lowell once exaggeratedly stylized – *pro patria* – as having done "more for the great poet's memory than any man since [Thomas] Tyrwhitt," believed that the study of poetry needed to be distinguished from the study of scientific subject matter.[33] Child held that "[w]hen the charm of poetry goes […] it seems best to me not to stay. If the world is nothing but Biology and Geology, let's get quickly to some place which is more than that."[34]

Frederick Norris Robinson (1871–1966) found his place in the academic world of Harvard University during a time when the German philological influence was still strong. While Harvard University did not produce anything like a veritable "school" in medieval studies, there can be little doubt that the study of medieval English at Harvard had "a far more extensive influence on the study of Old and Middle English than any other group of scholars from a North American university, an influence that has spread as much through published works as through the training of successive generations of doctoral candidates."[35] Francis James Child (1825–96), first appointed as college tutor in 1846 and named Harvard's first professor of English in 1876, was succeeded by Kittredge (1860–1941), who began teaching as a lecturer in 1888 and became the first Gurney Professor of English in 1917. Robinson, after taking his A.B. in 1891, his A.M. in 1892, and his Ph.D. in 1894, in turn, succeeded his teacher, Kittredge, as Gurney Professor of English in 1936, after appointments as instructor (1894), assistant professor (1902), and full professor (1906).[36] Like his teachers, Robinson was thoroughly immersed in philological practices through his year abroad at the University of Freiburg (1895).[37] At Freiburg, Robinson studied with Rudolph Thurneysen, one of the founders of Celtic philology, and, upon his return, would himself become the founder of Celtic studies in the United States.[38] Under the supervision of Kittredge, Robinson wrote a thoroughly philolog-ical/linguistic doctoral dissertation, "On the Modal Syntax of Finite Verbs in the *Canterbury Tales*" (1894). This dissertation also reflects the period's concentration on individual authors as admission ticket to prestige and the various awards that accompanied it.[39] However, except for one single review of Robert Kilburn Root's 1926 edition of *Troilus and Criseyde*, he had not produced any scholarship on Chaucer before 1933, and his only other publication in the area of medieval English language or literature was little more than a chance offshoot of his more prevalent concentration in Celtic philology.[40]

This absence of published activity in Chaucer and Middle English studies was the reason why Brandl, the German reviewer of his *Complete Works* in 1933, thought he was dealing with a *homo novus*. What Brandl did not comprehend is that Chaucer was (and still continues to be) an exception among British cultural exports to the United States because he depends on the classroom for his survival as an author who deserved to be read and studied.[41] If the obvious linguistic and historical connections between Britain and the United States and a certain degree of Anglophilia can explain the reading of any British writer in North America, and if the degree of linguistic and

editorial difficulty of medieval texts served to position English literature study against the established departments of classical language and
literature in the late nineteenth century, F. N. Robinson, educated by
Child, Kittredge, and Thurneysen as a scientistic philologist, found
himself challenged not only by the (to some extent anti-German)
opposition to a dry-as-dust and rigid philology, but also by gradually
changing student demographics and attitudes. While the study of
medieval English literature had replaced the classics partly because it
was old and difficult, while still being native English, it had itself gradually become the established, dusty canon that obstructed the path
toward the study of modern literature and especially American literature. Thus, by 1933, "Chaucer studies had to compete again, this time
not with Latin, but with Tennyson and Whitman."[42] Practically all the
contexts sketched above as well as his publisher's profit-driven financial
strategies to produce a one-volume edition of the medieval poet would
converge in shaping Robinson's specific response to existing (British)
editions and (German) philological scholarship. In fact, the 1933
Complete Works of Geoffrey Chaucer is not only an example of the interplay of these contexts, but the very publication to bring about and
signal the *translatio* of Chaucer study to the United States.

"Some Good Words are due the Publisher": Outmarketing the Europeans

The *Complete Works* appeared in one of Houghton Mifflin's most
successful book series, "The Cambridge Poets," a title implying – like
Cambridge, Massachusetts itself – the historical and linguistic filiation
with the British tradition as well as American pride in moving forward
and beyond that tradition. The series had the goal of publishing the
major writers of the Anglo-Saxon/British canon in new U.S. editions.
By 1933, it included volumes on (Robert) Browning, Burns, Byron,
Dryden, Keats, Milton, Pope, Shakespeare, Shelley, Tennyson, and
Wordsworth, established British worthies whom it proudly joined
with several American classics, namely three actual "Cambridge
Poets," Longfellow, Lowell, and Whittier, and all volumes were edited
by U.S. scholars. There can be little doubt that Robinson's shrewd
publishers wanted to tap into the dominant patriotic Anglo-American
mentalité that conceived of reading these poets' works as an aesthetically valuable part of patriotic duty and citizenship training. Carefully

avoiding stirring up possible anti-American feelings with this major
U.S. publication of the "father of 'English' poetry," the volume on
Chaucer was printed, marketed, and sold in Britain, continental
Europe, and the Commonwealth by Oxford University Press.[43] This
strategy, although recognized and discussed as such by the *Times
Literary Supplement*, contributed to making the *Complete Works* the
most widely accepted edition of Chaucer all over the world within
only a few years of its publication. Although the *TLS* reviewer does his
best to stress the achievements of his countryman Sir William
McCormick, whose study *The Manuscripts of the Canterbury Tales* had
been published earlier in the same year, and calls U.S. Chaucer scholarship "ruthless" for emphasizing "the great gaps which Chaucer left
in his work and the uncertainties of his plans for filling them up," he
admits that McCormick heavily depended on American support
(John M. Manly), that in recent years "a much greater amount of
original work on Chaucer has been done in the United States than in
England," and that the edition's "cheapness and lightness in the hand
will doubtless ensure [...] continued popularity."[44] J. S. P. Tatlock's
comment, in his review for *Speculum*, that "some good words are due
the publisher," while similarly meant to praise the quality of print and
paper, should be extended to the area of effective national and international marketing.[45] As the numerous letters from grateful recipients
of the *Complete Works* at the Harvard University Archives attest, a
very large number of complimentary and review copies were sent out
in a global effort to obliterate all existing editions. Dozens of these
recipients indicate in their appreciative responses that they immediately decided to adopt "Robinson" as their new classroom text.[46] Most
German universities and scholars, perhaps as much for financial as for
patriotic reasons, avoided purchasing and using the *Complete Works*
and continued working with the existing British and German editions
until the 1950s, thereby isolating themselves even more from the new
center of Chaucer studies in North America.[47] However, considering
how small the German market for a Chaucer edition was in comparison with the ever-increasing U.S. and British/Commonwealth
markets, losing a few German customers was not a concern for
Houghton Mifflin. In the end, Houghton Mifflin and Robinson's
Complete Works neutralized British scholars and readers, who could
stake the most direct claim to "owning" Chaucer, by coopting Oxford
University Press into their project, and they marginalized German

scholars, who had colonized Chaucer as a Germanic author, by outpublishing and outmarketing them.[48] Publisher and editor had "conspired to make a remarkable volume," as Raymond D. Havens of Johns Hopkins's English Department put it.[49] And Hyder Rollins, one of Robinson's Harvard colleagues, identifies an important motive for producing the *Complete Works*: "If this book doesn't make you [Robinson] famous as well as rich, then I'll never make predictions again."[50]

A "Monument" Providing "Pleasure": Chaucer's Teachability and Accessibility as a Modern Classic

Since in 1933 the only other one-volume edition of Chaucer in print, Skeat's 1894 *Student Chaucer*, was based on dated scholarship and contained few textual and almost no explanatory notes, Robinson's sections of extended textual and comprehensive explanatory notes were an ideal compromise satisfying the need for scholarly reliability and a more general audience's desire for accessibility, a syncretistic effort that was praised by U.S. reviewers but that would have scandalized German Anglicists, most of whose foundational efforts resulted in drawing demarcation lines between scholarly and more public-oriented discourses.[51] Robinson avoided even the appearance of such demarcation lines when addressing all "readers of Chaucer" as the intended audience of his edition and when placing Chaucer's most popular text, the *Canterbury Tales*, first.[52] Further, in the introduction, philological or technical matters are kept brief, a decision lamented by some critics, of course. Although Robinson, unlike earlier modern editors, did not try to resolve the inconsistencies inherent in the ordering of tales in existing manuscripts of the *Canterbury Tales*, his banning of textual and explanatory notes to the end of the volume and its title, the *Complete Works of Geoffrey Chaucer*, suggest a finality about medieval texts that modern readers expect from perusing modern and contemporary poets' complete and authorized works, but that occludes the particular difficulties inherent in the editing and reading of medieval texts. Like the illustration gracing the paperback edition of Houghton Mifflin's current *Riverside Chaucer* (which shows a number of Canterbury pilgrims, perhaps Chaucer among them, from a manuscript of John Lydgate's *Siege of Thebes*), these features pretend to satisfy a desire in modern readers that Chaucer's work and its manuscripts prevent time and again: "to witness the poet in the prime imaginative site of the *Tales*, meeting and speaking with his fictional creations."[53]

Small wonder, then, that non-academic readers in the 1930s most commonly emphasize their "pleasure" at being able to peruse the earliest canonical English writer in their homes as a coffee-table book or call the volume a veritable "monument," indicating how the medieval poet had – in their eyes – become available in something like an authorized edition, just like the modern classics whose editions already graced their bookshelves.[54] And even well-published Chaucerians thought that Robinson had come closer than any to what Sylvia Tomasch described as the "editorial Elysium, the place where readers encounter authors, even after their deaths."[55] Chaucerians deemed it "unlikely that either newly discovered manuscripts or fresh approaches to textual problems will ever bring us much closer to Chaucer's actual words."[56]

In general, scholarly reviewers and readers appreciated the teachability of the revised text and praised the survey of scholarship. Aware of the degree to which Chaucer's popularity in the U.S. depended on successful classroom teaching, scholars were greatly enthusiastic about an edition that promised to maintain and even increase the importance of Chaucer the author and, at the same time, the prestige of their own specialty area.[57] They, too, express their satisfaction about having the "definitive one-volume edition of the works of our great poet," indicating both the inclusion of Chaucer as a classic in the English canon of the United States (visible in the use of the personal pronoun) and the finality of an edition that made Chaucer's texts available like those of modern and contemporary poets.[58] Pedagogical usefulness and general accessibility had reached a powerful symbiosis in this edition. Since the U.S. academy, to a much higher degree than the German philological tradition, favored the amalgamation of scholarship with civic, aesthetic, and practical teaching needs, Robinson's "scholarly Chaucer in one volume – a book that a person might keep conveniently at hand for constant reading as one might the collected words of a modern poet," met with general approval in the United States.[59]

"A Critical Edition" or Simply "Common Sense"? Robinson's Editorial Practice

In his introduction to the *Complete Works*, Robinson indicates that his edition of the *Canterbury Tales* is based on ten manuscripts and there-fore "may be called a critical edition, with one reservation. In the case of some of the more important works, including the *Canterbury Tales*, the manuscript materials accessible to the editor have not been exhaus-tive."[60] Clearly an integumentary formula intended to anticipate criti-cism from German and other philologically-minded colleagues, the reservation was apparently disallowed by Alois Brandl, who chided Robinson for not having been "enlightened by the spirit of Karl Lachmann" and pretending to a "critical" edition when his actual basis of editorial decision-making had been "his common sense." Robinson, said Brandl, had limited his work to "prints" and "poor copies" and completely underestimated the various issues of manuscript filiation, on which Lachmann focused "by teasing out scribes' positive errors."[61] Similarly, J. S. P. Tatlock, who praised Robinson's decision to take a "*via media*" between Walter W. Skeat's eclecticism ("the literary man") and the strict textual genealogist method of John Koch ("*a priori* theory"), nonetheless remarked that Robinson demonstrated "little awareness of the inaccuracy" of the existing printed editions.[62]

As Roy Vance Ramsey has demonstrated, Robinson, far from presenting an entirely new text of the *Canterbury Tales* based on the ten manuscripts he referenced, showed intriguingly little interest in original manuscripts and their relations. Rather, Robinson depended – just as Brandl had intimated – heavily on earlier printed editions, first and foremost Skeat's printed text, the one authority "universally accepted as standard throughout the twenty-nine years that Robinson worked on his own edition."[63] While the resulting text would not have been massively different, especially since his sources included, in Robinson's words, "the best copy, the Ellesmere MS.,"[64] his editing by primary resort to earlier editions effectively achieved the opposite of the genealogical method as championed by Lachmann and the German Chaucerians in the nineteenth and early twentieth centuries:

> The principal reason for an initial attempt to work out the rela-tions of the manuscripts is that by doing so an editor can have objective help in detecting and removing the changes to which an

author's text has been subjected since he wrote it. By choosing among earlier editorial choices of readings with little regard for their basis in the manuscripts and their relationships, Robinson piled his own particular set of choices upon those made by earlier editors, in their turn based upon others, often in a chain all the way back to the earliest editions.[65]

It appears, then, that Robinson's practice, while paying lip service to the German tradition of "critical" editing, was actually in flagrant opposition to that tradition.[66] At the same time, Robinson's silence about the central importance of Skeat's text(s) for his own edition manifestly obliterates Skeat's achievement, perhaps in an act of revisionary editorial anxiety.[67]

In fact, his *via media* of establishing "[t]rustworthy texts" by shunning the "strict constructionists" as well as "mere eclecticism" resembles an important feature of modern U.S. medievalism whose representatives, because of their geographical distance from European ideological battlegrounds, have continued to propose new, mediating, pragmatic, and common-sensical solutions to long-standing European scholarly aporias.[68] Not surprisingly, U.S. reviewers diagnose and applaud Robinson's "kindly consideration" and "good sense," while German ones denounce that same "common sense" as a problematic editorial guide.[69] The same pragmatic approach can be observed in his short introductions to "Language and Meter" (pp. xxv–xxvi), "Pronunciation" (pp. xxvi–xxviii), "Inflections" (pp. xxviii–xxxi), and "Versification" (pp. xxxi–xxxii), which, accordingly, are found wanting by European philologists, but find approbation among most U.S. scholars, who place more importance on the content and literary qualities of historical texts than on extensive, let alone exclusive, consideration of historical linguistics.[70] Those U.S. Chaucerians who tried to beat the German and English philologists at their own game, especially John Manly, were thought of as genial scientistic specialists, but their work was lacking the cherished pragmatic characteristics and pedagogical usefulness. Henry B. Hinckley of Yale University, for example, assured Robinson that his *Complete Works* had nothing to fear from the forthcoming Chicago edition:

> [...] Manly seems to specialize in what is brilliant, startling, even revolutionary – more so than any other Chaucerian in the world. But without denying that his work has value, and even great value,

I find myself moving for several years toward the conclusion that a part of the greatness is spectacular. I can't help thinking that your work will be more useful than his; also that it has its own peculiar charm, which will endure longer than the commotion which his work is likely to cause.[71]

Robinson avoided such commotion by basing much of his decision-making about individual textual passages not on a strict comparison of manuscript testimony, but on pragmatic and "very neat and rigid ideas about Chaucer's meter and grammar" that, he believed, "fully matched" Chaucer's own (unerring) grammatical and metrical regularity.[72]

"Facts are in High Esteem": Robinson's "Explanatory Notes"

As its reception history reveals, the major feature granting authority to Robinson's *Complete Works* is the lengthy section containing the "Explanatory Notes" (751–1000). Their lucid commentary on the text received unreserved praise from all reviewers and correspondents as "an amazing achievement" (Tatlock), "a first-rate compendium of Chaucer scholarship" (Ruud), "a storehouse of information" (Ferguson), and "enough reason to urgently recommend the book for purchase to all German Anglicists" (Brandl).[73] While establishing the "trustworthy" texts of the *Complete Works* must have taken a considerable effort, it is the collecting, reading, and synthesizing of the vast amounts of scholarly opinion that took the lion's share of his work between 1904 and 1933 and made the edition, as James A. S. McPeek wrote, "the Bible of every Chaucer scholar." Like McPeek, a former student of Robinson at Harvard and then English professor at Connecticut State College, hundreds of Chaucerians "hunted assiduously" for their own names and perhaps viewed them "in the notes with a vain interest which very shortly gave way to a feeling of grave responsibility at being thus in the shadow of greatness."[74] And those who, like the famous French medievalist Emile Legouis, had "striven however imperfectly to keep up with the works of Chaucerian scholars" and found their work cited and summarized could appreciate and "duly estimate the sum of labour represented" by Robinson's "monumental edition."[75] Even Brandl approvingly remarks that Robinson converted all existing scholarship together with his own readings into an impressive "mosaic." The German scholar realized that Robinson's commentary distinguishes itself by a "strict" adherence to "facts" that allows its author to include only results based on "sober" deliberation. Brandl explains: "Facts are in high esteem [...]. Many of the things usually included in the poet's biographies and literary criticism are left out as theoretical rubbish. Imagination is the poet's domain, but truly not the critic's." Robinson's desire for facts appears, at first sight, to parallel with the demands German philologists developed for dispassionate and distanced academic work. However, when one considers that practitioners of serious philology, including Brandl, fought quite heatedly over their investigations and lived up to Jacob Grimm's dictum of philology as "prouder, nobler, disputatious, or less merciful to error" than all other academic subjects, the explanatory notes in the *Complete Works* reveal themselves as born out of a typically "American" mentality to avoid dispute by concentrating on what appears factual and, therefore, sound.[76]

In an essay on Hemingway's 1932 *Death in the Afternoon*, a non-fiction book published only one year before the *Complete Works* and "a mammoth treatise on the art [...] of killing specially bred fighting bulls," Edward Said diagnoses a general kind of "how-to-ism" in U.S. culture, an attitude that reveals the regular "dismissal of opinion and interpretation," but also the:

> cult of "objectivity" and expertise, the spread of consultancy as a profession, and the institutionalization of the "news," which in America, it is believed, has been [...] separated from the burden of subjectivity. [...] The assumption underlying the [twenty-four-hour] news is that a tight little product, billed as pure "information" with all opinion removed and flashing across our vision for no longer than thirty seconds per item, is convincing beyond question. That this form of news is "fact" few people will dispute: what gets excluded is the tremendously sophisticated process of selection and commodification which makes bits of information into unassailable "fact."[77]

Henry B. Hinckley was impressed with Robinson's similar handling of "an exceedingly large number of facts and ideas, many of them matters that have been disputed for decades" and the "politeness" with which he had treated some of these disputes.[78] Robinson achieved this feat by fashioning himself as a simple purveyor of facts, as when he calls his concise surveys of scholarship "brief digest[s]," mentions his "extremely brief" "account" of the history of Chaucer's "ideas," or speaks of his plan to "register fully, though in brief form," Chaucer's sources.[79] As with his shaping of Chaucer's works into an edition resembling that of a modern or contemporary poet, such fore-grounding of factual and brief information, again according to Said, "is in many ways to say that what matters can be pushed up to the surface, and that history, insofar as it is out of easy reach, is better forgotten or, if it can't be forgotten, ignored. Experience of the here-and-now – the relevant – is therefore given priority."[80]

This is not to imply that Robinson's fact-enamored commentary (or his "Bibliography," 743–47) does not mention all kinds of international and older sources, but there is a conspicuous emphasis on recent publications by U.S. scholars, which were most easily accessible to him and in whose work he might also have felt a certain sense of national pride.[81] With many of these U.S. scholars he consulted via hand-written letters, even as the *Complete Works* was already "in press," and there can be little doubt that it is the writing of the "Explanatory Notes" more than the establishing of the "critical" text that obliged him to procrastinate the final publication of his edition until 1933, when he had begun the project as early as 1906.[82] Moreover, by providing English syncretic summaries of German and other non-English scholarship, he achieved a large-scale Englishing of Chaucer scholarship, making it much less necessary to read the original historical criticism often enough written in German and sometimes in French, an effort in concert with Dudley David Griffith's and Willard E. Martin's Chaucer bibliographies (1926, 1935, and 1955) or Eleanor Hammond's *Chaucer. A Bibliographical Manual* (1908).[83] In addition, by citing other scholars' English surveys and summaries of earlier research, for example Aage Brusendorff's 1924 English translation of his originally Danish monograph on the *Chaucer Tradition*, he further silenced the non-English-speaking originators of various theories on Chaucer's texts.[84] In the end, Robinson's pragmatic efforts at presenting a comprehensive, fact-based, now fully Englished digest of existing scholarship on Chaucer resulted in the kind of "Explanatory Notes" that, "instead of being necessary evils, as so many notes are, [...] have a kind of fascination, even when read without the text."[85] The updating of factual novelty was hailed by reviewers as Robinson's main achievement even for the revised second edition of 1957.[86]

Supplanting Predecessors, Repressing Rivals: The Complete Works as a
"Matter of Pride to All American Scholars"

After what has been said about some of the "American" contexts and
features of Robinson's *Complete Works*, it should come as no surprise
that his colleagues in the United States agreed that the edition was "a
worthy monument to cap the 75 years of work done on the poet at
Harvard" (Ernest P. Kuhl), "a monument of American philological
scholarship," and that it "should be a matter of pride to all American
scholars that what is by far the best text of a first-grade English poet is
the work of an American editor" (Henry N. McCracken).[87] And
Vernon P. Helming, in his review of the second, 1957 edition,
summarizes:

> [S]carcely a single scholarly paper published in this country since
> 1934 has referred its readers to any other text of Chaucer. Six
> generations of our college students, so far as they have made any
> serious study of this poet, have been introduced to him exclusively
> through this edition. One suspects that "Robinson" is more inevi-
> tably associated with Chaucer in the United States than
> "Geoffrey." Except for one or two texts in the classics of Greece
> and Rome, no "Student's Edition" of any author has so completely
> supplanted its predecessors and so long repressed possible rivals.

Thus, the review continues, the 1957 edition, like its 1933 prede-
cessor, "remains the starting point for all Chaucerian investigations,
the text that all American and most British scholars cite, the unap-
proached marvel of literary erudition and taste in the Middle English
realm."[88] By 1933, certainly by 1957, Chaucer studies and medieval
scholarship in general had become naturalized as "American":
"Robinson" had become a brand name better known than the first
name of the poet he had edited, and American medieval scholarship,
continuing but also substantially transforming nineteenth-century
German philological practices under the umbrella of the Medieval
Academy of America (1925–) and its interdisciplinary periodical,
Speculum: A Journal of Medieval Studies (1926–), had gradually
absorbed, Englished, and outpublished its German or British
colonizers.[89] By the middle of the twentieth century, Robinson's
academic postcolonial medievalism was universally recognized as one

of the most potent factors in reaching U.S. hegemony in Chaucer and medieval studies, and it certainly played a role in his election as President of the Medieval Academy in 1950. Most notably, it empowered Albert C. Baugh to claim, in the 1951 issue of *Speculum*, as a "simple statement of fact" and "in no unworthy spirit of self-esteem," that "the bulk of scholarly work [...] done on Chaucer in the last fifty years and the most significant achievements in this field of literary study have come from American scholars."[90] Thus, by the 1950s the colony had not simply written back, it had (and here's to you, F. N. Robinson!) veritably turned the tables on its former Old World colonizers, preparing for the founding of the mostly U.S.-based New Chaucer Society (1977) or for the publishing of a volume like *Editing Chaucer. The Great Tradition* (1984) that, equating "Great" with Anglo-American, completely erased the foundational influence of German *Chaucerphilologie*.[91] Accompanying their country's quick rise to economic, military, and political hegemony between 1870 and 1950, U.S. Chaucerians had moved from a position on the colonized margins to a colonizing dominance in the field of Chaucer (and medieval) studies. Robinson's edition was the most significant result of and – at the same time – an essential catalyst for this ascent to hegemony.

Epilogue: Filiations and the Writing of the History of Medieval Studies

It can be a daunting experience to delve into the history of one of the most influential publications in twentieth-century medieval scholarship: One of the (only) two medievalists who have so far undertaken essay-length investigations into the historical and methodological foundations of Robinson's *magnum opus* before me, Roy Vance Ramsey, was so thoroughly awed by his experience that he felt obliged to include an apology at the end of his essay, in which he professed how "deeply indebted" he was to Robinson's editions, "especially their introductions and notes," but that, as "Professor Robinson would have agreed," he had a "greater obligation" to present "the closest possible versions of what Chaucer originally wrote."[92] A second colleague who similarly focused on the editorial principles governing Robinson's texts in the *Complete Works*, George F. Reinecke, was in fact one of Robinson's closest collaborators for the second edition. He prepared, in Robinson's own words, "the typescript for the press, attended to the verification of new references, and read all the proofs, submitting changes to me, of course, for final decision," and provided the kind of reliable "secretarial service" considered "above and beyond the call of duty."[93] This close affiliation was not conducive to an independent but, as Joseph Dane has suggested, to a somewhat "celebratory" perspective.[94] Unlike Reinecke (1925–2000; Ph.D Harvard University, 1960; advisor: Bartlett Jere Whiting) and Ramsey (1933–; Ph.D University of Oklahoma, 1964; advisor: Paul G. Ruggiers), who collaborated with Robinson himself and/or with numerous of Robinson's collaborators, students, and friends, my own age (1961–) and education and teaching experience in Germany and the United States affords me, I would like to think, a view that regards the *Complete Works* not as an iconic and hence untouchable monument in the history of U.S. medieval studies, but as one, albeit major, source illustrating the genesis and development of today's medievalist practices.[95] By historicizing Robinson's edition within the context of its precursors, contemporaries, and immediate and intermediate national and international reception, I was able to reveal some of the conditions accompanying and influencing its foremost features.

This investigation shows Robinson as a rather typical representative of the mentalité governing his generation of U.S. medievalists. Although he was educated by American and German philologists and generally published and taught according to philological paradigms,[96] his pragmatic leanings, the post-World War I conditions of American higher education, and his publishers' marketing strategy swayed him to produce a one-volume edition that would be welcomed by scholars, college students, and the numerous non-academic readers who desired to read Chaucer's texts like those of a contemporary poet. These guiding principles, as well as the quickly growing importance of U.S. scholarship and English as the global academic *lingua franca*, led him to create a volume that Englished and thereby diminished the foundational achievements of German-speaking Chaucerians. I very much doubt that Robinson, whom his correspondents address as "Fritz" as often as "Rob" or "Fred," had any conscious plan to "write back" and openly declare America's academic independence from Germany, Britain, or Old Europe in general. However, a good many of the features of his edition and certainly the patriotic pride expressed about it by his U.S. colleagues and friends would suggest that he readily participated in the process bringing about and showcasing this very independence. His "Preface," in which he exclusively thanks American colleagues for support and assistance, and the absence of even a single letter indicating collegial collaboration or consultation with a German or British Chaucerian might be further indication of the postcolonial – perhaps already neocolonial – American subconscious shaping his academic medievalism.[97]

NOTES

1. Sacvan Bercovitch, "Discovering America: A Cross-Cultural Perspective," in *The Translatability of Cultures. Figurations of the Space Between*, ed. Sandford Budick and Wolfgang Iser (Stanford, CA: Stanford University Press, 1996), 145–68, here 157. – An early version of this article was presented at the 21st International Conference on Medievalism at Ohio State University in the fall of 2006. My research on this topic could not have been completed without the competent assistance of two graduate research assistants at the University of Northern Iowa, Lucie Bukalova and Jewon Woo, who collected a vast array of bio-bibliographic data. I would also like to acknowledge the kind collegial input I received on various issues from Jacek Fisiak (Adam Mickiewicz University), Renate Haas (University of Kiel), Daniel W. Mosser (Virginia Polytechnic Institute and State University), Elizabeth Scala (University of Texas at Austin), and Sylvia Tomasch (Hunter College). Furthermore, I would like to thank Kelly Kunert (Houghton Mifflin Publishers), Gerald L. Peterson and Barbara Weeg (Donald O. Rod Library, University of Northern Iowa), Peter Arcado and Timothy Driscoll (Houghton Library, Harvard University), Kathryn Hodson (University of Iowa Libraries), and Donna Vaughn (National Library of Australia) for their assistance in accessing copies of the sources discussed in this essay. Finally, I would like to express my sincere gratitude to Jesse Swan (University of Northern Iowa) and Kathleen Verduin (Hope College), who took it upon themselves to read complete draft versions of my work and provided substantial critical commentary on language, style, and content, and to the three anonymous *SiM* referees. Any remaining gravamina are, of course, solely my responsibility.

2. Alois Brandl, *Archiv* 146 (1933): 266–68, here 266.

3. For full bio-bibliographical data, see Gunta Haenicke and Thomas Finkenstaedt's *Anglistenlexikon 1825–1990. Biographische und bibliographische Angaben zu 318 Anglisten* (Augsburg: Universität Augsburg, 1992), 42–44. Brandl also wrote a fascinating autobiography, *Zwischen Inn und Themse. Lebensbeobachtungen eines Anglisten. Alt-Tirol / England / Berlin* (Berlin: Grote, 1936), which reveals much about the professional mentality

of German academics from Imperial Germany and Austria through the beginnings of the Nazi era.

4. For the rest of this essay, *Complete Works* (in a few cases: "Cambridge Edition") will be used to refer to *The Complete Works of Geoffrey Chaucer*, ed. F. N. Robinson (Boston and New York: Houghton Mifflin; Oxford: Oxford University Press, 1933); the second, revised edition, also edited by Robinson, was entitled *The Works of Geoffrey Chaucer* and published in 1957; in 1987, a third edition, revised by an entire team of scholars and entitled the *Riverside Chaucer* (a reference to the Riverside Publishing Company founded by Henry Houghton in 1852, now a subsidiary of Houghton Mifflin Company) was published under the general editorship of Larry D. Benson of Harvard University. This most recent edition is sold exclusively in a hardback edition in North America and in hardback and paperback editions in the United Kingdom and Europe. Other editions and studies of editions frequently mentioned in this essay are the "Globe edition" (*The Works of Geoffrey Chaucer*, ed. Alfred W. Pollard, H. Frank Heath, Mark H. Liddell, and W. S. McCormick [London: Macmillan, 1898]); the "Oxford Chaucer" (*The Complete Works of Geoffrey Chaucer*, ed. Walter W. Skeat [Oxford: Clarendon Press, 1894–97], 7 vols.); the "Student's Chaucer" (*The Student's Chaucer*, ed. Walter W. Skeat [Oxford: Clarendon Press, 1895]); *Canterbury Tales*, ed. John Matthews Manly (New York: H. Holt, 1928); and *The Text of the Canterbury Tales*, ed. John Matthews Manly and Edith Rickert (Chicago: University of Chicago Press, 1940), 6 vols., usually referred to as the "Chicago edition."

5. On Ten Brink's appointment and the establishing of English studies as elements of a concerted policy of cultural Germanization by the Imperial government, see Thomas Finkenstaedt, *Kleine Geschichte der Anglistik. Eine Einführung* (Darmstadt: Wissenschaftliche Buchgesellschaft, 1983), 58–59. Renate Haas and Albert Hamm have recently elucidated the various contexts of this appointment in bilingual Alsace in *The University of Strasbourg and the Foundation of Continental English Studies* (Frankfurt: Lang, 2009), esp. 47–76.

6. Henry Sweet, *The Oldest English Texts* (London: EETS, 1885), v–vi.

7. Walter W. Skeat, preface to his edition of *Chaucer. The Minor Poems* (Oxford: Clarendon Press, 1888), vii.

8. Arthur S. Napier, "On the Study of English at German Universities," *Educational Review* 2 (1892): 66–69, here 65 and 69.

9. See the chapter, "Philology's Man in Palo Alto: Ewald Flügel's 'Mission Impossible,'" in Richard Utz, *Chaucer and the Discourse of German Philology. A History of Reception and an Annotated Bibliography of Studies, 1793–1948* (Turnhout: Brepols, 2002), 127–58.

10. On the German influence on U.S. institutions, see the chapters on

the "New University" in Gerald Graff's *Professing Literature. An Institutional History* (Chicago: University of Chicago Press, 1987), 55–80. So pervasive was the reputation of German philological study that Mark Twain, when registering with the police during his stay in Heidelberg in 1878, listed his occupation as "philologist and artist," to impress his hosts. See Robert Sattelmeyer, "The Awful German Influence, or How the Blue Jay Got to Heidelberg," *American Literary Realism* 35/3 (2003): 262–69.

11. The central document conflating and rejecting military and political Germanity together with German "philology" was the so-called *Newbolt Report* (*The Teaching of English in England. Being the Report of the Departmental Committee Appointed by the President of the Board of Education to Inquire into the Position of English in the Educational System of England*, ed. Sir Henry Newbolt, et al. [London: HMSO; New York: Harcourt, Brace, 1922]). On the role of the Newbolt Report for the history of medieval English language and literature study, see David Matthews, *The Making of Middle English, 1765–1910* (Minneapolis: University of Minnesota Press, 1999), xxviii; and Utz, *Chaucer and the Discourse of German Philology*, 177–81. On the general British rejection of German(ic) Philology before and after World War I, see Richard Utz, "*Englische Philologie* vs. English Studies: A Foundational Conflict," in *Das Potential europäischer Philologien. Geschichte, Leistung, Funktion*, ed. Christoph König (Göttingen: Wallstein, 2009), 34–44.

12. For an illustrative example of a young German Anglicist's hubris against established British scholarship, see the reception history of the fifteenth-century poem *Thomas of Erceldoune*. Only five years after James A. H. Murray, who would later become editor of the *New English Dictionary*, edited the text, Alois Brandl reedited it with a heavy focus on dialect study, rhyme, word study, and the interrelations and history of all extant manuscripts. In this specific case, if one believes later authorities on the poem, Brandl's "philological" investigation did indeed advance knowledge about the late medieval text beyond the level originally established by Murray. For a detailed discussion, see Richard Utz, "Medieval Philology and Nationalism: The British and German Editors of *Thomas of Erceldoune*," *Florilegium* 23/2 (2006): 27–45.

13. Arnold Schröer, "Aus der Frühzeit der englischen Philologie. I. Persönliche Erinnerungen und Eindrücke," *Germanische Romanische Monatsschrift* 13 (1925): 33–51, here 34.

14. For numerous examples of this kind of criticism, see my *Chaucer and the Discourse of German Philology*, 61–158.

15. John Koch, "Der gegenwärtige Stand der Chaucerforschung," *Anglia* 49 (1926): 193–234, here 195. Koch's use of the Canon's Yeoman's proverb, "But al thyng that shineth as the gold/ Nis nat gold," may have wanted to suggest to readers that, like the Yeoman's Canon, who dabbles

unsuccessfully in alchemy, U.S. Chaucerians dabbled in things they did not fully understand. On John Koch's Chaucerian publication record, which includes about a dozen book-length studies and editions and hundreds of reviews, see Richard Utz, "Editing Chaucer: John Koch and the Forgotten Tradition," in *"And gladly wolde he lerne and gladly teche." Studies on Language and Literature in Honour of Professor Dr. Karl Heinz Göller*, ed. Wladislaw Witalisz (Cracow: Jagiellonian University Press, 2001), 1726.

16. John Koch, *Englische Studien* 61 (1926–27): 440–41, here 440.

17. John Koch, "Rev. of John Matthews Manly, ed., *Geoffrey Chaucer: Canterbury Tales*, (1928)," *Englische Studien* 64 (1929): 100–13, here 104.

18. Koch, "Rev. of John Matthews Manly," 108. On the reactions of French scholars against German attempts at hegemonizing French (medieval) philology, see for example Alain Corbellari, "Joseph Bédier, Philologist and Writer," and Per Nykrog, "A Warrior Scholar at the College de France," both in *Medievalism and the Modernist Temper*, ed. R. Howard Bloch and Stephen G. Nichols (Baltimore, MD: John Hopkins University Press, 1996), 269–85 and 286–307, respectively. The direct philological altercations with France began earlier and quickly grew fiercer because of the Franco-German war of 1870–71.

19. An excellent example of Koch's sharp criticism are his remarks ("Neuere Chaucer-literatur," *Anglia Beiblatt* 22 [1911]: 265–82, here 276) on Harold C. Goddard's claims ("Chaucer's *Legend of Good Women*," *Journal of English and Germanic Philology* 7 [1908]: 87–129), that the *Legend of Good Women* might be a literary travesty. Koch asks the rhetorical question if "one should be more flabbergasted by the author's impertinence to give his opinion without any in-depth study of the poet, whom he imagines like the editor of a Yankee job-pamphlet, or by his complete inability to understand medieval thought." For further examples, see Koch's treatment of U.S. scholarship in his review essay "Die Chaucerforschung seit 1900," *Germanisch Romanische Monatsschrift* 1 (1909): 490–507; and his reviews of Wilbur Owen Sypherd's *Studies in Chaucer's Hous of Fame* (1908) and Karl Young's *The Origin and Development of the Story of Troilus and Criseyde* (1908), in *Englische Studien* 41 (1910): 113–21, and 121–26.

20. See specifically the section "The War Climate," in Graff's *Professing Literature. An Institutional History* (Chicago: University of Chicago Press, 1987), 128–32. See further, Carol S. Gruber, *Mars and Minerva: World War I and the Uses of the Higher Learning in America* (Baton Rouge: Louisiana State University Press, 1975), and John A. Walz, *German Influence in American Education and Culture* (Freeport, NY: Books for Libraries, 1969).

21. Mark Sullivan, *Our Times*, 6 vols. (New York: Charles Scribner's Sons, 1926–33), 5:468; *The Great Tradition: Selections from English and American Prose and Poetry, Illustrating the National Ideals of Freedom, Faith,*

and Conduct, ed. Edwin Greenlaw and James Holly Hanford (Chicago: Scott, Foresman, 1922), xiii.

22. On these early critics of German methodologies on U.S. soil, see the section "Germanity in Retreat," in Graff, *Professing Literature,* 100–4.

23. The citations are from Daniel Kilham Dodge, "English at the University of Illinois" (71–73, here 72), and Albert H. Tolman, "English at the University of Chicago" (86–91, here 88), in *English in American Universities,* ed. William Morton Payne (Boston: D. C. Heath, 1895).

24. Learned's speech, "Linguistic Study and Literary Creation," was published in *PMLA* 24 (1909): xlvi–lxv, here lxv.

25. J. R. R. Tolkien, "Philology: General Works," *The Year's Work in English Studies* 4 (1923): 20–37, here 36–37.

26. On the "stranglehold" of German philological paradigms and foundational information in the 1930s, see Walter Jackson Bate, "The Crisis in English Studies," *Harvard Magazine* (September/October 1982): 46–53, here 49: "If you took a Ph.D. here [at Harvard] as late as the 1930s, you were suddenly shoved – with grammars written in German – into Anglo-Saxon and Middle Scots, *plus* Old Norse (Icelandic), Gothic, Old French, and so on. I used to sympathize with the Japanese and Chinese students who had come here to study literature, struggling with a German grammar to translate Gothic into English! William Allan Neilson, the famous president of Smith College, had been a professor of English here for years. Forgivably, he stated that the Egyptians took only five weeks to make a mummy, but the Harvard English Department took five years."

27. After World War I, Chaucer study (and the study of medieval English literature) in Germany lost much of its importance as the study of contemporary English literatures gained ground, often in an effort to strengthen Germans' knowledge of the culture and mentality of the Anglo-Saxon nations who had managed to defeat Germany. The result for German Chaucer study was that fewer and often less qualified scholars entered into endless and futile philological debates. On perhaps the most infamous of these altercations, Viktor Langhans and Hugo Lange's epic twenty-year-long "discussion" of the authenticity of the two versions of Chaucer's *Legend of Good Women,* see Richard Utz, "Eminent Chaucerians? Continuity and Transformation in German-Speaking Chaucer Philology, 1918–1948," in *Anglistik: Research Paradigms and Institutional Policies, 1930–2000,* ed. Stephan Kohl (Trier: Wissenschaftlicher Verlag, 2005), 25–43; an earlier version of this essay, "*Translationes Imperii*: Swan Songs, Adaptations, and New Beginnings in Third-Reich Chaucer Philology," was published in *Anglistentag 2001 Wien, Proceedings,* ed. Dieter Kastovsky, Gunther Kaltenböck, and Susanne Reichl (Trier: Wissenschaftlicher Verlag, 2002), 253–63.

28. For examples of such practices by U.S. scholars, see the chapter "*Ceterum Recenseo*: John Koch, the School Teacher," in Utz, *Chaucer and the Discourse of German Philology*, 159–90. As an undated, machine-typed proforma among the Robinson materials regarding the *Complete Works* suggests (Robinson was a member of the Advisory Board for the project), U.S. scholars were confident enough of their experience to work without any non-U.S. contributors for W. F. Bryan and Germaine Dempster's *Sources and Analogues of Chaucer's Canterbury Tales* in the late 1930s (the finished volume was published with the University of Chicago Press in 1941). The publication was part of the efforts of the MLA's "Chaucer Group," and Robinson was a member of the "Editorial Committee and Advisory Board" of the group, which consisted of Albert C. Baugh, Beatrice Daw Brown, Carleton Brown, John M. Manly, Robert K. Root, J. S. P. Tatlock, Karl Young, and W. F. Bryan.

29. Candace Barrington, *American Chaucers* (New York: Palgrave, 2007). M. B. Ruud's statement, in his 1935 review of the *Complete Works* for *Modern Language Notes* (vol. 50, 329), indicates that while U.S. scholars have been generally "troubled by the state of higher studies in our universities," they "have long taken comfort in the achievements of American Chaucerians; for here more conspicuously than in any other field of English studies we have more than held our own."

30. Kittredge's confidence in disinterested scholarship is visible in his famous essay on "Chaucer's Lollius" in *Harvard Studies in Classical Philology* 28 (1917): 47–132, here 47. Instead of "discordant conjectures," Kittredge proceeds "to examine certain obvious phenomena [...] in an orderly and logical manner, in the light of reason and common sense."

31. George Lyman Kittredge, "Supposed Historical Allusions in the Squire's Tale," *Englische Studien* 13 (1889): 1–25, here 4 and 24. Brandl's own essay, "Über einige historische Anspielungen in den Chaucer-Dichtungen," had appeared in *Englische Studien* 12 (1889): 161–86. See further Kittredge's critical commentary on Eugen Kölbing's 1889 edition of *Ipomadon* and Karl Bülbring's commentary on the *Alexander* fragments and *Robin Hood and the Monk* ("Anmerkungen zum mittelenglischen Ipomadon A. Zu Ipomadon B. Zu Ipomadon C," Cf. *Englische Studien* 14 [1890]: 386–92; "Zwei Berichtigungen," *Englische Studien* 14 [1890]: 392–93). Interestingly, both essays were written in German. On the importance of *Englische Studien* (1877–1944), the first journal in the world concentrating on English studies, and the role of medieval studies in its success, see Richard Utz, "Medieval Scholarship in *Englische Studien*, Part I: Eugen Kölbing and the Foundational Period (1877–1899)," *Erfurt Electronic Studies in English* 12 (2006): <http://www.uni-erfurt.de/eestudies/eese/artic26/richard/2_2006bb.html>, accessed 20 September 2009. On Kittredge's biography and careers, see John

C. McGalliard, "George Lyman Kittredge (1860–1941)," in *Medieval Scholarship: Biographical Studies in the Formation of a Discipline*, ed. Helen Damico and Joseph B. Zavadil, 3 vols. (New York: Garland 1998), 2:241–52.

32. Lowell does so, for example, in his extensive review essay, entitled "Chaucer," discussing several publications of the Chaucer Society, E. G. Sandras's *Étude sur Chaucer considéré comme imitateur des Trouvères* (1859), W. Hertzberg's *Geoffrey Chaucer's Canterbury-Geschichten* (1866), and A. Kissner's *Chaucer in seinen Beziehungen zur italienischen Literatur* (1867), for the July 1870 edition of the *North American Review*, 155–99. About Lowell's essay, see Richard J. Utz, "Will it *do* to say anything more about Chaucer?," *North American Review* 291/6 (November/December 2006): 50.

33. Lowell, "Chaucer," 160.

34. Child's statement is recorded by Gamaliel Bradford, *As God Made Them. Portraits of Some Nineteenth-Century Americans* (Boston: Houghton Mifflin, 1929), 223–24.

35. Daniel Donoghue, "The History of English Medieval Studies at Harvard University," *Medieval English Newsletter* 28 (June 1993): 1–3, here 1. On Harvard's pervasive influence during this period, see further William J. Courtenay, "The Virgin and the Dynamo: The Growth of Medieval Studies in North America 1870–1930," in *Medieval Studies in North America. Past, Present and Future*, ed. Francis G. Gentry and Christopher Kleinhenz (Kalamazoo, MI: Medieval Institute Publications, 1982), 5–22, here 13–14.

36. On Robinson's life and career, see Donoghue, "The History," 1–2; F. P. Magoun, B. J. Whiting, and H. M. Smyser's eulogy, "Fred Norris Robinson," in *Speculum* 42.3 (1967): 591–92; and George F. Reinecke, "F. N. Robinson," in *Editing Chaucer. The Great Tradition*, ed. Paul G. Ruggiers (Norman, OK: Pilgrim Books, 1984), 231–51. Anita Obermeier's short bio-bibliographic entry on Robinson, forthcoming in *Handbook in Medieval Studies: Concepts, Methods, Historical Developments, and Current Trends in Medieval Studies*, ed. Albrecht Classen (Berlin: de Gruyter, 2010), was not yet available for inclusion.

37. Child spent two years in Berlin and Göttingen studying with among others, Jacob Grimm; Kittredge one year in Leipzig and Tübingen working with, among others Eduard Sievers.

38. On Robinson's role as founder of Celtic studies, see "The Story of Celtic at Harvard," <http://www.fas.harvard.edu/~celtic/storyofceltic/index.htm>, accessed 15 September 2009.

39. Michael Warner, "Professionalization and the Rewards of Literature: 1875–1900," *Criticism* 27/1 (1985): 1–28, here 16, discusses Robinson's

career at Harvard as a typical example of his generation of academic critics.

40. *The Book of Troilus and Criseyde by Geoffrey Chaucer*, ed. Robert Kilburn Root, was reviewed by Robinson for *Speculum* 1/4 (1926): 461–67. In 1898, although misnamed "J. N. Robinson," he published a research note on the relationship between the Celtic versions of the Middle English romance *Bevis of Hampton* in response to Eugen Kölbing's 1886 edition, *The Romance of Sir Beues of Hamtoun* ("Celtic Versions of *Sir Beues of Hamtoun*," *Englische Studien* 24 [1898]: 463–64).

41. On this topic, see Alan Baragona's excellent survey on "Chaucer in American Higher Education, Past and Present," in *Chaucer: An Oxford Guide*, ed. Steve Ellis (Oxford: Oxford University Press, 2005; companion website <http://www.oup.com/uk/booksites/content/0199259127/>; additional materials: <http://www.oup.com/uk/booksites/content/0199259127 /resources/usuniversities.pdf>, accessed 15 September 2009), 1: "Shakespeare as a general rule may first be introduced to modern Americans in high school, but his work has a life outside school in the theater, and it is possible for an American to discover Shakespeare first on the stage rather than on the page. British music, classical or folk, is known primarily in the concert hall and on radio; British films, in the movie houses; British art, in the museums. None of these really needs the classroom to be transplanted across the Atlantic. Although it is true that Chaucer is distinguished from his contemporaries like Gower and Hoccleve because he continues to appeal to modern sensibilities in a variety of ways, it is also true that, in the United States even more than in England, Chaucer depends on teachers to cultivate those sensibilities so that his work continues to be read."

42. For a survey of the social, demographic, and methodological changes in U.S. Chaucer study from Child and Kittredge through Robinson, see Baragona, "Chaucer in American Higher Education," 8–9.

43. Brandl, for example, in his review for *Archiv* (266), assumed that the entire project belonged with Oxford University Press, the world's "biggest publisher in English studies," because his review copy came from Humphry Milford, Oxford.

44. Anon., "A New Chaucer," *Times Literary Supplement* (23 February 1934): 123, made a point of comparing the *Complete Works* with its "English predecessors," Walter W. Skeat's "Oxford Chaucer" (1894) and the Globe edition (1898), and to offer "a warm welcome" to "this American one, published by Houghton Mifflin company, of Cambridge, Massachusetts, and sponsored here by the Oxford University Press, despite its connexion with Professor Skeat's." In fact, Oxford University Press, intent on capitalizing on both editions, republished Skeat's edition in the very year it co-published Robinson.

45. J. S. P. Tatlock, Review of F. N. Robinson's *Complete Works*, *Speculum* 9/4 (1934): 459.

46. Where not otherwise indicated, all letters mentioned and cited in this essay were kindly made available to me in copy by the Harvard University Archives: Papers of "Fred Norris Robinson." Correspondence, 1900–1960. HUG (FP) 40.15. Box 2. "Chaucer: Correspondence regarding the Chaucer edition." Letters that indicate immediate adoption of the *Complete Works* are by Kemp Malone (Johns Hopkins University; 21 May 1933); Joseph Robinson (Mercer University; 23 June 1933), Harold C. Goddard (Swarthmore College; 20 September 1933), Albert K. Potter (Brown University; 27 September 193[3]), Helen Pearce (Willamette University; 23 February 1934), William J. Calvert, Jr. (Jacksonville Teachers College; 12 December 193[4]), Anon. (Columbia University; 21 December 1934); H[enry] N[oble] McC[racken] indicates in his review for the *Saturday Review of Literature* 10 (1933): 311, that he has been "using the book in daily classroom practice"; and Vernon P. Helming, in his review of the second edition (1957) for *Speculum* 33/1 (1958): 123, remembers that "[o]n its publication in 1933" the volume "[a]lmost at once [...] became the *vade mecum* of American Chaucerians everywhere." By 1957, when the second revised edition was published, the volume had long become "the ever-indispensable Robinson," as John Lawlor (University College of North Staffordshire) expressed to Robinson in a letter dated 11 October 1957.

47. A check of representative examples from German-speaking literary and linguistic criticism published between 1933 and 1950 demonstrates that most scholars keep using Skeat's and the Globe editions. Will Héraucourt (*Chaucer's Wertwelt. Die Wertwelt einer Zeitwende* [Heidelberg: Winter 1939]) cites all textual passages according to Skeat, but prefers Robinson's "Explanatory Notes," which he includes as "Notes" among his frequently cited abbreviations. One of the most internationally-minded and progressive German Anglicists, Walter F. Schirmer, first mentions Skeat's seven- and one-volume editions and the Globe edition in his 1945 history of English literature (*Kurze Geschichte der englischen Literatur* [Tübingen: Max Niemeyer]), then Robinson's edition, followed by the exclamation "(excellent!)" as recommending commentary (47).

48. Houghton Mifflin did send review copies to some of the German journal editors, as the reviews by Brandl and Lange indicate. According to my search of German and Austrian libraries via the Karlsruhe Virtual Catalog, only seven university libraries currently hold (and probably bought in the 1930s) the *Complete Works* (<http://www.ubka.uni-karlsruhe.de/hylib/en/kvk.html>, accessed 1 September 2009). On the partially self-sought isolation of German Chaucerians after World War I, see Richard Utz, "*Translationes*

Imperii", 253–63; this essay was republished, with slight revisions, as "Eminent Chaucerians? ...".

49. Raymond D. Havens (1880–1954), in a letter to Robinson dated 13 March 1934.

50. Hyder [Edward] Rollins (1889–1958), in a letter to Robinson dated 14 May 1933. Robinson was also approached by Maynard T. Smith (Letter dated 27 October 1953) from the Department of Cinema at the University of Southern California. Smith wanted to enlist Robinson's "help in the making of our educational film on *The Canterbury Tales* in arriving at a [Middle English] sound track that will be agreeable to the majority of Chaucerian scholars." The textual basis for the sound track was to be the *Complete Works*.

51. Tatlock, for example, contends at the end of his 1934 review for *Speculum* (464): "Mr Robinson's edition is the soundest, most stimulating, and most agreeable edition in existence, for both the general reader, the serious student, and the proficient scholar." Martin B. Ruud, in his 1935 review for *Modern Language Notes*, similarly praises Robinson for having prepared, "with rare distinction," a "dependable edition, fully abreast of modern scholarship, of the poet's complete works" for "the student, teacher, and amateur of Chaucer" (329). For examples of the various demarcation techniques used against "journalists, essayists, and feuilletonists" (often summarily dismissed as "aesthetes" and "dilettantes") by German Anglicists, see Utz, *Chaucer and the Discourse of German Philology*, 61–126.

52. Robinson, "Preface," vii.

53. Stephanie Trigg, *Congenial Souls. Reading Chaucer from Medieval to Postmodern* (Minneapolis, MN, and London: University of Minnesota Press, 2002), xv.

54. On Robinson's *Complete Works* serving as a coffee-table book or otherwise displayed as a "monument," see the letter by Patty [?], of 11 May 193[3], which reads: "We are all tremendously pleased to be the joint owners (along with the guest room) of such a complete works of Chaucer, edited by one we know! – and are very proud to know, and will be sure to let others know we know, by giving this very fine book a front seat in the guest room." Patty [?] even indicates next to which other volume the *Complete Works* would find itself: Ellen Churchill Semple's 1931 study of *The Geography of the Mediterranean Region*, a monograph that had stimulated much debate about the interconnections between geography and history. Sarah L. Slattery, wife of Charles Lewis Slattery, a former Massachusetts Episcopal Bishop and preacher at Harvard University, indicates in a letter dated 9 May 1933 how it would give her "the greatest pleasure to add it to the poetry section of Charles's library." And Charles M. Thompson (14 May 1933) announced he would "put it on the shelf next to Jebb Fletcher's Dante" (i.e., the 1931

translation of Dante's *Divine Comedy* by J. B. Fletcher). For other instances
of the "pleasure" the edition elicits, see the following letters to Robinson: T.
Spencer (19 April 1933); Ruth Crosby (22 April 1933); James A. S.
McPeeck (25 April 1933); Nathan C. Starr (1 May 1933); Alwin Thaler (7
May 1933); L[e] B[aron] R[ussell] Briggs (9 May 1933); Sarah L. Slattery (9
May 1933); Theresa Coolidge (10 May 1933); Nancy Toy (11 May
[1933]); Cornelia Le Boutillier (12 May 1933); Chas. H. Taylor (13 May
1933); Edmund T[aite] Silk (14 May 1933); Laura Gustafson (16 May
1933); Hannah [C.V.] (20 May 193[3]); Kemp Malone (21 May 1933);
Deborah Webster (25 May 1933); H. B. H. (29 May 1933); Dorothy I.
Morrill (5 January 1934); Barklie Henry (2 February 1934). See further
James H. Powers's review in the *Boston Daily Globe* (Saturday, 13 May
1933). – For examples of readers praising the "monumental" character of
Robinson's edition, see: James A. S. McPeeck (25 April 1933); J. McG.
Bottrol (26 April 1933); Wilbur Owen Sypherd (1 May 1933); Sarah L.
Slattery (9 May 1933); Eleanor H. Hinckley (10 May 1933); Emile Legouis
(12 June 1933); Clare Allen Haskins (10 June 1933); Tarquinio Vallese (24
June 1933); Wirt A. Cate (7 August 1933); E[rnest] P[eter] Kuhl (no date,
193[3]); Harold C. Whitford (1 October 1935).

　　55. Sylvia Tomasch, "Editing as Palinode: The Invention of Love and
the Text of the *Canterbury Tales*," *Exemplaria* 16/2 (2004): 457–76, here
465. Walter Clyde Curry, for example, in a letter to Robinson, dated 19
October 1933, states that "[h]ere at last, we may reasonably suppose, is
Chaucer's work." Interestingly, the 1942 report of the committee awarding
the Medieval Academy of America's Haskins Medal to the strictly philological *The Text of the Canterbury Tales*, withheld similar praise from John M.
Manly (see Tomasch, "Editing as Palinode," 462–63).

　　56. This is the verdict by Vernon P. Helming (University of Massachusetts, Amherst) in his review of the revised 1957 edition for *Speculum* 33/1
(1958): 123–25, here 124. C[harles] H. Grandgent, a professor of Romance
literatures and languages at Harvard University, had described his desire for a
"contemporary" Chaucer in a letter to Robinson dated May 12 193[3]:
"Congratulations are due also to Geoffrey Chaucer if, as I like to believe, he
is still cognizant of mundane affairs."

　　57. See, for example, the letters to Robinson by Anon. (Washington
and Jefferson College), 25 April 1933 ("All Chaucer scholars, particularly
teachers, will find it of great value."); Thomas E. Ferguson (Stephen F.
Austin State Teachers College), 14 January 1935 ("I wish to express to you
my gratitude for this storehouse of information for students and teachers of
Chaucer."), as well as the letters announcing the adopting of the *Complete
Works* for their classes listed in footnote 46. Five years after its publication,
Dorothy Everett (*Medium Aevum* 7 [1938]) mentions that the volume had

become "the edition most commonly referred to in scholarly work on Chaucer" (213). J. Burke Severs of Lehigh University (31 May 1933) predicted that Robinson's would "be the standard edition of Chaucer for many years to come." And J[efferson] B[utler] Fletcher, the Columbia University medievalist and Dante specialist (9 November 1933), contended that "[s]urely Chaucer is edited for good and all."

58. W[ilbur] O[wen] Sypherd, letter to Robinson written on 1 May 1933.

59. Wirt A[rmistead] Cate in a letter to Robinson dated 7 August 1933. James H. Powers, reviewing the edition for the 13 May 1933 issue of the *Boston Daily Globe*, called it "as humanly interesting in its commentaries as the poet himself continues to be in his verses." The editor of the *Globe*, Charles H. Taylor, to whom Robinson had sent a personal copy of the *Complete Works*, immediately sent him "100 copies" of the review "printed with the Globe slug on them" (letter to Robinson, 13 May 1933). See further L[e] B[aron] R[ussell] Briggs's letter to Robinson of 9 May 1933, in which Robinson's former colleague and Dean stresses how the *Complete Works* would "help every reader from the Chaucerian down to the solitary and untrained lover of poetry;" and Paull F. Baum's letter to Robinson of 20 April 1933, in which he states that the volume "is a splendid work which will lighten the labor of many teachers of Chaucer and be a boon to every reader" (Baum was a Chaucerian at the University of North Carolina, Chapel Hill). Herbert Drennon, although not a Chaucerian specialist, wrote a review of the *Complete Works* for *Englische Studien* (69 [1935]: 406–7). In a letter to Robinson accompanying a copy of that review (dated 1 March 1935), he confirms how Robinson had rendered a "splendid service" to "all interested readers of that noted fourteenth-century writer."

60. *Complete Works*, xxxii.

61. Brandl, in his *Archiv* review, 267–68.

62. Tatlock, *Speculum*, 459–60. M. B. Ruud, in his review for the *Modern Language Notes*, similarly situates the editorial principles governing the *Complete Works* between "easy eclecticism of Skeat" and "the rather excessive conservatism of Mr. Manly" (330).

63. Roy Vance Ramsey, "F. N. Robinson's Editing of the *Canterbury Tales*," *Studies in Bibliography* 42 (1989): 134–52, here 148. Ramsey confirmed his findings about Robinson in his 1994 monograph, *The Manly-Rickert Text of the Canterbury Tales* (Lewiston, NY: Edwin Mellen), esp. 22–43. A German reviewer, Hermann Heuer (*Anglia Beiblatt* 45 [1934]: 201–4, here 202–3), had already indicated the discrepancy between Robinson's claims and the reality of his editorial practice: "The examples mentioned on p. xxxiii [of Robinson's "Introduction"] do not attest to much methodological audacity, because in almost all cases Skeat and the respective

editors of the Globe edition or even both had established the same text. I found a similar result during a random check (C.T. A 165–269) where only the rhyme *whelp:help* (A 257/258) presents a change from the other editors."

64. Robinson, "Introduction," xxxiii.

65. Ramsey, "F. N. Robinson's Editing," 150. Kathleen M. Hewitt-Smith's "Transcript Error and the Text of Troilus," *Studies in the Age of Chaucer* 13 (1991): 99–119, would support Ramsay's caveat about the unnoticed transmission of errors from earlier into later editions of Chaucer.

66. Reinecke, "F. N. Robinson," 238, comments on Robinson's use of such expressions as "critical," "superior archetype," and "trustworthy" in the "Introduction": "This is a little disconcerting, because of the ambiguities and subtle guardedness of 'due regard to critical principles,' 'best copies,' and 'enough others.' It is just this paragraph that the reviewers tended to fall upon. Surely Robinson knew that when he spoke of archetypes and critical editions nearly all would take him to mean what the German textual-criticism tradition had meant for a century."

67. The instance in which Robinson appears to have gone beyond Skeat and the printed tradition is in his collation of these printed sources with the Cardigan and the Morgan manuscripts of the *Canterbury Tales*. According to Daniel W. Mosser ("Witness Descriptions," *The Nun's Priest's Tale on CD-ROM*, ed. Paul Thomas [Birmingham, UK: Scholarly Digital Editions, 2006]; see further A. S. G. Edwards, "The Case of the Stolen Chaucer Manuscript," *The Book Collector* 21 [1972]: 380–85), the Cardigan manuscript (Cardigan HRC Pre-1700 MS 143) was stolen from the library of George L. Brudenell in Deene Park, Peterborough, England, in 1915, and later sold to Henry Noble MacCracken, acting for Vassar College, in 1923. It was recovered by the Brudenell family with the assistance of a detective in 1925, then deposited by the family in the British Museum for the use of John M. Manly and Elisabeth Rickert in 1935, and placed on indefinite loan to the Museum in 1937. It was sold through Sotheby's to the New York dealer H. P. Kraus and purchased by the Stark Library of the University of Texas at Austin (now part of the Harry Ransom Humanities Research Center at the University of Texas) in 1959. Robinson received access to the manuscript during its short stay at Vassar because of his close friendship with Henry McCracken, Vassar's President from 1915 to 1946 (see Robinson's "Preface," viii). However, unlike Clara Marburg, "Notes on the Cardigan Chaucer Manuscript," *PMLA* 41/2 (1926): 229–51, Robinson does not appear to have asked and/or have been granted permission by the actual owner of the manuscript, Major Robert Brudenell-Bruce, to publish the results of his collation. Robinson gained access to the Pierpont Morgan Manuscript of the *Canterbury Tales* through Belle da Costa Greene, the director of the Morgan Library (see "Preface," viii).

68. Robinson, "Introduction," xxxii–xxxiii. Patrick Geary's *Before France and Germany. The Creation and Transformation of the Merovingian World* (New York and Oxford: Oxford University Press, 1988) is a fine medievalist example of such a mitigating American perspective. Geary, whose goal was to extend the audience interested in Merovingian culture beyond the small group of academic specialists, challenges the dominant understanding of this crucial period, formulated long ago and "under the twin influences of nostalgia for the high cultural tradition of antiquity and of modern nationalistic fervor fanned by the fires of French-German hostilities. To the French, the Merovingian period has too often been seen as the first time (of many) when crude and faithless Germanic hordes would invade and occupy Gaul, plunging this civilized and urbane world into three centuries of darkness. For some German scholars of the past, the Merovingians represented the triumph of new and vigorous peoples over the decadent successors of Rome. The elements of these viewpoints have been eroded bit by bit, and little now remains. However, word of this demise has not reached much beyond academic circles, much less word of the new understanding of this crucial period which has taken its place. I hope to present the results of these important reappraisals and evaluations to a wider audience with little or no previous familiarity with this period of Continental history." A similarly illustrative example of the American medievalist *via media* from the beginning of the twentieth century is Josephine Burnham's decision to point out the futility of the altercation about the Englishness or Scottishness of the late medieval border romance *Thomas of Erceldoune*, when the dialect of the poem clearly showed both so-called English and Scottish forms ("A Study of Thomas of Erceldoune," *PMLA* 23 [1908)]: 375–420).

69. H[enry] N[oble] McC[racken], *Saturday Review of Literature* 10 (1933): 311. Brandl, *Archiv*, 267. Dorothy I. Morril of Hood College, MD (5 January 1934), compliments Robinson on the "sanity [...] of your judgment in the midst of conflicting theories."

70. Dorothy Everett, in her discussion in "Middle English," in *The Year's Work in English Studies*, 16 (1936), 103–23 [104], calls these sections "dubious": "The discussion of Chaucer's pronunciation seems hardly likely to content any kind of reader. It hints at unsolved problems in a manner calculated to disturb the unlearned without satisfying them, and it is not detailed enough to interest the philologist. The accounts of Chaucer's grammar and of the general principles underlying his versification are rather too brief even for a beginner." Brandl (*Archiv*, 268) finds fault with a host of features, especially the discussion of the "difficult issues of open and closed long e," which are "shrugged off" in two or three lines and the complete exclusion of pre-Middle stages of the language. Even its successor volume, the 1957 edition, was deemed "linguistically a little weak" by D. S. Brewer

(*Modern Language Review* 54 [1959]): 252; similarly, R. W. Zandvoort (*English Studies* 43 [1962]: 111 and 113) deemed the "linguistic apparatus" the "one weak spot" and thought that the section on pronunciation "leaves something to be desired" in both the first and the second edition.

71. Letter to Robinson, dated 7 June 1933. About one week earlier, on 29 May 1933, Hinckley had already assured Robinson that his edition would "not be superseded by Manly's. I predict that Manly will have a larger number of brilliant and original remarks, but that he will commit two, or perhaps even three, indiscretions where you have committed one. Indeed I am tempted to express this last point even more strongly. He will, of course, profit greatly by your work." Derek Pearsall, "Editing Medieval Texts: Some Developments and Some Problems," in *Textual Criticism and Literary Interpretation*, ed. Jerome J. McGann (Chicago: University of Chicago Press, 1985), 92–106, here 93, indicates that Robinson's "pragmatism" as editor led to the neglect of the "monumental edition of the *Canterbury Tales* by J. M. Manly and Edith Rickert (1940), which is rarely cited or used by Chaucer scholars. [...] [I]t makes clear [...] that Robinson's choice of base manuscripts was mistaken, and that the order of the tales he presents is not Chaucer's."

72. Ramsey, "F. N. Robinson's Editing," 151. See Robinson's "Introduction," xxxiv–xxxv: "[T]he editor has tried to give special consideration to old grammatical forms or idioms which might have been lost or corrupted by the scribes. [...] [T]hroughout all Chaucer's works [...] the spellings of the manuscripts have been corrected for grammatical accuracy and for the adjustment of rimes." Ramsey, *The Manly-Rickert Text*, 23, contends that Robinson's pragmatism even went so far as to neglect "Harvard's duplicate set of the same photostats of all the manuscripts [of the *Canterbury Tales*] that John Livingston Lowes had arranged for and that Manly, Rickert and their students were working with in Chicago." Robinson ("Introduction," xxxiii) declares that the only place in which these "photographs" have been "brought together" is the "University of Chicago, by Professor Manly and his associates, who are preparing a great critical edition."

73. Tatlock, *Speculum*, 460; Ruud, *Modern Language Notes*, 331; Ferguson, letter to Robinson, 14 January 1935; Brandl, *Archiv*, 267.

74. Letter to Robinson, 25 April 1933. Several others, among them Edmund T[aite] Silk of Yale University (14 May 1933) and Walter Clyde Curry of Vanderbilt University (19 October 1933), similarly remark on how much they appreciated finding their scholarship mentioned in the "Explanatory Notes", and Howard R. Patch of Smith College (11 May 1933) could "only add that as I turn the pages I am proud to be involved in any way" in the volume's "production." In fact, so closely did some of the scholars check for the inclusion of their achievements that they complained to Robinson if

they felt they had not been given proper credit for a specific idea. Henry B. Hinckley (29 May 1933), for example, was visibly disappointed that "you credit [Hyder] Rollins rather than myself with pointing out the resemblance between 'a whetstone is no kervyng instrument' [in *Troilus and Criseyde*] and the passage in the *Ars Poetica* of Horace."

75. Letter to Robinson, 12 June 1933.

76. Tom Shippey, translating Jacob Grimm's definition of "philology" from the *Deutsches Wörterbuch* in *The Road to Middle Earth* (Boston: Houghton Mifflin, 1983), 9. One of the most widely noticed of these altercations is the Nibelungenstreit between Germanists at the Universities of Berlin (Karl Müllenhoff, Karl Lachmann, Wilhelm Scherer) and Leipzig (Karl Bartsch, Friedrich Zarncke) about the question of the appropriate philological principles for a critical edition of the German epic. On this topic, see Rainer Kolk, *Berlin oder Leipzig? Eine Studie zur sozialen Organisation im "Nibelungenstreit"* (Tübingen: Max Niemeyer, 1990).

77. Edward Said, "How Not to Get Gored," in his *Reflections on Exile and Other Essays* (Cambridge: Harvard University Press, 2000), 230–38, here 230–32.

78. Henry B. Hinckley, letter to Robinson, 29 May 1933.

79. Robinson, "Preface," viii. Albert K. Potter (Brown University) expresses his appreciation for the "brief adequacy" of the explanatory notes in a letter to Robinson dated 27 September [1933]. Phyllis Portnoy ("The Best-Text/Best Book of Canterbury: The Dialogic of the Fragments," *Florilegium* 13 [1994]: 161–72, here 170) indicates that although "a critical edition purports to present the full range of critical opinion, the editor's introduction can effectively preclude such critical debate if this prime space is used as a forum for interpretative comments that are not identified as such." While Robinson is not guilty of such interpretive comments, his insistence on fashioning himself as harmless *compilator* without any interpretive intentions appears to have helped engender a similar silence as to his exact editorial practice.

80. Said, "How Not to Get Gored," 231.

81. This tendency to concentrate on recent studies, especially by U.S. scholars, is noted by Hugo Lange (*Deutsche Literaturzeitung* 10 [11 March 1934]: 450), who complains, in a review published in the section on "Germanische Literaturen," that Robinson had not cited essays Lange had published several years prior to 1933, but included Russell Krauss, Haldeen Braddy, and C. Robert Kase's *Three Chaucer Studies* of 1932. Dorothy Everett ("Middle English," 105, indicates that Robinson "is perhaps too inclined to give space to opinions merely because they are recent." Consequently, since U.S. scholars had published the lion's share among recent work on Chaucer, George R. Noyes, a professor of Slavic languages at the

University of California, Berkeley, in a long letter dated 16 May 1933, felt that Robinson's introductions and notes demonstrated that "the largest part of the advance [of Chaucer studies] seems due to American scholars – and the smallest to those in Great Britain."

82. See, for example, Robinson's letter of 12 July 1932 to Ernest P. Kuhl at the University of Iowa (Papers of Ernest Kuhl, Special Collections, University of Iowa Libraries, Iowa City, Iowa: RG 99.0064, Box 3). Reinecke, "F. N. Robinson," 232, suggests that his secure position at Harvard, his dedication to teaching, and his numerous professional responsibilities (for example, his presidency of the Modern Language Association of America) are the reasons why Robinson took twenty-nine years to finish the project.

83. Eleanor Prescott Hammond, *Chaucer. A Bibliographical Manual* (New York: Macmillan, 1908); interestingly, the volume was reprinted in New York with Smith Publishers in 1933); Dudley David Griffith, *A Bibliography of Chaucer: 1908–1924* (Seattle: University of Washington Press, 1926); Willard E. Martin, Jr., *A Chaucer Bibliography: 1925–1933* (Durham, NC: Duke University Press, 1935); Dudley David Griffith, *A Bibliography of Chaucer: 1908–1955* (Seattle: University of Washington Press, 1955).

84. Robinson, "Preface," vii, specifically mentions Brusendorff's *Chaucer Tradition* as helpful in "the further reconsideration of many matters." Robinson was attracted to Brusendorff's monograph (Oxford: Oxford University Press, 1925) because it provided authoritative surveys and bibliographies of entire areas of earlier scholarship, notably many of the philological specialty areas. The 1925 English monograph Robinson used was a revised and translated version of Brusendorff's originally Danish doctoral dissertation (University of Copenhagen, 1921). Unlike German Anglicists, who still thought they might retain German as one of the dominant languages in medieval studies, Brusendorff realized that the audience for a book on Chaucer written in Danish would be extremely limited. Sometimes, Robinson erased even long-standing altercations on a topic, as when he completely obliterates the twenty-odd-year altercation between Viktor Langhans and Hugo Lange on the priority of the "F" or the "G" version of the *Prologue* to the *Legend of Good Women*. Quite understandably, he must have regarded the vicious philological argument as futile, but his omission of a major Chaucerian conflict that consisted of one monograph and more than thirty essays and reviews was a judgment call that throws an interesting light on his definition of a factual survey of scholarship. Albert C. Baugh, in his bibliographic essay surveying the first "Fifty Years of Chaucer Scholarship" in the twentieth century (*Speculum* 26 [1951]: 659–72, here 667), agreed with Robinson on the futility of the conflict, but nevertheless described and

evaluated it for his audience: "There would be little point in following here the long controversy between Hugo Lange and Viktor Langhans which ran through ten years of *Anglia* before the editor finally closed the journal to it. Langhans' view that only the G-Prologue, preserved in a single manuscript, is genuine is fantastic. Lange, though accepting the priority of the F version, maintained the view, widely held in the nineteenth century, that the God of Love and Alceste represent Richard and Anne, merely adding to the heraldic argument. The objections to this view were pointed out by Lowes […] and by Kittredge […]." J[ohn] M. Steadman, Jr., in his review of Willard E. Martin's 1935 *A Chaucer Bibliography: 1925–1933* (*South Atlantic Bulletin* 2.1 [1936]: 3–4, here 4), also notices the German obsession with this aporia. On the Lange-Langhans conflict, see the chapter "Duelling Philologists: Viktor Langhans vs. Hugo Lange," in Utz, *Chaucer and the Discourse of German Philology*, 191–204.

85. L[e] B[aron] R[ussell] Briggs in his letter to Robinson of 9 May 1933.

86. See, for example, Arthur Sales's telling comment in the *Cambridge Review* of 18 January 1958, 233, that "[a]dditions [to the second edition] tend to be new references rather than explanations." Similarly, the anonymous reviewer in the *Times Literary Supplement* of 13 June 1958, 327, observes: "The bulk of the notes in the former [1933] edition remain unchanged; it is a tribute to Professor Robinson's care and accuracy that only amplifications and no alterations appear to have been necessary." The only voice to disagree with the general chorus of praise about the explanatory notes was Frederick Tupper, who ("Chaucer and the Cambridge Edition," *Journal of English and Germanic Philology* 39 [1940]: 503–26) accused Robinson of "critical excesses […] committed in the name of caution" (503). Tupper saw in Robinson's pragmatic précis of his scholarship on the seven deadly sins in the *Canterbury Tales* a falsification of facts, things "I have never and at any time claimed" (513).

87. The first quotation is by E[rnest] P[eter] Kuhl (1881–1981), in an undated letter (written on a "Sunday," presumably in the second half of 1933) to Robinson on "State University of Iowa" letterhead and indicating that "[f]or months it has been on my mind to tell you about your edition of Chaucer." H[enry] N[oble] McCracken made the remark in the second quote during his 1933 Commencement speech as President of Vassar College (reported by Chester N. Greenough, a Harvard English professor and former Dean of Harvard College, in a letter to Robinson dated 15 June 1933), and the remark in the third quotation in his review of the *Complete Works* for the *Saturday Review of Literature* 10 (1933): 311. McCracken had congratulated Robinson in a personal letter as early as 1 May 1933, in which he calls the *Complete Works* "a great achievement, and an honor to *our*

scholarship" (my emphasis). For a recent example of the significance some
U.S. Chaucerians attach to the first edition of the *Canterbury Tales*
"published by an American," see the web pages of Arnold A. Sanders,
Goucher College, Baltimore, MD (<http://faculty.goucher.edu/eng330/
chronological_view.htm>, accessed 20 September 2009).
    88. Helming, *Speculum* 33.1 (1958): 123–25, here 123 and 124.
George R. Noyes (16 May 1933) had predicted this success: "All in all your
edition will definitely supersede Skeat and the Globe [edition] as that for the
average man and the average student – and as a key to the subject for the
professional student. It ought to have this success even in England."
Carleton Brown, Chaucerian and secretary of the Modern Language Association of America, stated in a letter to Robinson, dated 17 May 1933: "Hence-
forth we shall use the Robinson Chaucer." As Joseph A. Dane ("Copy-Text
and its Variants in Some Recent Chaucer Editions," *Studies in Bibliography*
44 [1991]: 164–83, here 177) has argued, Larry D. Benson's third edition
(1987), rather than superseding the authority of Robinson's first and second
editions, actually enhanced their status as the canonical edition(s) of Chaucer's works. Houghton Mifflin Publishers, on the title page of the current
Riverside Chaucer, memorialize Robinson's "author function" by reminding
readers that this third edition is "based on *The Works of Geoffrey Chaucer.*
Edited by F. N. Robinson."
    89. One could include in this process of "Americanization" the final-
izing of the *Chaucer Concordance* by J. S. P. Tatlock and Arthur G. Kennedy
(published through the Carnegie Foundation in 1927) after the sudden
death of Ewald Flügel, the Stanford philologist from Leipzig to whom Frederick James Furnivall had entrusted the project and who had intended it not
only as a Chaucer concordance but a fully blown dictionary with sample
quotations from a large number of other Middle English texts and texts from
other languages. Brandl, in his *Archiv* review (153 [1928]: 264–66, here,
265) of the *Concordance*, stresses somewhat jealously how "the power of capitalist funding" rendered possible the completion of the mega-project and
resignedly underlines the role of Flügel, who embodied the "enormous entre-
preneurial spirit that characterized our countrymen" before World War I.
Another publication indicative of the gradual American colonization of
Medieval Studies during this period is J. E. Wells's *A Manual of the Writings
in Middle English* (New Haven, CT: Yale University Press, 1916–). Finally, as
the attractiveness of the U.S. academy for the British Chaucerian Caroline
Spurgeon (1869–1942) demonstrates, the increasing American hegemony
over medieval studies and marginalization of European scholars and their
foundational achievements led, at the same time, to a democratic inclusive-
ness within U.S. medieval studies for women scholars. On this phenomenon, see Renate Haas, "Caroline Spurgeon, English Studies, the United

States and Internationalism," *Studia Anglica Posnaniensia* 38 (2002): 215–28.

90. Baugh, "Fifty Years," 659–60. Baugh underlines that U.S. scholars reached their supremacy "undaunted by the achievements of the nineteenth century" (659). Robinson, in his "Anniversary Reflections" (*Speculum* 25.4 [1950]: 491–501) began writing the glorious "pre-history" of "American" medieval scholarship just as the German Anglicists had begun writing the genealogies of their founding fathers thirty years into the existence of their discipline: "There were strong men before Agamemnon and worthy American medievalists before the Academy," he opines, and then praises a list of "[p]ioneers" from Child through Kittredge and Manly (493–94). Steadman, in his review of W. E. Martin's *A Chaucer Bibliography* (1935) for the *South Atlantic Bulletin* (2/1 [April 1936]: 3–4, here 4), revels in listing the numbers of studies on Chaucer according to the authors' countries of origin and lists "outstanding contributions to Chaucer scholarship between 1924 and 1933," including ten titles by Americans, one by a Dane (Brusendorff), and one by a British scholar (McCormick).

91. Already in 1951 ("Fifty Years," 659), Baugh had made the *pro domo* claim that "[i]n Germany Chaucer studies never really flourished," although his own bibliography lists fifty reviews, fourteen scholarly notes, almost fifty articles, five textual editions, and more than forty doctoral dissertations in the first fifteen years of the twentieth century alone. Paul Ruggiers (1918–98), who founded the New Chaucer Society, the *Variorum Chaucer*, and edited *Editing Chaucer*, rightly canonizes William Caxton, William Thynne, John Stow, Thomas Speght, John Urry, Thomas Tyrwhitt, Thomas Wright, Frederick James Furnivall, Walter W. Skeat, Robert K. Root, John M. Manly, Edith Rickert, and F. N. Robinson, but his Anglo-American prejudice – it is ironic that the volume's subtitle, *The Great Tradition*, should be the same as the title of the patriotic textbook edited by Edwin Greenlaw and James Holly Hanford in 1922 – made him disregard John Koch (1850–1934), who published more criticism and did more editorial work on Chaucer than any other Chaucerian except Walter W. Skeat. In the assumption that Chaucer exclusively belongs to the Anglo-American (great) tradition, Ruggiers and his collaborators join Skeat's own defensively patriotic reaction against the German(ic) philological invasions into British textual territory. Ruggiers ("Introduction," 2) calls his volume an "attempt to provide an overview of the evolution of the editions of Chaucer." By implication, then, the numerous contributions of German Chaucerians to the history of editing Chaucer are evolutionary dead ends.

92. Ramsey, "F. N. Robinson's Editing," 151.

93. Robinson, "Preface to the Second Edition," *The Works of Geoffrey*

Chaucer, x. For some of the central lacunae of Reinecke's findings, see Ramsey, *The Manly-Rickert Text*, 23–37.

94. Joseph A. Dane, "Copy-Text and its Variants in some Recent Chaucer Editions," *Studies in Bibliography* 44 (1991): 164–83, here 183, fn. 30. In fact, Bartlett Jere Whiting, Reinecke's Harvard thesis advisor, worked as Robinson's "secretary" for the 1933 edition (see Reinecke, "F. N. Robinson," 233).

95. I was educated in Germany, at the University of Regensburg (1981–85; 1986–90; Dr. phil., 1990; advisor: Karl Heinz Göller) and Williams College (1985–86) and have taught English language and literature at the Pädagogische Hochschule Dresden (1990–91), the University of Northern Iowa (1991–96; 1998–2007), the University of Tübingen (1996–98), and Western Michigan University (2007–09). As I found out, one cannot be too careful about claiming independence from Robinson's pervasive influence and hegemony: The edition in which I first encountered Chaucer, a brightly orange dual-language volume (Middle English and German) by Reclam publishers, Stuttgart, which accompanied Karl Heinz Göller's lecture course on "Chaucer" in the summer term of 1982 at the University of Regensburg, used Robinson's second edition as the source for its Middle English text. During the academic year abroad at Williams College, Sherron Knopp assigned "Robinson II" to a dozen eager students taking her "Chaucer" seminar. During our first class meeting, she distributed a copy of a *Peanuts* cartoon meant to calm our fears about reading Middle English. In it, Peppermint Patty says to Franklin: "It's really good stuff once you crack the code." I sincerely hope to have done so, belatedly, in this essay. National mentalities are, of course, still palpable in some current medieval studies, as Elizabeth Scala's review of A. C. Spearing's *Textual Subjectivity* (2005) suggests (*The Medieval Review*, 4 August 2007, <http://hdl.handle.net/2027/spo.baj9928.0804.007>, accessed 23 September 2009). My goal with this investigation is not a revisionist critique of the very Chaucer industry in which I work, but to historicize some of that industry's unspoken assumptions by a comparison of mentalities and their accompanying practices in Germany, the United States, and Britain.

96. For the clearly philological orientation of his teaching, see, for example, the lecture notes by Ernest G. Moll, an M.A. student in Robinson's lecture course on "Historical English Grammar" during the academic year 1922–23 (MS 9238 Ernest G. Moll [1900–97] Box 12, Folder 21, housed in the National Library of Australia). Moll's notes indicate Robinson's dedication to historical linguistics from the Celtic through the late Middle English period and his ample reliance on German and other European scholarship. I am grateful to Mr. Richard E. Moll for granting me permission to copy and read his father's 78-page manuscript.

97. For the *Complete Works*, one single letter from a British colleague, the famous historian George C. Coulton (3 June 1933) remains. Only two other Europeans, Emile Legouis (France; 12 June 1933) and Tarquinio Vallese (Italy; 24 June 1933) appear to have acknowledged receipt of complimentary copies. While Robinson acknowledges British institutions and their librarians for providing photocopies of manuscripts, he acknowledges "assistance" and "advice" exclusively from U.S. colleagues and friends ("Preface," viii).

False Memories:
The Dream of Chaucer and Chaucer's Dream in the Medieval Revival

Richard H. Osberg*

Introduction

In 1892, when Thomas Lounsbury published in his *Studies in Chaucer* a chapter, "The Chaucer Legend," systematically debunking the spurious elements that had accreted in the Chaucer biography from Leland to Godwin and beyond, the scholarly evidence he marshaled had been available, in some cases, for more than fifty years; and the de-accession of inauthentic works from the Chaucer canon, upon which many of these narratives were founded, was by that time rapidly accelerated. Nonetheless, Lounsbury notes, "no fictitious story connected with Chaucer's career has ever been wholly abandoned. It may be modified, but it is never contemptuously cast aside."[1] This resistance to biographical scholarship suggests that what Stephanie Trigg has called the "cultural formation and institutional force of Chaucer" in the nineteenth century[2] – that is, the Chaucer represented, for instance, in Arthur Burrell's 1908 modernized Everyman edition, *Chaucer's Canterbury Tales for the Modern Reader* – was significantly different from that of the twentieth-century Chaucer embodied in the Riverside edition:[3] he is a nineteenth-century Chaucer whose biography and poetic oeuvre say much about how the medieval revival

---

* This article was completed by Alan Gaylord following Richard H. Osberg's untimely death in 2007. See the Appendix for an appreciation and a list of Professor Osberg's writings.

intersected with popular and literary conceptions of the fourteenth century and its foremost poet.[4]

Ironically, Chaucer's cultural formation in the nineteenth century may well be indebted less to his poetry, which almost everyone agrees was not widely read, than it is to the Chaucer biography and its ancillary materials – Prefaces, Books of Days, Birthday Books, and so on – that made up the popular body of Chaucer representations.

In 1841, a volume of Chaucer selections began its introduction with the issue of Chaucer's unfamiliarity:

> The present publication does not result from an antiquarian feeling about Chaucer, as the Father of English poetry [...]; but from the extraordinary fact, to which there is no parallel in the history of the literature of nations, – that although he is one of the great poets for all time, his works are comparatively unknown to the world. Even in his own country, only a very small class of his countrymen ever read his poems.[5]

Works like Charles Cowden Clarke's *The Riches of Chaucer*[6] create the nineteenth-century "Dream of Chaucer," and continue to exert influence on twentieth-century cultural constructions of Chaucer. On regarding Chaucer as a nature poet, for instance, Burrell remarks, "Other poets write about the beauties of the outer world. To none of them does Chaucer yield; as a lover of sunlight, of birds, of the golden world he stands with the Psalmists and with Wordsworth" – here echoing Thoreau's 1843 comparison of Chaucer to that Romantic nature poet *par excellence*.[7] Burrell's edition, too, takes as its epigraph Longfellow's sonnet, "An old man in a lodge within a park,"[8] one of several by the poet that associates Chaucer with Woodstock Park, and with what now has become a critical cliché of neo-literary history: "romantic isolation."[9]

That is, the Chaucer represented in Burrell's edition is a nineteenth-century Chaucer whose biography and poetic oeuvre say much about how the medieval revival "remembered" the fourteenth century and its foremost poet. Two false memories in particular – the first, "Chaucer's exile to Zealand" and, upon his return to England, "his imprisonment in the Tower" (both the result of his putative involvement in the affairs of John of Northampton against Sir Nicholas Brember for election as Lord Mayor in 1382); and second, "Chaucer in retirement in the park at Woodstock" – provide opportunities for examining the specific cultural formations associated with long-lived conceptions of Chaucer in the popular imagination. Although at first blush these two spurious accounts seem unrelated, they are, as I hope to show, part of a larger pattern of meaning that maps onto the fourteenth century a number of nineteenth-century ideals about sincerity and honor (elements of middle-class Victorian patriarchal ideology) as well as romantic isolation and rural Englishness – a pattern that, as one biographer put it, "gives us a moving picture of the poet's sufferings, but at the same time displays the unconquerable power and energy of his mind, the harmony and tranquillity of which no outward circumstances were able to disturb."[10]

Dreaming Backwards

The voice here, however, could hardly be called that of a biographer, even though it is the author's, writing the 32-page "A Life of Geoffrey Chaucer," placed after Horne's long introduction, and before the Chaucerian material begins. But no better spokesman could be discovered for the Patriarchy – guardians of the literature and the morality of the British Empire – than the person of "Professor Leonhard Schmitz." The name is rarely invoked in histories of Chaucerian scholarship, probably because the professor wrote no books, edited no editions, and gave no lectures on Geoffrey Chaucer. But he was a thoroughly educated and prolific scholar of the Latin classics and Roman history, which no doubt gave him unquestioned authority as a writer on Chaucer. An examination of his obituary in the *Annual Register* for 1890 (158–59) recounts his German birth and education (Bonn Ph.D.), his move to England, and his fame as a scholar and schoolmaster (tutoring Prince Albert at one point); but in the listing of his many books there is no mention of medieval literary studies, let alone of Chaucer.

There are two issues regarding his treatment of Chaucer's life, the one dealing with Schmitz's accuracy, the other with his attitudes. In his biography he deals forcefully with the first of our "false memories," as he establishes the context for the Northampton affair as a plot by "adherents of the old Church" to destroy the influence of John of Gaunt and Wicliffite reformers. "In one of these contests," Schmitz continues:

the life of Chaucer was endangered, and he only saved himself by seeking shelter in a foreign land. In the year 1384 two men, Sir Nicholas Brember and John of Northampton, were brought forward as candidates to the mayorship of the city of London. The former was supported by the government, the latter, a man of great integrity, and a declared friend of the Wickliffites, by the popular party. When the contest grew hot, and the people broke out in open rebellion, Chaucer joined the party of Northampton. But the insurrection was soon suppressed; John of Northampton was taken into custody, and an active search was made after his confederates. Chaucer, in fear of being likewise imprisoned, and of being compelled to betray those of his friends who had taken a prominent part in the riot, fled from England.[11]

This is almost entirely fabrication, or even worse, supposition.

The persistence of these false memories that map nineteenth-century medievalist ideals and concomitant codes of patriarchy onto the constellation of texts representing "Chaucer" ultimately reflects medievalism's own dreaming of a Middle Ages as refuge from nineteenth-century industrialism, commerce, spiritual aridity, and moral compromise.

Chaucer's supposed role in the Northampton affair and its aftermath was first described in John Dart's biography, prefixed to Urry's 1721 edition,[12] and was derived in large measure from the fifteenth-century "Testament of Love" by Thomas Usk, often (but no longer) attributed to Chaucer. The narrative is given full expression in the first volume of William Godwin's 1803 *Life of Chaucer*, of which Lounsbury writes: "Godwin's life of the poet may indeed be declared to deserve the distinction of being the most worthless piece of biography in the English language – certainly the most worthless produced by a man of real ability."[13] And yet there is some value in this apparently wasted work, taken in the sense of something foundational, something that was so influential that not only its assumptions about Chaucer and his age, but also his style of eloquence, were influential for more than half a century.

From the point of view of early Chaucer studies, Godwin's book might be called huge, though in several ways – even as it reveals itself – somewhat disingenuously, as being limited and even superficial. It is in two thick quarto volumes, and its aims are large and wide. For my present study, its stated aims are more informative than definitive, for his preface (1803) lays out a program of medievalism that is ambitious, non-academic, and amateur. It is also an appeal to the many readers he hoped to have, that they would follow him in recuperating a too-much-neglected and too-often-misunderstood author. Here are some telling parts of his program:

> Chaucer fixed and naturalised the genuine art of poetry in our island. (vii)

> The first and direct object of this work, is to erect a monument to his name, and, as far as the writer was capable of doing it, to produce an interesting and amusing book in modern English, enabling the reader, who might shrink from the labour of mastering the phraseology of Chaucer, to do justice to his illustrious countryman [...]. Many might by its means be induced to study the language of our ancestors, and the elements and history of our vernacular speech [...]. (vii–viii)

> We must observe what Chaucer felt and saw, how he was educated, what species of learning he pursued, and what were the objects, the events and the persons, successively presented to his view, before we can strictly and philosophically understand his biography. (viii)

> I can pretend only to have written a superficial work [...]. It was my purpose to produce a work of a new species. Antiquities have too generally been regarded as the province of men of cold tempers and sterile imaginations [...]. It was my wish [...] to carry the workings of fancy and the spirit of philosophy into the investigation of ages past. I was anxious to rescue for a moment the illustrious dead from the jaws of the grave, to make them pass in review before me, to question their spirits and record their answers. I wished to make myself their master of the ceremonies, to introduce my reader to their familiar speech, and to enable him to feel for the instant as if he had lived with Chaucer. (ix, x–xi)

If such ambitions, or at least the ambitious imagery, verge on necrophilia, it must be said that Godwin had intended to go into the historic written records to revive these words from the dead, and that although he would have preferred to take his sources to his room for study, he resigned himself to working in the British Museum; and yet, he confesses, under pressure from his "bookseller," he had to stop his

excavations before he came to the period of the *Canterbury Tales* and
threatened to overflow into a third quarto![14] Thus, cut off more or less
at the knees, Godwin joins the company of well-intentioned but
handicapped amateurs who, for part of a century, stood as "authorities" in things medieval and Chaucerian ... until the rising tides of
philology, scholarship, and academe flooded over their copious but
shallow publications. And yet, so many of their ideologies, their attitudes, and their factoids had at the very least a half-life, even a potent
memory, of events falsely construed and communicated!

Clearly, Lounsbury did not find all this amusing: "Even when his
facts were accurate, the conclusions that he allowed himself to found
upon them bore about the same relation to the truth that the incidents of a dream do to the actual events that may have inspired
them."[15]

It is the nature of that "dream" and particularly its persistence that
I wish to interrogate.

Alterity Nationalized

The sometimes hilarious compositions derived from a patchwork of
distorted facts and factoids litter the landscape of biography I want to
explore, but the "dream" is a larger, less cohesive, but culturally more
profound phenomenon.[16] It was neither static nor fossilized, as illustrated by Schmitz's "Life of Chaucer," affixed in 1841 to *The Poems of
Geoffrey Chaucer Modernized* (an edition that included translations by
Wordsworth, Leigh Hunt, Elizabeth A. Barrett, and Richard Hengist
Horne). The category of "modernization" reveals at once the medieval
revival's desire to install Chaucer and his writings (incorrectly multi-
plied) near the top of the canon of medieval English literature, and
also the recognition that many readers were put off from encountering
his poetry by its archaic language.[17] Lounsbury dismisses this enter-
prise of Horne's as a disaster, whose principal failing was simply a lack
of sufficient intelligence. Since accuracy is his theme here, all he has
for Schmitz is this scornful sentence: "[the volume contains a] life of
Chaucer by Leonhard Schmitz, which was particularly careful to
retain every misstatement of fact that the craziest conjectures of
previous biographers had succeeded in imposing upon the world as
actual incidents in the career of the poet."[18]

In the speculative mode that drove Lounsbury to distraction, Schmitz avers, contradicting Godwin:

> It is not clear whether he was accompanied by his wife in his exile, and we may therefore reasonably conclude that she was not living, because, from their well-known attachment to each other, it is not likely she would have left him at a time when her tenderness was more than ever necessary to render his life endurable.[19]

This instance of supposititious "reasonable concluding" is nugatory; but more relevant here is the preoccupation with Chaucer and Phillipa's relationship in various of these accounts that reinforces the pattern of patriarchal ideology – one, according to Anthony Harrison, that "promulgated a belief in the spiritual power of love and in the positive moral influence of women."[20]

Schmitz's conclusion regarding Chaucer's deportment in the Northampton fiasco:

> It is indeed not difficult for a moralist to lay down general rules of conduct, but he too often forgets to take into account the real character of human nature, and to consider that a thousand circumstances may render an action, in itself blameable, if looked upon in the abstract, not only excusable, but even justifiable, because it has become a matter of physical necessity.[21]

in fact, echoes Godwin's, and will itself be quoted at length in the 1896 edition of Charles Cowden Clarke's *Riches of Chaucer*.[22]

In 1844, the antiquarian Sir Nicholas Harris Nicolas published a "memoir" on Chaucer (prefixed the following year to the Aldine edition) presenting documents proving Chaucer had, in the period 1380 to 1388, received half of his pension, semi-annually, with his own hand, and so could not have been in exile in Zealand in the period 1384–86;[23] furthermore, Nicolas shows that in 1386, when Chaucer was reputedly in prison, he was in fact a member of Parliament and a knight of the shire from Kent.

Despite these documents, the false memory of Chaucer's exile persisted, altered subtly to accommodate where possible the inconvenient facts. The dates, for instance, were pushed back to the period 1386 to 1388 (when Chaucer had lost his position at Customs); Cowden Clarke maintains that Chaucer received his remuneration by deputy (a phrase he italicizes);[24] and as late as 1894, in a new and revised edition with illustrations from the Ellesmere MS, an edition dedicated to Furnivall "in grateful acknowledgment of his work on Chaucer and his help in the present revision," John Saunders writes of the Northampton affair, "Sir Harris Nicolas certainly shows that the story as it stands, cannot possibly be true; on the other hand, the passages of Chaucer's *Testament of Love*, on which Godwin chiefly relies, do, it appears to us, show that there is truth of some kind in it."[25]

Even four years after Lounsbury published "The Chaucer Legend," the fourth edition of Charles Cowden Clarke's *The Riches of Chaucer* (1896) still offers its "new" memoir of 1835 that repeats the fictitious story: "It appears, from collateral evidence, that his wife Philippa, accompanied him in his exile."[26] Clarke also praises Chaucer's selflessness in attempting to "screen his accomplices," and he quotes from the following from Godwin to draw his moral:

> If Chaucer, who had witnessed the anarchy of his country, and the tragical scenes which were transacted almost in his presence, who had been reduced to barter his last resources for bread, and who saw an affectionate wife and a cherished offspring in danger to perish for want, felt at length subdued and willing to give up somewhat of the sternness of his virtue, we may condemn him as moralists, but we cannot fail in some degree to sympathize with feelings which make an essential part of our nature.[27]

Franklin Court has suggested that a philosophical foundation in Adam Smith's *The Theory of Moral Sentiments* makes possible "the formalized study of biographical models and characters in literary texts as examples of ethical behavior,"[28] and in their attachment to this account of Chaucer in exile, the biographers reveal their underlying motives as ethicists. On the one hand, the poet's beliefs and mode of conduct are encoded in a medievalist discourse largely governed by patriarchal ideology. Anthony Harrison argues that these terms include "such patriarchal ideals as chivalry, manliness, selflessness, gallantry, nobility, honor, duty, and fidelity (to the crown as well as to a beloved)."[29] On the other hand, the converse is suggested by Schmitz's phrase "the real character of human nature." As Charlotte C. Morse has noted, "Politically, Cowden Clarke was always a reformer. The circles within which he moved were forming up before the 1820s,

the time by which, Gerald Newman argues, English culture had
converted to the new model of sincerity, the complex virtue at the
heart of Victorian middle class culture."[30] Sincerity is, indeed, one of
the hallmark virtues associated with Chaucer, as in James Russell
Lowell's remark: "so sweet is it to mark how his plainness and
sincerity outlive all changes of the outward world."[31] This understanding of sincerity as a common bond, evidence of a trans-historical
human nature that links the poet sympathetically to his readers
despite the obscurities of language and the barbarism of his age,
furthermore, is constructed from Chaucer's decision to sacrifice his
honor for the sake of his family: in Godwin's words, we sympathize
"with feelings which make an essential part of our nature."[32]

Escaping to Live with Mother

"Chaucer's Dream" (now known as "The Isle of Ladies"[33]), too, has its
role in what Lounsbury terms "The most widespread and enduring
[…] of all the legendary stories connected with Chaucer […] the one
which makes him a resident of Woodstock."[34] For it is in this poem
that Godwin finds a description that:

> sufficiently answers to the geography of Woodstock Park; in which
> are contained a spring of water, called Rosamond's Well from the
> celebrated Rosamond Clifford, mistress to Henry II; and another
> (not far from the house still denominated in the deeds and legal
> instruments in which it is described, Chaucer's House) called
> Queen's Pool in memory of Philippa queen to Edward III.[35]

Originating in a passing reference in Leland's life ("He left Lewis
as the heir of his fortunes, whatever they were, and especially of his
villa at Woodstock, adjoining the palace of the king." [l. 141]), as well
as from confusion with his son Thomas (who did own property at
Woodstock), the association of the poet with the town took various
forms. "For centuries," writes Lounsbury:

> the story was generally accepted and widely repeated on the
> authority originally of Speght, that "the place of his most abode
> was a fair house of stone next to the king's place," and that he
> "took great pleasure to lie there, in regard of the park, in sundry of

his writings, much by him commended as also to be near the court where his best friends were, and they who were able to do him most pleasure."[36]

Lounsbury notes that:

> near the royal park was a tenement which, as late certainly as 1436, was called Hanwell House. In the sixteenth century it had acquired the title of Chaucer's House, and under that name was disposed of several times during the reigns of Elizabeth and of James I. As late as 1871 the residence, on changing hands, was advertised under the name of Chaucer's House.[37]

It is still called "Chaucer's House" today.

E. G. Stanley argues that "The memory of Chaucer at Woodstock has faded away, or, rather, it survives only, not undelightfully, in minor verse of the eighteenth century and in enthusiastic or foolish prose in the century that followed."[38] Nonetheless, the cultural trajectory of that prose should not be underestimated, for it shaped two powerful ideas about Chaucer. First, the Woodstock myth projected the image of solitary Chaucer, for whom the invention of the *Canterbury Tales* was entirely a recuperative exercise of imagination and fancy. Second, the Woodstock myth perpetuated the idea of Chaucer as a nature poet, whose solitary morning walks, memorializing the landscapes of Blenheim, helped to codify a sense of pastoral Englishness, even as that rural landscape became inscribed on a medievalized London.

The myth of poetic recuperation, found both in would-be serious scholarship – as in J. Hales's 1882 essay, "Chaucer at Woodstock,"[39] for instance – and in more popular venues like *Chambers' Book of Days* (1869) and John Lord's *Beacon Lights of History* (Vol. 3. Part 2, 1902) (both still available on the web), is clearly limned in Hales's assertion that Chaucer "had a reverse of fortune [...] and was even imprisoned in the Tower;" and Robert Chambers seems to know even more:

> Here, it is said, either faltering in courage through the rigour of his confinement, or provoked by the ingratitude of certain accomplices, he informed against the rest, and regained his liberty. For some time after, though he retained apparently many of his grants, Chaucer seems to have been in rather low water. He describes himself as "being berafte out of dignitie of office, in which he

made a gatheringe of worldly godes."(Oct. 25th); – but [returning
to Hales] "at fifty-one he gave up his public duties ... and retired
to Woodstock and spent the remainder of his fortunate life in
dignified leisure and literary labors."[40]

Godwin further elevates the poet from his retirement at Woodstock to
a later residency at Doddington Castle (another false memory in the
biographical apocrypha! – this one a Gothic nightmare), but Peter
Brown offers a modern critical framework for analyzing these
Godwinian flights of fancy and their cultural/anthropological implications:

> Many of the rural descriptions in his works have been traced to
> this favourite scene of his walks and studies and it is at Woodstock
> that Chaucer wrote the *Canterbury Tales* [...]. Such connections
> may strike us as tenuous and specious, but in a sense that is not the
> point. What we are dealing with here is the sanctioning of place by
> virtue of its association with a writer presumed to have lived there,
> a place which is supposed to have prompted the thoughts, feelings,
> and descriptions that eventuated in great poetry. It is an attempt to
> get nearer to the mysteries of the creative process, while idolizing
> the individual through whom they were channeled [...]. A large
> part of the appeal of the places he describes stems from their state
> of ruin or absence, which stirs nostalgia in the contemplation of
> change and decay, and romantic feelings of desolation and
> sadness.[41]

Thus the period "at Woodstock Park" remains for the biographer
both a natural reaction to the stress of Chaucer's political misadventures in the Northampton affair and the culmination of his poetic
genius and career:

> Being now more than sixty years of age, he retired to his favourite
> residence of Woodstock. He was tired of business and of courts,
> and wished to enjoy the pleasures of privacy and nature. He did
> not however retire to a life of indolence. As he had begun his
> literary career early, so he finished it late. In a green and vigorous
> old age he planned and undertook *The Canterbury Tales*. One of
> the most extraordinary specimens of active genius and various
> talent which England has produced, thus appears to have been the
> fruit of a period of life, when common men think themselves
> excused from further exertion.

Chaucer was probably satisfied with his modest roof at Woodstock. *The Canterbury Tales* may be seen to have been the production of a serene, a cheerful and contented mind, buffeted by the world, but not broken, and carrying off from all its defeatures and misadventures whatever is most valuable in man.[42]

Godwin suggests here that without adversity, without political exile and misfortune, without "defeatures," Chaucer could not have winnowed out "whatever is most valuable in man." Note, too, the underlying metaphor of vegetable growth: Chaucer is "green and vigorous"; his poetry is "fruit." This romantic vision of Chaucer rooted in the park at Woodstock, in tranquility recollecting the hard lessons of court and his personal failures is, of course, completely at odds with a contending nineteenth-century view of Chaucer as an urbane, sophisticated man-of-the-world, but the idea of romantic isolation continued, nonetheless, to exert considerable influence in popular conceptions of the poet.

The cultural force of these false memories can be seen, for instance, in Edward Burne-Jones's illustration of Chaucer for the Kelmscott edition with which Steve Ellis begins his study of Chaucer's reception in the late nineteenth and twentieth centuries. Quoting Derek Brewer, Ellis notes the "'isolation' of the Kelmscott Chaucer," and how its "Romantic medievalising [...] is at odds with the predominant interest in Chaucer's humor and realism that characterizes Victorian responses."[43] He notes that Chaucer's "gregariousness, his urbanism, his 'man-of-the-world' status – find no echo" in the Kelmscott illustration. In fact, just the opposite is the case, as in this quotation from *Tales from Chaucer in Prose, designed chiefly for the use of young persons by Charles Cowden Clarke* (London, 1870 [2nd ed.]) (See also his *The Riches of Chaucer.*) Especially useful are the passages on nature and the defense of Chaucer's betrayal of friends:

Few persons not wholly indifferent to the charm and sentiment of association, would pass Blenheim (Woodstock) without turning their steps to this Mecca of our poet, there to offer the simple homage of admiration and gratitude due to extraordinary genius. Here may still be traced in his lines, as by a chart, the walks he was accustomed to take in the prime of the day, when the sun looked "ruddy and brode" through the morning vapour; when the dew "like silver shining" was upon the "sweet grass," and his beloved

daisy was beginning to unfold its pinky lashes. Here is still the
rivulet by which he coasted, with its water "clear as beryl or
crystal," and the "walled park of green stone:" – here is the "fresh
hawthorn in white motley, that so sweet doeth ysmell;" and the
birds are here cropping the "small buds and round blossoms;" and
the "little well under the hill, with its quick streams and cold, and
the gold gravel, and the banks environing, soft as velvet." How
exquisite are these rural associations with the mind and habits of a
great poet, compared with those of the artificial world! Who in
thinking of Chaucer connects him with the comptrollership of the
Customs, or as page to Edward III? Yet these employments, with
all their temporal benefits, brought with them much labour and
anxiety; while the beneficent spirit of nature rewarded him during
life with untroubled calm and happiness for his decoction at her
shire, and after death with a crown of glory as fresh and vivid as
the recurring flowers that she sprinkles over her green lap.[44]

In light of the false memories of Chaucer at Woodstock, however,
the Burne-Jones portrait is highly intelligible, depicting the solitary
poet writing tranquilly in the enclosed park next to Rosamund's Well.
   Laura Valentine's *Picturesque England: Its Landmarks and historic
haunts as described in lay and legend, song and story* (1894), for
instance, avers that:

> many of the rural descriptions in Chaucer's poems are evidently
> taken from Woodstock Park. He tells us that a park he describes
> "was a park walled with green stone," and Woodstock was the first
> walled park. The description in "The Cuckoo and the Nightin-
> gale," of the morning walk he takes, was an exact picture of the
> way from Chaucer's house, through the park to the brook in the
> vale, under Blenheim. Woodstock is therefore classic ground.[45]

In Retreat

Indeed, Schmitz describes that morning walk in language that
hearkens back to originary impulses from an earlier "biographer":

> He went to rest with the sun, and rose before it, and by that means
> enjoyed the pleasures of the better part of the day, his morning
> walk and fresh contemplations. This gave him the advantage of
> describing the morning in so lively a manner as he does every
> where in his Works; the springing sun glows warm in his lines, and

the fragrant air blows cool in his descriptions; we smell the sweets of the blooming haws, and hear the musick of the feathered choir, whenever we take a forest walk with him. The hour of the day is not easier to be discovered from the reflection of the sun in Titian's paintings than in Chaucer's morning landscapes.[46]

Valentine quotes a poem by Kent, "Chaucer at Woodstock," that contains the key elements of this romantic isolation. Chaucer is pictured in the garden as a "great poet-soul," "a dreamful man was he," who "calmly broods alone" over the "flowering waste."[47] And this is published in 1894.

Guidebooks aside, the false memory of Chaucer at Woodstock had a further half-life in the characterization of medieval London. As late as 1859, Woodstock was urged as Chaucer's birthplace on aesthetic grounds, as Lounsbury quotes from an anonymous source in *Dublin University Magazine*: "We have been assured that Woodstock was a more becoming birthplace than the roar and smoke of London for one who loved the forest and sketched so well the wild wood with its song of birds."[48] As it became increasingly clear, however, that Chaucer's association with Woodstock was tenuous at best, those for whom Chaucer was preeminently a nature poet, "the flower and leaf school," as Ellis denominates them, reinvented London in the rural mode.[49] If Chaucer could not be brought to Woodstock, then Woodstock would be brought to Chaucer, and so occurs the rustication of London, as epitomized by H. Snowden Ward's *The Canterbury Pilgrimages* (1904).[50] Chaucer is "essentially the poet of Springtime" whose "verse breathes of birds and sunshine, daisies and open air." Of greater importance, perhaps, is the "Englishness" of this love of the rural countryside, expressed, for instance, in J. M. D. Meiklejohn's *The Prologue to the Canterbury Tales* (London 1880 [with examination papers, a school text]), whose description of medieval London is as much a protest against the nineteenth-century industrial and commercial racket of the city as it is evocation of a pastoral urban garden:

> But London in the fourteenth century was not the vast province covered with houses – filled with smoke and harassed by unceasing noise – that London now is. It was a clean, quiet, almost noiseless city, full of shady gardens, every house different in character from every other, permeated by green lanes, and the short streets divided

and refreshed by green fields. The quiet meadows were within a few minutes walk of the very heart of the city. There were no cars or carriages, no part of the endless grind and roar that now fill the main arteries of London; but the slow leisurely rumble of a market-cart intensified the sweet silence. It was, indeed, as Mr. Morris [William Morris] says:

> London, small, and white, and clean.
> The clear Thames bordered by its gardens green.
>   [*The Earthly Paradise*]

You could hear the songs of the birds clear and trilling in the streets; and the citizens had the English love of the country so thoroughly in their blood, that on the morning of the First of May, they rose at daybreak, with songs in their mouths and in their hearts, to do honour to the coming summer.[51]

This rustication of London is found frequently in children's Chaucer; Mary Seymour's *Chaucer's Stories simply told* (1884), for instance: "In the London of olden time – the city as it was five hundred years and more ago – when houses were fewer far than fields and gardens, when birds sang in the trees and flowers might be culled from the wayside [...]."[52] Mrs. H. R. Haweis, in *Chaucer for Schools* (1877) uses medieval London to condemn the blight of industrialization: "I dare say, when Chaucer walked in the streets, the birds sang over his head and the hawthorn and the primrose bloomed where now the black smoke and dust would soon kill most green things."[53] In these descriptions, the medieval park of Woodstock where Chaucer took his morning walk has become the medieval city of London itself.

Taking Leave(s)

I return to Arthur Burrell's Everyman edition of 1908 and particularly its epigrammatic use of Longfellow's poem invoking Chaucer at Woodstock, which, in connection with Burrell's comparison of Chaucer to Wordsworth, perpetuates the romantic image of Chaucer in isolation. This conjunction suggests that the poet in retirement (experiencing powerful emotions recollected in tranquility) invents the Canterbury pilgrimage from the recesses of his fancy in a way that

mirrors the nineteenth-century poets' and painters' reinvention of the
Middle Ages from their own fancy and imagination:

> An old man in a lodge within a park;
> The chamber walls depicted all around
> With portraitures of huntsman, hawk, and hound,
> And the hurt deer. He listeneth to the lark,
> Whose song comes with the sunshine through the dark
> Of painted glass in leaden lattice bound;
> He listeneth and he laugheth at the sound,
> Then writeth in a book like any clerk.
> He is the poet of the dawn, who wrote
> The Canterbury Tales, and his old age
> Made beautiful with song; and as I read
> I hear the crowing cock, I hear the note
> Of lark and linnet, and from every page
> Rise odors of ploughed field or flowery mead.[54]

Particularly interesting here is the ekphrasis of the hunt; Woodstock
was created as a royal forest by Henry I around 1110, the manor originally constructed as a hunting lodge – Chaucer is envisioned
surrounded not with the natural world here, but indoors, surrounded
by art, by the history of the hunt; even the song of the lark comes to
him through the "dark of painted glass." That is, Chaucer (like any
clerk, any writer, like Longfellow himself) records the Middle Ages
not from experience, but from pre-existing art, from the ekphrasis of
the hunt and the hues of stained glass, a process that replicates how
medievalists of the nineteenth century proceeded, necessarily recreating the medieval from art and the comfortable scholarship of the
patriarchy, rather than from experience.

In his 2004 popular biography of the poet, Peter Ackroyd writes
that Chaucer "was the poet of sunrise rather than of sunset" (4), that
his poetry "is often conceived to be of springtime rather than of
autumn" (9), and that "his was a thoroughly native genius" (14).[55]
These sentiments are, in no small part, the long refraction of the
dream of Chaucer in which the nineteenth-century medievalists
vested their romanticized reactions to industrialization, commercial-
ization, and the urban erasure of the natural world. This is the
Chaucer, I think, to be found in Burne-Jones's final Kelmscott illustration, at the end of "Troilus and Criseyde." Here a clearly older

Chaucer, his hood covering his head and obscuring his face, is pictured in a walled garden, echoing Kent's poem: "Half reclined by garden terrace,/ In a careless hood drawn upward./ Swathing half his hoary head."[56] Holding a large closed folio volume, the poet is looking intently at a winged figure holding a lyre and standing in, indeed, seeming to grow out of, a bushy tree. This is a portrait of the poet for whom the Muse, the God of Love, and Nature are one and the same; he is in the garden at Woodstock – that is, a portrait drawn not from Chaucer's poetry but from that dream of Chaucer, the false memories of his biography that construct him, as Sir Walter Scott epitomized him, as the "Bard of Woodstock."

NOTES

1. Thomas R. Lounsbury, *Studies in Chaucer. His Life and Writings*, 3 vols. (New York: Russell & Russell, Inc., 1962 [1892]), 1:175.

2. Stephanie Trigg, *Congenial Souls. Reading Chaucer from Medieval to Postmodern*, Medieval Cultures, vol. 40 (Minneapolis: University of Minnesota Press, 2002); on pages 159–85, Trigg examines Furnivall's contribution to Chaucer studies; but, as Charlotte C. Morse has observed: "For over sixty years, versions of Cowden Clarke's modernized Chaucer dominated the popular market for Chaucer," "Popularizing Chaucer in the Nineteenth Century," *Chaucer Review* 38/2 (2003): 99. Trigg, of course, was focusing on academic and scholarly studies of Chaucer.

3. Arthur Burrell, *Chaucer's Canterbury Tales for the Modern Reader*, prepared and ed. by Arthur Burrell, M.A. Everyman's Library. #307, Poetry and the drama (London: J. M. Dent & Co.; New York: E. P. Dutton, 1909); *The Riverside Chaucer, Third Edition*, gen. ed. Larry D. Benson (Boston: Houghton Mifflin, 1987).

4. My title is meant to evoke both Alice Chandler's seminal work on the medieval revival, *The Dream of Order: The Medieval Ideal in Nineteenth-century English Literature* (Lincoln: University of Nebraska Press, 1970), and the poem originally entitled "Chaucer's Dream" (now called "The Isle of Ladies"), one of the sources of the Woodstock myth, discussed below: "The Isle of Ladies," ed. Derek Pearsall, in *The Floure and the Leafe, The Assembly of Ladies, and The Isle of Ladies* (publ. for TEAMS [Consortium for the Teaching of the Middle Ages, Inc.] by Medieval Institute Publications, Western Michigan University [Kalamazoo], 1990), 63–140.

5. *The Poems of Geoffrey Chaucer, Modernized*, ed. R. H. Horne (London: Whittaker & Co., 1841), v. Even as late as 1909, Burrell remarks

(5) that for English men and women "Chaucer is a sealed book." Cf. Morse, "Popularizing Chaucer," 100: "[…] signs of a very broad readership do not emerge until the 1860s, the very decade when schools and universities begin to encourage the reading of Chaucer's poetry."

6. Charles Cowden Clarke, *The Riches of Chaucer In Which His Impurities Have Been Expunged; His Spelling Modernised; His Rhythm Accentuated; And His Obsolete Terms Explained. Also Have Been Added A Few Explanatory Notes And A New Memoir of the Poet* (London: Effingham Wilson, Royal Exchange, 1835). Several reprintings or editions followed, until the 4th "edition" of 1896 (London and New York: Macmillan & Co.) – a stereotyped reprint from the 1870 edition, itself reprinted in 1877. Unless otherwise noted, subsequent page refs. will be from the first edition (1835), from which later editions varied little. The "new" life appeared in 1835, and was "new" in later printings.

7. Burrell, *Chaucer's Canterbury Tales*, 6; Thoreau: "Such pure and childlike love of Nature is hardly to be found in any poet […]," in *Five Hundred Years of Chaucer Criticism and Allusion, 1357–1900*, ed. Caroline F. E. Spurgeon, 3 vols. (New York: Russell & Russell, 1960 [orig. 1908–17]), II, 2, 251. Thoreau's published lecture is given in full in *Geoffrey Chaucer: The Critical Heritage*, ed. Derek Brewer (London & New York: Routledge, 1995 [1978]), 50–57.

8. *The Masque of Pandora, and Other Poems, by Henry Wadsworth Longfellow* (Boston: J. R. Osgood & Company, 1875). The poem is given in full, below.

9. Cf. Derek Brewer's version of this idea: "The outstanding example of Romantic 'medievalism' associated with Chaucer is remarkable as much for its isolation as its beauty: Morris's great Kelmscott Chaucer with the Burne-Jones illustrations," *Geoffrey Chaucer: The Critical Heritage*, 2, 21.

10. Leonhard Schmitz, "A Life of Geoffrey Chaucer, by Professor Leonhard Schmitz," cvii–cxxxviii (cxxx), in *The Poems of Geoffrey Chaucer, Modernized*.

11. Schmitz, "A Life of Geoffrey Chaucer," ccxxiv–ccxxv.

12. *The works of Geoffrey Chaucer, compared with the former editions, and many valuable mss. out of which, three tales are added which were never before printed; by John Urry […]. together with a glossary […] to the whole is prefixed the author's life, newly written, and a preface, giving an account of this edition* (London: Printed for Bernard Lintot, 1721). Lounsbury's discussion of this seminal dream of a life appears in "The Chaucer Legend," *Studies in Chaucer*, 1:186–91, and contains information about Dart's work on the biography, and its revision by William Thomas. On pages 189–91 of "The Chaucer Legend," Lounsbury also offers a useful "abstract" of the "Northampton" core of the Legend.

13. Lounsbury (*Studies in Chaucer*, 1:194–95) cites in passing a severe treatment of Godwin's *Life* by Sir Walter Scott in the *Edinburgh Review*, January 1804 (reprinted in *The Miscellaneous Prose Works of Sir Walter Scott*, vol. 6, "Periodical Criticism" [Paris: Baudry's European Library, 1838], 30–43). It is a wittily savage dismembering, but for all its points and arguments, including allusions to Godwin's unsavory politics, it seems to have had no effect on the long life of the Legend.

14. Godwin, *Life of Geoffrey Chaucer, the early English poet: including memoirs of his near friend and kinsman, John of Gaunt, Duke of Lancaster: with sketches of the manners, opinions, arts and literature of England in the fourteenth century / by William Godwin*, 2 vols (London: printed by T. Davison, for Richard Phillips, 1803).

15. Lounsbury, *Studies in Chaucer*, 1:193.

16. Franklin E. Court, *Institutionalizing English Literature: The Culture and Politics of Literary Study, 1750–1900* (Stanford, CA: Stanford University Press, 1992), 14–15, 168–69. Court shows how Adam Smith's *The Theory of Moral Sentiments* (1759) "lays a philosophical foundation for a way of reading that will be appropriated for *CT* and one already adumbrated by Dryden." See Kevin Pask, *The Emergence of the English Author: Scripting the Life of the Poet in Early Modern England* (Cambridge: Cambridge University Press, 1996), 48–49.

17. Many, if not most, of the popular editions of Chaucer published during this era of the medieval revival advertise such aims in their titles; as for example: *The Riches of Chaucer: in which his impurities have been expunged, his spelling modernised, his rhythm accentuated and his obsolete terms explained; also have been added a few explanatory notes and a new memoir of the poet/ by Charles Cowden Clarke* (London: E. Wilson, 1835.)

18. Lounsbury, *Studies in Chaucer*, 1:217–18.

19. Schmitz, "A Life of Geoffrey Chaucer," cxxv.

20. Anthony H. Harrison, "Medievalism and the Ideologies of Victorian Poetry," *Studies in Medievalism* 4 (1992): 219–34.

21. Schmitz, "A Life of Geoffrey Chaucer," cxxviii.

22. Clarke, *Riches of Chaucer*, 24–27.

23. *The poetical works of Geoffrey Chaucer/ with memoir by Sir Harris Nicolas*, The Aldine edition of the British poets (London: W. Pickering, 1845). The text of the *Canterbury Tales* is from Tyrwhitt's edition (1775–78), the other texts from the Chiswick Chaucer, 1822.

24. Clarke, *Riches of Chaucer*, 4th ed.

25. John Saunders, *Chaucer's Canterbury tales, annotated and accented, with illustrations of English life in Chaucer's time, by John Saunders*, new and rev. ed. with illustrations from the Ellesmere ms. (London: J. M. Dent, 1904), 149.

26. Clarke, *Riches of Chaucer*, 23.

27. Clarke, *Riches of Chaucer*, 28. Clarke quotes long passages from Godwin throughout this memoir, treating it admiringly as an authority.

28. Court, *Institutionalizing English Literature*, 13, 21–23.

29. Harrison, "Medievalism and the Ideologies of Victorian Poetry," 220.

30. Morse, "Popularizing Chaucer," 100. The reference is to Gerald Newman, *The Rise of English Nationalism: A Cultural History, 1740–1830* (London: Macmillan, 1997).

31. James Russell Lowell, *Conversations on Some of the Old Poets*, 3rd ed. (Boston: Ticknor & Fields, 1862), 20.

32. In Clarke, *Riches of Chaucer*, 26.

33. One poem in the Chaucer apocrypha (now usually titled "The Isle of Ladies") is indeed entitled "Chaucer's Dreame" (Brown-Robbins index 3947), first appearing in Speght's edition (1598). In William Thynne's 1532, 1542, and 1550 folio editions, the Book of the Duchess is entitled "The Dreame of Chaucer," and these titles continued to be confused in the early editions. See Kathleen Forni, " 'Chaucer's Dreame'; A Bibliographer's Nightmare," *Huntington Library Quarterly* 64 (2003): 139–49.

34. Lounsbury, *Studies in Chaucer*, 1:176.

35. From "supposed allusions to the park in the Parliament of Fowls," in the "Death of Blanche" and in the so-called "Dream," now better styled "The Isle of Ladies," and, finally, from a direct reference to the place in the poem entitled "The Cuckoo and the Nightingale," to wit: "Under the maple that is fair and green/ Before the chamber window of the queen/ At Woodestock upon the greene lay." Godwin, *Life of Chaucer*, 1:389–90.

36. Lounsbury, *Studies in Chaucer*, 1:177.

37. Lounsbury, *Studies in Chaucer*, 1:175–76.

38. E. G. Stanley, "Chaucer at Woodstock: A Theme in English Verse of the Eighteenth Century," *Review of English Studies* new series 48/190 (1997): 157–67.

39. "Chaucer at Woodstock" from *The Gentlemen's Magazine* for April 1882, reprinted in John W. Hales, *Folia Litteraria: Essays and Notes on English Literature* (London: Seeley & Co., 1893), 70–75.

40. Robert Chambers, *Chambers' Book of Days* (London and Edinburgh: W. & R. Chambers, 1869), 75.

41. In *Chaucer: An Oxford Guide*, ed. Steve Ellis (Oxford and New York: Oxford University Press, 2005), 4, 586–87. Godwin, *Life of Chaucer*, 2:515–21.

42. Godwin, *Life of Chaucer*, 2:565.

43. Steve Ellis, *Chaucer At Large: The Poet in the Modern Imagination* (Oxford and New York: Oxford University Press, 2005), 1.

44. Clarke, *Tales from Chaucer*, 33–34.
45. Laura Valentine, *Picturesque England: Its Landmarks and historic haunts as described in lay and legend, song and story* (London and New York: Frederick Warne & Co., 1894), 192. The association of poet and place is repeated most ardently in William Howitt's *Homes and Haunts of the Most Eminent British Poets* (1847), with many subsequent editions. In the opening essay on Chaucer, Howitt makes the case for Chaucer at Woodstock, "where the king held court on numerous occasions. Chaucer would have attended him, and so must have had a house there, which became his favourite abode. It was a square stone house near the park gate, and long retained the name of Chaucer's house" (4). See Brown's essay in *Chaucer: An Oxford Guide* on the relationship between "ground" and "poet."
46. This imagery has its origins in Dart's biography in Urry.
47. W. Charles Kent, "Stereoscopic Glimpses: XII. – Chaucer at Woodstock," *The New Monthly Magazine* 121 (1894): 97.
48. *Dublin University Magazine* (1859), 247, quoted in Lounsbury, *Studies in Chaucer*, 1:161.
49. Ellis has noted the persistence of what he calls the "flower and the leaf" school, associating it with pre-Raphaelite romanticism; despite all evidence to the contrary, and Furnivall's scorn, for instance, Swinburne persisted in ascribing to Chaucer the "Court of Love," "Chaucer's most beautiful of young poems," as late as 1906 (Ellis, *Chaucer at Large*, 2), and in 1902 appeared C. R. Ashbee's beautiful limited edition of "Chaucer's Flower and the Leaf" from the Essex House Press, which Ashbee viewed as a successor to, but not an imitator of, Morris's Kelmscott Press.
50. H. Snowden Ward, *The Canterbury Pilgrimages* (London: A. C. Black, 1904).
51. J. M. D. Meiklejohn, *Chaucer, The Prologue to the Canterbury Tales, With Notes, Plan of Preparation, Examination Papers and Glossary* (London and Edinburgh: W. & R. Chambers, 1885).
52. Mary Seymour, *Chaucer's Stories Simply Told* (London: Thomas Nelson & Sons, 1884), 7.
53. H. R. Haweis, *Chaucer for Schools* (London: Chatto & Windus, 1877), 7. The remarkable medievalism of Haweis has been recently presented by Mary Flowers Braswell from unpublished materials: " 'A Completely Funny Story': Mary Eliza Haweis and the Miller's Tale," *Chaucer Review* 42/3 (2008), 244–68.
54. See n. 8 above.
55. Peter Ackroyd, *Chaucer*, Ackroyd's Brief Lives (London: Chatto & Windus, 2004).
56. "A great poet-soul lay basking/ In the sunny atmosphere [...]"; Kent, "Stereoscopic Glimpses," 97.

A Note about Richard Osberg

Richard Osberg was Professor of English at Santa Clara University, California, and Director of the University Honors Program, having been Chair of the Department, 1997–2003; at the age of 60, he was stricken with a virulent brain tumor and died soon after, in October 2007. As one who knew Dick when he was a student at Dartmouth, and had him in my courses on Arthurian Romance and on Chaucer, and then enjoyed watching his career as a medievalist unfold, I take his life as exemplary of a kind of academic whose arc and rich development – strong but quiet – should be noticed and studied with more assiduity than is presently the case in medieval studies. He was strongly connected to post-medieval literature and culture, discovering for himself the category of Medievalism; he became a member of the Editorial Advisory Board of *Studies in Medievalism*. Dick Osberg was a craftsman, and making fine furniture in Shaker and Arts & Crafts styles was more than a hobby. He was a careful worker, whether gardening, assembling a harpsichord, or doing research. At his death he was constructing a sabbatical proposal to be called "The Dream of Chaucer and 'Chaucer's Dream' in the Medieval Revival," which was to bring to a head his gathering interests in medievalism, with special focus on William Morris and C. R. Ashbee, as part of an arts context for Victorian re-definitions of Chaucer's poetics. A long essay with the same title of his proposal was discovered by his wife, Sally Osberg, on his computer. She was able to transmit that draft to me so I could fill in the unfinished citations and forward it for posthumous publication.

A. Gaylord
Dartmouth College, Princeton University

Richard H. Osberg: Selected Publications

"Alliterative Technique in the Lyrics of MS Harley 2253," *Modern Philology* 82,2 (Nov. 1984): 125–55.

Sir Gawain and the Green Knight: A New Edition and Verse Translation (New York: Peter Lang, 1990).

"The Maimed King, the Waste Land, and the Vanished Grail in Iris Murdoch's *The Green Knight*," *The Year's Work in Medievalism for 1995* 10 (1995): 124–34.

"Pages Torn From the Book: Narrative Disintegration in Terry Gilliam's *The Fisher King*," *Studies in Medievalism* 7 (1995): 194–224.

"The Prosody of Middle English Pearl and the Alliterative Lyric Tradition," in *English Historical Metrics*, ed. C. B. McCully and J. J. Anderson (Cambridge: Cambridge University Press, 1996), 150–74.

"Rewriting Romance: From Sir Gawain to *The Green Knight*," in *The Future of the Middle Ages and the Renaissance: Problems, Trends, and Opportunities for Research*, ed. Roger Dahood (Turnhout: Brepols, 1998), 93–108.

"Language Then and Language Now in Arthurian Film," in *King Arthur on Film: New Essays on Arthurian Cinema*, ed. Kevin J. Harty (Jefferson, NC: McFarland, 1999), 39–66.

"'I kan nat geeste': Chaucer's Artful Alliteration," in *Essays in the Art of Chaucer's Verse*, ed. Alan T. Gaylord (New York: Routledge, 2001), 195–227.

Contributors

DR. LESLEY COOTE is a professor of medieval and early modern literature and culture in the English department of the University of Hull, U.K. As well as Arthurian and outlaw myth, prophecy and courtly literature, she teaches film and media theory, and literature through film. She has written a book and articles on political prophecy in later medieval England, and has also written widely on medievalism and "neo"medievalism in film, in addition to producing a student-friendly edition of Chaucer's *Canterbury Tales*. Her work features both "traditional" and "neo"medievalist methodologies and theories; her latest articles explore the marginality of greenwood outlaws, prophecy and art in genealogical texts, violence in medievalist film, and Arthurian "art house" cinema.

ALAN T. GAYLORD is a Senior Scholar, English, at Princeton University, and Winkley Professor of English, Emeritus, Dartmouth College. His major work has been on Chaucer's poetry, especially his prosody, and that has included recording Chaucer and Middle English poetry for The Chaucer Studio. He will be publishing an essay, "What is Prosodic Criticism and Why Should It Matter?," in a Festschrift for Chick Chickering. He has a project on "The Medievalism of William Morris," using materials at the Huntington Library on Morris and Arts & Crafts. This will include a monograph, "A Cultural History of the Morris Chair."

CORY LOWELL GREWELL is an Assistant Professor of English at Thiel College in Greenville, PA. His scholarly work has focused on medieval and Renaissance drama as well as contemporary medievalisms. He has written on the latter topic for *The Year's Work in Medievalism* and contributed an article co-written with Amy Kaufman to: *The Medieval in Motion: Neomedievalism in Film, Television and Video Games*.

AMY S. KAUFMAN is Assistant Professor of English and Women's Studies at Wesleyan College. She has published articles on gender in medieval Arthurian literature in *Arthuriana* and *Parergon*, and her work on medievalism in contemporary culture has appeared in *Studies in Medievalism*, *The Year's Work in Medievalism*, and the upcoming MEMO anthology entitled *The Medieval in Motion*. She is area chair of Arthurian legend for the National Popular Culture Association, is currently editing *The Year's Work in*

Medievalism 2009, and is in the process of finishing a monograph on Malory's women.

DAVID W. MARSHALL is Assistant Professor of English at California State University, San Bernardino, where he teaches courses in medieval literature, medievalism, and adaptation studies. His edited collection, *Mass Market Medieval*, encourages the study of medievalism as a broad phenomenon gathering myriad genres and media. He works on English collective identity and literature around the Rising of 1381 and has published on the John Ball letters. He has also published on the use of dragon legends in Creationism and is working on a book-length study of *Beowulf* in popular culture.

LAURYN S. MAYER is Associate Professor of English at Washington and Jefferson College, where she teaches medieval literature. She is the author of *Worlds Made Flesh: Reading Medieval Manuscript Culture*. She has published articles on early modern rhetoric and medievalism in online communities. She is currently working on a book on the *Polychronicon*.

BRENT MOBERLY received his Ph.D. in Medieval Literature from Indiana University, Bloomington. His dissertation examined changing representations of labor in late medieval England. His current scholarly work focuses on neomedievalism, romance, labor, and spectacle in contemporary role-playing computer games. He currently works as a software developer for Indiana University, Bloomington.

KEVIN MOBERLY is an Assistant Professor of Rhetoric at Old Dominion University in Norfolk, Virginia. His research focuses on understanding how computer-enabled manifestations of popular culture reflect, contribute, and transform contemporary cultural and political discourses. In particular, he is interested in the way that contemporary computer games represent labor, often blurring already uneasy distinctions between work and play.

GLENN PEERS is Professor in the Department of Art and Art History at the University of Texas at Austin. He is collaborator with Barbara Roggema on the forthcoming book *Orthodox Magic in Trebizond and Beyond: On A Fourteenth-Century Greco-Arabic Amulet Roll in America*, and is currently pursuing projects on medieval Syracuse and Byzantine materiality.

TISON PUGH is an Associate Professor in the Department of English at the University of Central Florida. He is the author of *Queering Medieval Genres and Sexuality* and *Its Queer Discontents in Middle English Literature*, and his edited volumes include *Approaches to Teaching Chaucer's* Troilus and

Criseyde *and the Shorter Poems*; *Race, Class, and Gender in "Medieval" Cinema*; *Men and Masculinities in Chaucer's* Troilus and Criseyde; and *Queer Movie Medievalisms*.

E. L. RISDEN, Professor of English at St. Norbert College, teaches medieval and Renaissance literature and Classical myth. He has published thirteen books, including most recently *Heroes, Gods, and the Role of Epiphany in English Epic Poetry*, *A Living Light*, and *Hollywood in the Holy Land* (co-edited with Nick Haydock). He is currently working on projects on medieval narratology, the transition from medieval to Renaissance mind, and Tolkien's ideas.

M. J. TOSWELL, Associate Professor of English at the University of Western Ontario, works principally on Old English psalm translations and Anglo-Saxon psalters, but her magpie tendency has led to articles on Tacitus, Earle Birney, and W. H. Auden; editing for six years the journal *Florilegium*; courses on fantasy literature after Tolkien, Arthurian literature, and neomedievalism; and many byways in administration.

RICHARD UTZ is Professor and Chair in the English Department at Western Michigan University. He is the author and/or editor of more than a dozen book-length publications, including: *Early Women Scholars and the History of Reading Chaucer* (2009), *Culture and the Medieval King* (2008), *Falling into Medievalism* (2006), *Speculum Sermonis* (2005), *Postmodern Medievalisms* (2005), *Chaucer and the Discourse of German Philology* (2002), *Medievalism in the Modern World* (1998), and *Literarischer Nominalismus im Spätmittelalter* (1990). His work in the area of medievalism focuses on the roles of nationalism, memory, and academic discourse in the reception of medieval culture.

Previously published volumes

Volume I

1. Medievalism in England
Edited by Leslie J. Workman. Spring 1979

2 Medievalism in America
Edited by Leslie J. Workman. Spring 1982

Volume II

1. Twentieth-Century Medievalism
Edited by Jane Chance. Fall 1982

2. Medievalism in France
Edited by Heather Arden. Spring 1983

3. Dante in the Modern World
Edited by Kathleen Verduin. Summer 1983

4. Modern Arthurian Literature
Edited by Veronica M. S. Kennedy and Kathleen Verduin. Fall 1983

Volume III

1. Medievalism in France 1500–1750
Edited by Heather Arden. Fall 1987

2. Architecture and Design
Edited by John R. Zukowsky. Fall 1990

3. Inklings and Others
Edited by Jane Chance. Winter 1991

4. German Medievalism
Edited by Francis G. Gentry. Spring 1991
Note: Volume III, Numbers 3 and 4, are bound together

IV. Medievalism in England
Edited by Leslie Workman. 1992

V. Medievalism in Europe
Edited by Leslie Workman. 1993

VI. Medievalism in North America
Edited by Kathleen Verduin. 1994

VII. Medievalism in England II
Edited by Leslie J. Workman and Kathleen Verduin. 1995

VIII. Medievalism in Europe II
Edited by Leslie J. Workman and Kathleen Verduin. 1996

IX. Medievalism and the Academy I
Edited by Leslie J. Workman, Kathleen Verduin, and David D. Metzger. 1997

X. Medievalism and the Academy II
Edited by David Metzger. 1998

XI. Appropriating the Middle Ages: Scholarship, Politics, Fraud
Edited by Tom Shippey and Martin Arnold. 2001

XII. Film and Fiction: Reviewing the Middle Ages
Edited by Tom Shippey and Martin Arnold. 2002

XIII. Postmodern Medievalism
Edited by Richard Utz and Jesse G. Swan. 2004

XIV. Correspondences: Medievalism in Scholarship and the Arts
Edited by Tom Shippey and Martin Arnold. 2005

XV. Memory and Medievalism
Edited by Karl Fugelso. 2006

XVI. Medievalism in Technology Old and New
Edited by Karl Fugelso with Carol L. Robinson. 2007

XVII. Defining Medievalism(s)
Edited by Karl Fugelso. 2009

XVIII. Defining Medievalism(s) II
Edited by Karl Fugelso. 2010